Perspectives on Social Ontology and Social Cognition

Studies in the Philosophy of Sociality

Volume 4

For further volumes:
http://www.springer.com/series/10961

Mattia Gallotti • John Michael
Editors

Perspectives on Social Ontology and Social Cognition

Springer

Editors
Mattia Gallotti
School of Advanced Study
University of London
London, United Kingdom

John Michael
Central European University
Budapest, Hungary

ISBN 978-94-017-9146-5 ISBN 978-94-017-9147-2 (eBook)
DOI 10.1007/978-94-017-9147-2
Springer Dordrecht Heidelberg New York London

Library of Congress Control Number: 2014942846

Printed on acid-free paper

Springer is part of Springer Science+Business Media (www.springer.com)

Preface and Acknowledgements

Perspectives on Social Ontology and Social Cognition brings together contributions from researchers with a highly diverse range of disciplinary backgrounds – from philosophy to anthropology, economics, psychology, neuroscience and linguistics. Although the concepts and the methods that shape their contributions differ greatly, one thing that they all share in common is that they have been inspired in one way or another (indeed, in many ways) by John Searle's pioneering and foundational work in the philosophy of language and mind and, more recently, society. In order to provide a rich and varied source of ideas, arguments and empirical material for people interested in social ontology and social cognition, the editorial board and guest editors have placed great weight upon the inclusion of a diverse range of views from heterogeneous perspectives – in some cases even views with which they themselves would not agree. If, as a result, the reader should find some arguments or some formulations controversial, either in tone or in substance, the editors request that she bear this in mind and interpret it as a testimony to the broad and engaged interest that John Searle's work continues to generate.

The project of editing a collection of essays on some of the most pressing and fascinating questions in current research on social ontology and social cognition started to take shape at the *Interacting Minds Centre* at the University of Aarhus in Summer 2011. Some of the essays included in this volume were first presented in the context of *Objects in Mind*, the first Aarhus-Paris conference on social ontology and social cognition, which was held at the Centre of Functionally Integrative Neuroscience at the University of Aarhus on June 25–26, 2012. We owe a special debt to the *Interacting Minds Centre* at Aarhus and to the European ORA Project "NESSHI" (the Neuro-turn in European Social Sciences and Humanities: Impact of neuroscience on economics, marketing and philosophy) for providing us with generous support to organize the event. We particularly want to thank Sacha Bourgeois-Gironde and Andreas Roepstorff for their inspiration and their generous support.

We would also like to express our gratitude to a number of friends and colleagues who agreed to act as anonymous referees in reviewing contributions to the volume.

To Raimo Tuomela we owe a particular debt. In his capacity as the Editor-in-Chief of the Springer book-series *Studies in the Philosophy of Sociality*, Raimo oversaw a rigorous and constructive review process and offered valuable advice and guidance throughout the editorial 'journey'.

Contents

Chapter 1
Objects in Mind

Mattia Gallotti and John Michael

Abstract In this editorial introduction, we provide some background to the discussions in social ontology and social cognition which form the context for the papers collected together in this volume. In doing so, we also briefly sketch how the individual contributions fit together within this broader context.

When we cast a philosophical glance upon the social world around us, one thing that is likely to jump out at us is that so many of the entities that we deal with and depend upon depend, in turn, upon us. Parliamentary commissions, computers, and works of art, in contrast to bacteria, minerals, and plants, are entities which would not exist without us. This is not to deny that such entities are materially constituted. However, it is not their material substrate that makes them what they are but, rather, something about the way in which we relate to them. How, then, are we to conceptualize the "way in which we relate to them"? One proposal, which dates back to John Searle's highly influential work on social ontology (1995, 2010) and is offered in a fresh formulation in this volume, is that institutional facts are an important subset of social facts, broadly understood, in virtue of having the status functions we intend them to have (Chap. 2). So, for example, it is because we all collectively accept that slips of paper printed by the Central Bank have the status of dollar bills that these slips of paper can function as dollar bills. If people did not accept that these slips of paper had the status of dollar bills, then they would not *be* dollar bills.

M. Gallotti (✉)
School of Advanced Study, University of London, Stewart House,
32 Russell Square, London WC1B 5DN, UK
e-mail: Mattia.Gallotti@gmail.com

J. Michael
Central European University,
Frankel Leo Ut 34, 1023 Budapest, Hungary
e-mail: michaelj@ceu.hu

M. Gallotti and J. Michael (eds.), *Perspectives on Social Ontology and Social Cognition*, Studies in the Philosophy of Sociality 4, DOI 10.1007/978-94-017-9147-2_1,

By highlighting the importance of our intentional attitudes for social ontology, Searle's intentionalist framework points toward the possibility that social cognition research and social ontology could be mutually informative and mutually constraining. For example, if facts of social-institutional reality depend upon our collectively intending certain entities to have particular functions, this raises the question whether understanding, learning about, or using them relies upon distinct mechanisms from those which underpin our dealings with other kinds of entity, notably natural kinds. Similarly, one might ask whether the conventional creation of institutional facts entails that learning about them during development involves psychological processes and brain areas postulated in current research on the development of social cognition. Do individuals with social cognition deficits, such as autism spectrum disorder or an impaired understanding of the distinction between moral rules and conventions, have difficulties in recognizing and/or reasoning about institutional facts?

However, as some critics of John Searle have pointed out, it is also important not to overstate the role of our attitudes in establishing and sustaining facts of the social realm. Indeed, although the material substrates of institutional entities, such as money, appear to be more or less arbitrary, materiality is of far greater importance for some other entities, such as screwdrivers, which have physical affordances that facilitate the recognition of their purpose and offer potentials for action. Moreover, although some can be brought into existence right here and now by consensus or fiat, many others appear to have emerged through gradual historical processes, during the course of which humans' attitudes toward them evolved. Some theorists, following Ruth Millikan (1984), have therefore proposed that social entities owe their existence to their functional history rather than to anyone or any group assigning particular functions to them. It seems likely, in fact, that in some cases, institutions may evolve without anyone ever having a concept of them or an intentional attitude that is specifically related to them. However, far from severing the link between social ontology and social cognition research, proposals that relativize the role of intentions in creating, sustaining, and/or constituting the social-institutional reality in fact open up a diverse array of subtle questions about how social cognition and social ontology might be interrelated.

The contributions in this volume approach the issue of how human attitudes, material substrates, history, norms, and convention relate to each other in different ways and form multiple disciplinary perspectives. Some of the contributions focus on fundamental philosophical questions about the nature of institutional facts, whether this implies dependence upon the mental, notably collective intentionality, or not, and how an adequate theory of social ontology ought to address the question of mind dependence (if any). Some, on the other hand, focus on more specific ideas about how intentional attitudes shape and are shaped by social institutions, how social factors modulate our attitudes toward and potentials for interacting with physical objects, or how the intentional attitudes of multiple individuals are coordinated in order to establish a common ground for planning joint actions and for communication about social facts.

Perspectives on Social Ontology and Social Cognition explores these and related issues, being loosely based upon the contributions to the first Aarhus-Paris conference held at the University of Aarhus in June 25–6, 2012. In the remainder of this introduction, we would like to provide some background to the discussions in social ontology (Part 1) and social cognition (Part 2) which form the context for this collection of papers and, in doing so, also to briefly sketch how the individual contributions fit together within this broader context.

1.1 Part I: Perspectives on Social Ontology

In order to grasp the issues that are at stake in the field of social ontology and to assess their methodological significance for empirical research in social cognition, it is useful to begin by demarcating the domain of phenomena to be investigated: social kinds in contrast to natural kinds. What is it for an object to be of a certain *kind* in general? Kinds are systems of classification by which we divide up the world of naturally and nonnaturally occurring entities into groups. Doing so enables us to formulate general statements about groups or kinds of entity, and thus to draw inferences about entities based upon what kinds they fall into. For example, galaxies and viruses are natural kinds which have general features in common based on their kind membership. Importantly, they do not depend on there being human minds for their constitution and maintenance. Should we as humans disappear, there would still be galaxies and viruses. But this appears not to hold for social kinds, like artifacts and institutions.

Historically, discussions about the nature of social kinds developed out of sustained interest about natural kinds in the philosophy of language and mind (Margolis and Lawrence 2007). By natural kind terms, we mean referring to terms like "water" as well as thoughts about water, used by competent speakers of English to pick out naturally occurring exemplars of the kind *water*. In the 1970s, a novel approach to the semantics of natural kind terms began to emerge which was to have relevant implications in areas of philosophical inquiry such as social ontology. The central question of the debate was about the mechanisms of reference by which natural kind terms refer to genuine exemplars of their extension (Bird and Tobin 2012). The received view, back then, was that the reference of natural kind terms works along descriptivist lines: water terms reach out to their referents in the world in virtue of there being members of the kind that satisfy a description commonly associated with water as the kind of entity that comes across as an odorless, transparent, and so forth entity.

Descriptivism came to be challenged famously by Kripke and Putnam's causal-historical accounts of natural kinds (Kripke 1972/1980; Putnam 1975). As the story goes, if the reference of a natural kind term is fixed by a commonly accepted description of the referred-to substance, then the sort of odorless, transparent, etc., entity that looks identical to water and surrounds our physical duplicates on Twin Earth – subjects populating twin planets with the same history and body structure and, therefore, psychological experiences as ours – would indeed be water. But

Putnam (1975) invites us to think about that substance as having a different chemical structure from water. By stipulation, just as we call water on Earth "water," our twins also call "water" the substance that surrounds them on Twin Earth (call it "t-water" for the sake of clarity). Do water terms refer to the same thing on Earth and Twin Earth? If descriptivists were right, then the same description of water and t-water would suffice to fix the reference of "water" on Earth as well as Twin Earth. But Putnam submits that if t-water has a different chemical composition from water, then surely "water" refers to water but *not* to t-water[1]! But, then, if the same description fits both water and t-water, clearly reference works along different lines than those suggested by descriptivists.

Causal-historical theorists generally agree that the reference of a term is fixed by applying the term ostensively to refer to the naturally occurring cause of a set of events and that users of the term refer successfully to that cause by being linked to it through a causal-historical connection that traces back to when the cause was originally given that name. "Ostension" here refers to some event, or process, by which a language user acquires a causal relation to an entity or kind in the world. This can be as simple as pointing to a phenomenon and assigning it a natural kind term or naming a putative unobservable causal agent that produces the phenomenon. Thus, returning to the locus classicus of causal theories of reference, the reason why our twins on Twin Earth do not actually mean water by referring to t-water as "water" is that they entertain a causal relation with a (water-like) substance that bears a different atomic structure from water. So, the stereotype or description associated with water-like substances does not play a role in fixing the reference of the term "water" in the following sense: only the relation between the very essence and the agent, of the kind *water*, which causally explains the properties of the phenomenon, the phenomenon itself, and the dubbing event, fixes the reference of the term "water."

What this tells us is that in order for some entity to qualify as a member of a particular natural kind, it is not sufficient that it accord with folk conceptions of it. A natural kind must have whatever observable or unobservable internal properties are decisive for membership in the kind in question. But it is not always the internal atomic structure that is decisive for kind membership. In the case of biological kinds, for example, genealogy is generally taken to be decisive for species membership (Ghiselin 1974; Hull 1994; Sterelny and Griffiths 1999). The difference is even more striking if we compare natural with social kinds, which rely on conditions other than their physical structure for creation and persistence over time. Interestingly for our purposes, questions about the conditions of membership of natural kinds have contributed significant insights into the ontology of social kinds. Why? What properties ground the reference of social kind terms? And what are the consequences for the way we acquire knowledge of, and make discoveries about, the facts that populate the social realm?

[1] Most, but not all, commentators share this linguistic intuition (Crane 1991). In fact, there is evidence of systematic cross-cultural differences in intuitions about this type of case (Mallon et al. 2009).

1.1.1 Intentionalism, Functions, and Human Kinds

The recent debate on social facts has grown from the pioneering work of John Searle, whose conceptual apparatus is now taken widely, though not unquestionably, as the starting point of most analyses of social ontology (Searle 1995, 2010). In his contribution to this volume and conversation with the editors, Searle reminds us that his analysis of social reality has a particular kind of social facts at its core: institutional facts. For a fact to be of an institutional kind, it must be the sort of thing that is collectively accepted as having a "status function"[2] where status functions are created and maintained by a class of linguistic representations with the logical structure of so-called status function Declarations and bring to light a texture of "deontic powers" including, notably, rights and obligations. If a deontology results from the assignment of a particular status function, then the fact is institutional. In his own terms, Searle describes the status function of institutional kinds as:

> a function that an entity or person performs not in virtue of its physical structure alone, but in virtue of the collective imposition or recognition of the entity or person in question as having a certain status (…). And the structure of that – logically speaking – is the collective imposition of a function of the form 'this entity X counts as having this status and therefore this function as Y in this context C.' (Searle 2007, 12–13)

Two aspects of this passage stand out. The first one is that the entities of institutional reality are "factitive" in structure, the reason being that status functions and deontic powers are brought about by representations of facts about the world and therefore have propositional structure. As Searle remarks with regard to the scope of his philosophical project, this is not a minor point of terminology. Many recent discussions of social ontology refer to "social *objects*," while Searle on the other hand maintains that the key explanatory unit in social ontology should be institutional *facts*. In brief, representations of facts about "objects" are propositional in structure, where it is the factitive rather than the "objective" status of the entities represented that matters for human institutional reality. The second aspect pertains directly to collective intentionality. Notice that the assignment of functions has to be effected in the requisite manner in fact. It is not sufficient that each person individually intend that a given bit of paper be assigned the function of a piece of legislature with legal value – think about a stimulus bill. For the bill to be a member of the relevant institutional sample, it must have the function that is collectively recognized as distinguishing the relevant kind of thing. The collective imposition and acceptance of social functions is thus a form of collective intentionality in this precise sense: the function that we recognize and accept as being assigned to an entity is one which we intend *together* (Gallotti 2012).

Searle's "intentionalist" conception of social ontology has served to pave the way for novel analyses of the ontology of technical and artistic kinds (Margolis and Lawrence 2007). Unlike institutional facts, however, it has been noted that the

[2] In the interview, Searle uses capital letters to name the building blocks of his conceptual apparatus. In the remainder of the chapter, we will use capital letters only if the terms refer to the interview.

decisive property of artifactual kinds may frequently be the function assigned by their individual creator rather than by any group of individuals taking a collective perspective (Thomasson 2003). All in all, intentionalism in social ontology is thus the view that facts about the intentionality of the "creator," be it a group of individuals holding collective attitudes or an individual intending to craft an artifact with a certain function, are the sort of property that sets the conditions for social kindhood.

In contrast to this, some critics of John Searle have been keen to admonish against overstating the role of human intentionality in establishing and sustaining the facts that populate the social realm, broadly conceived. So, although the specific material substrates of paradigmatic institutions, such as money, appear to be unimportant, materiality is of far greater relevance for some artifacts, such as telescopes and screwdrivers, which have physical affordances that facilitate the recognition of their purpose and offer potentials for action. Moreover, theorists inspired by Ruth Millikan's (1984) work have emphasized the role of functional history in establishing social kinds. In Millikan's picture, social kinds are a subspecies of historical kinds. Historical kinds are kinds that link together sets of properties by virtue of a common historical origin. Thus, for example, individual members of a species tend to exhibit many of the same typical properties simply because they inherit them from the same ancestors, that is, because they are members of the same "reproductive family."

Although Millikan has (until now) not written much directly tying her ideas to debates in social ontology, her theoretical framework has been drawn upon in this context as an alternative to Searle's approach to social ontology. Indeed, as many of the contributions to this volume clearly show, there is a tendency among philosophers of social ontology to situate themselves somewhere in between Searle's intentionalist theory and the approach to social kinds pioneered by Millikan. In her contribution to this volume, Millikan spells out a way of applying her conception of reproductive families to social kinds. On her view, social kinds are historical kinds insofar as they share typical properties in common because they have been copied from earlier social entities and activities. So neither individual nor joint intentions, but shared history, are directly decisive for demarcating the boundaries among social kinds. Intentions may of course play various roles in this social history, but not generally by virtue of anybody intending for particular entities to take on particular functions. For example, social kinds could sometimes happen to have been initially established by collective intentionality. However, Millikan defends the view that it is much more common for social kinds to arise gradually, being reduplicated and modified simply because they fulfill particular functions.

Several accounts of social ontology embrace Millikan's lesson without giving up on the intentionalist claim that social kinds are mind dependent in some respect. To see how this is possible, consider the claim that it is the function assigned to a piece of paper that determines whether or not the entity falls into the boundaries of the kind *money*. The literature provides a useful distinction between two ways to understand how intentional attitudes may be involved in the assignment of functions (Epstein 2012). One way is to say that there are conditions of application that must be met by any given piece of paper to be a member of the relevant kind, and among these conditions there can be concepts and intentions. The other is to say that the kind *money* displays such-and-such conditions of application in virtue of more fundamental facts of the world including, particularly, collective or individual attitudes. For example, as we have seen, it is in virtue of naturally occurring facts that water has the atomic structure it does. But those facts are not the same as the conditions that must be met by any substance to be an exemplar of water, namely, having the chemical composition H_2O.

What is evident from this is that human intentionality is involved in neither the application conditions of water nor the facts which establish those conditions. In contrast, one could argue that any artifact must bear the function that was intended by its creator(s) for it to be the kind of artifact that it was originally meant to be. If so, then, one might take the intention of the original maker to be the sort of "fundamental" fact that is decisive for establishing the conditions for kind membership. In addition to this, one might argue that intentionality is involved in the conditions *themselves* that must obtain for a thing to be of the relevant artifactual kind (Thomasson 2007). Thus, if you want to reproduce an artifact by making a copy with the same intended function, you must ensure that the new artifact bear the very same function that the maker intended for the original artifact to have. And this, in turn, requires that you have a certain understanding, or concept, of what the maker intended to do. In other words, whether the new artifact falls within the boundaries of the relevant kind, thereby fulfilling the conditions of application of the corresponding kind term, depends on your having the right idea as to what the creator intended to make at the outset.

The distinction between the conditions of instantiation of social kinds – the "grounding" facts – and the facts that put them in place – the "anchoring facts" – is central to the anchoring project pursued by Brian Epstein in Chap. 4 of this volume. To illustrate this, consider a dollar bill. The conditions for instantiating a dollar bill include the property of having been issued by the Bureau of Engraving and Printing. But why should paper bills printed by this particular institution count as dollar bills? To explain this, we need a separate explanation, namely, that Congress enacted legislation in 1874 which formally established ("anchored") these instantiation conditions ("grounds"). Interestingly, Epstein suggests that the accounts associated with Searle and Millikan are in fact not theories about the conditions of instantiation of social kinds, but theories about the processes that establish those conditions of instantiation, that is, the anchoring schemas. According to Epstein, it is the failure to make this distinction that leads to the idea that intentions or reproductive histories are constitutive of social kinds. Epstein marshals a series of interesting and compelling examples aiming to demonstrate that there is not likely to be any one particular anchoring schema that is common to all social kinds. Of course this does not exclude the possibility that social kinds share some common metaphysical structure, but it does surely cast doubt on this possibility. After all, each anchoring schema could be used to put in place a great variety of instantiation conditions. And if there are many different anchoring schemas at work in the social world, then there is all the more reason to expect heterogeneity in the instantiation conditions that underlie social kinds.

These theoretical considerations in fact have nontrivial methodological consequences. On the one hand, if we hold on to the intentionalist view that social facts involve collective intentionality at bottom, social kinds turn out to be mind dependent. But, then, how can it be that we do not already know everything there is to know about social facts? The claim that social kinds are wholly or partly dependent on mental attitudes does not imply that we cannot possibly be wrong about features of the institutional reality or that the structure of the social world can only be known a priori (Guala 2010). In order to articulate the role of empirical research in social ontology, then, it is necessary to identify in what ways our knowledge of social kinds might be incomplete or in error and thus in need of supplementation or correction by scientific investigation. On the other hand, if Millikan is right, then the functions which tie social facts together in reproductive families may be entirely unknown to us and lend themselves to the very same sort of naturalistic investigation as natural kinds. What new knowledge can be attained by pursuing objective and evidence-based scientific research along the lines of scientific research on natural kinds?

One way to deflate the difference between social and natural kinds, as well as to defend the scientific status of social science as a source of discovery and knowledge of social reality, is to argue that collective attitudes might play a role in the construction of social reality, though not a constitutive one. Intentionalism is associated with what Francesco Guala in Chap. 5 labels the "difference thesis," the view that, unlike natural kinds, for something to be a social fact, it must be *thought of* (intended, accepted, recognized, etc.) as such. This thesis enjoys a consensus that is unwarranted, according to Guala, because collective propositional attitudes are neither necessary nor sufficient for the constitution of social kinds. They are not necessary, since what people believe about social kinds often turns out to be massively mistaken, and they are not sufficient either, because what matters for social kindhood is not what conditions people think ought to be met for kind membership. All that matters is that people recognize and accept those conditions as coordination devices, namely, "tools" that facilitate the formation of shared beliefs and conventions among people. Intentional attitudes are thus not constitutively directed at the kinds themselves but, rather, *causally* directed at the attitudes of other people. And this is where social science turns out to be useful for better understanding what it takes to facilitate the convergence of actions and beliefs that sustains sociality.

One more concern with intentionalism regards the foundation of the collective attitudes that would be required to establish social facts. In Searle's philosophy of mind and society, intentional phenomena are underlain by a set of background capacities and dispositions known as the "Background." Searle's own thinking about the Background has evolved throughout the years and is now reflected in slightly different accounts which address challenges regarding, for instance, the normative dimension of intentionality and language (for a review see Schmitz et al. 2013). This is the key role of the Background, according to Terrone and Tagliafico (chapter 6), who offer a detailed and critical analysis of the two characterizations set out by Searle in *The Construction of Social Reality* (1995) and in *Making the Social World* (2010). Since neither version is satisfactory if considered alone, an alternative approach is needed to solve the tension between accounts of the

Background as intentional and/or non-intentional. On the approach pursued by Terrone and Tagliafico, the Background is rather constituted by the sort of pragmatic social interactions where implicit norms of conduct get formed, the same norms that enable to follow the constitutive rules that are responsible for the formation of institutional facts.

Moreover, as Édouard Machery points out in his contribution to this volume, even if and when social entities are dependent upon our attitudes, there is no guarantee that this dependency will be transparent to us. Thus, for example, although money does seem to depend on people having certain beliefs about what it can be used for, it is plausible that people do not need to realize this (let alone collectively recognize or accept those functions) in order for it to be the case. Indeed, reifying such social entities by effacing their human origins may in some cases increase their stability. Machery provides support for this suggestion by considering several examples of social entities, such as race and gender, which are social constructs (thus suggesting that they are dependent upon humans' attitudes), but which people generally take to be objective (i.e., to be independent of humans' attitudes). He goes on to reflect critically on a number of ways in which the Searlian intentionalist program could be shored up in response to the challenge of reification, such as stipulating that social entities depend upon the collective acceptance of their status functions by only some people (e.g., experts) rather than everyone or that only some social entities fall within the scope of the theory. Finding various problems with all of these possible solutions, Machery proposes that the best strategy for the intentionalist would be to give up on what he calls the "object-specific thesis," that is, that specific social entities depend upon humans' attitudes toward them, and to develop a nontrivial version of what he calls the "object-general thesis," that is, that (some) social entities depend upon more general features of human cognition, such as the capacity to share intentions or to mindread.

1.2 Part II: Perspectives on Social Cognition

If it is true that social facts, in general, involve the collective intentionality of two or more conscious animals, then a theory of social reality will include a theory of the mechanisms that underlie the capacity to share intentions and to coordinate actions together with others. Social cognition raises many interesting questions, which are closely connected with issues of social ontology, yet these connections remain a still largely unexplored topic to this day. Until recently, it was widely agreed that the most fundamental feature of social cognition is humans' ability to identify other people's mental states and that the primary function of this ability is to interpret and predict people's behavior. But the consensus view that mindreading is the clue to social cognition and agency is now under discussion in many quarters of philosophical and scientific research, and novel directions of research have emerged which rely on resources from the shared intentionality literature (Butterfill and Sebanz 2011; Gallotti and Frith 2013).

To see what is meant by the notion of collective intentionality and its implications for research in social cognition, consider the case in which we set out to have lunch outside on a sunny day. Clearly, there must be a difference between the case in which having lunch together is the result of an action that we intend to be collective, that is, joint, and merely lunching "together" as the result of sitting next to one another by happenstance. In the former case, our individual intentions are not enough to bring about truly joint behavior, unless we collectively intend to contribute to the task as something that is to be done *together*. However, although it has become customary to assume that joint action entails something like collective, or shared, or *we* intentions, the entailment relation still awaits clarification.

Perhaps, as Cédric Paternotte argues in Chap. 8, there are better points of departure to tackle the problem of joint action than a priori definitions of what it means to share intentions. In building definitions of joint action around fundamental ingredients, theorists of joint action tend to presuppose some understanding of what joint action is. But an alternative strategy to draw a minimal definition of joint action is to ask what we take joint action *not* to be and what sort of constraints should inform an empirically minded definition of joint action. Unsurprisingly, Paternotte shows that constraints such as the developmental and the motor constraints are implicitly endorsed by current research programs on the psychological and neural bases of joint action (Tomasello et al. 2005; Knoblich et al. 2011). Instead, it is somewhat disappointing that reflection on shared intentionality and agency has remained insulated from serious evolutionary considerations, despite the increasing number of studies on the evolution of cooperation.

In addition to an evolutionary account of collective intentionality, a satisfactory approach to social ontology will need to integrate such factors as the materiality and history of social objects and also the social interactions and social contexts in which we encounter them. And indeed, several recent trends in social cognition research provide exactly this kind of broader perspective. One of these trends is the rise of embodied and interactionist approaches to social cognition. In the 1980s and 1990s, it was considered relatively uncontroversial that the cognitive capacity to identify other people's mental states, that is, mindreading, was the fundamental building block of social cognition and that most or even all social understanding and competent social interaction depended upon this capacity. In recent years, however, social cognition researchers have increasingly appreciated the extent to which social understanding and coordination are scaffolded by embodied responses (Gallagher 2001; Reddy 2012; Michael et al. 2013), interactive patterns (Fusaroli et al. 2012; De Jaegher et al. 2010), and narratives (Hutto 2008).

This is important for social ontology insofar as other people's gaze direction, their actions, and indeed their mere presence induce cognitive and bodily responses in us that modulate our perception of objects (Samson et al. 2010), our degree of preference for objects (Becchio et al. 2008), and our assessment of our potentials for acting upon them (Obhi and Sebanz 2011). Thus, as Cristina Becchio and Cesare Bertone point out in Chap. 9 of this volume, apart from the question as to how our attitudes may create or sustain social objects, there are also subtler questions to be teased out about the kinds of embodied and interactive processes that structure our dealings with social objects. How do children develop an understanding of status functions? What role does shared intentionality play in this developmental process? What general features of social objects may be most important in understanding how the brain encodes them? For example, insofar as a social object has a functional character, the brain may tend to represent it as a tool, whereas the symbolic character associated with status functions may be reflected in a closer association with language in the brain.

Parallel to the emergence of embodied and interactionist approaches to social cognition, extended and situated approaches to cognition in general have become increasingly influential (Hutchins 1995; Menary 2010). These approaches emphasize the ways in which objects enable and perhaps even partially constitute cognitive processes. Thus, the relationship between material objects and cognition does not just go one way. Rather, as Tylen and McGraw emphasize in Chap. 10, material objects enable various kinds of cultural practices to arise which would not otherwise be possible and thus also shape the perceptual, cognitive, action-related, and social processes that arise within those cultural practices. Objects such as clocks, for example, enable more fine-grained planning and coordination than would otherwise be possible and thereby also provide a foundation for all manner of cultural activities. At the same time, of course, they also depend on us insofar as we must have the requisite dispositions to interpret and use them. Embodied and extended approaches not only uncover crucial elements that must be integrated into a balanced approach to social ontology, they also challenge us to think more carefully about the kinds of cognitive process that underpin our relations to social objects. As Michael et al. have argued (2013), an integrative approach to embodied social cognition need not conceptualize embodied or extended processes as alternatives to cognitive processes; rather it should start out from the working hypothesis that cognitive processes are likely to have been shaped phylo- and ontogenetically by the need to modulate, integrate, monitor, and compensate for embodied and extended processes. Thus, investigation of the latter should guide investigation of the former, not replace it.

Another way to conceptualize issues surrounding the relationship between social cognition and social ontology is to think in terms of the perception of affordances, as Anika Fiebich proposes in Chap. 11. She homes in on several ways in which social cognitive skills can modulate the perception of affordances. For example, such phenomena as social referencing and imitation in early childhood shape children's perception and evaluation of all sorts of objects, as well as their action repertoires for dealing with those objects. Importantly, this sort of social modulation of the perception of affordances is not limited to objects that were created by people. On the contrary, any objects at all can offer different affordances depending on how they are used and what roles they play in human sociality and can thus be considered social objects in this limited sense.

In the concluding contribution to the volume, Hohwy and Palmer also point out and examine a subtle nuance of the relationship between social cognition and social ontology. They observe that some objects can only play the roles that they play by virtue of people having common knowledge about them. To take one of their examples, people buy Listerine, thus sustaining the product's existence, because they reason that everyone knows what bad breath is and that it can be treated with Listerine and also that it is impolite to tell others that they have bad breath; hence, if you have bad breath, others will not tell you about it. They go on to consider some difficulties that individuals with autism may encounter in dealing with this kind of phenomenon and, in so doing, offer a groundbreaking demonstration of how a predictive coding framework can be fruitfully brought to bear upon social cognition and social interaction.

In sum, the time is ripe for an integrated exploration of social cognition and social ontology. It is therefore of crucial importance at this stage, as researchers in social ontology and social cognition increasingly discover interesting overlaps and engage with each other's work, that these foundational questions be raised and discussed together – not only in order to foster interdisciplinary research at the crossroads of social ontology and social cognition, but in order to maximize the chances of it generating novel and fruitful impulses for other fields too outside philosophy and cognitive science.

References

Becchio, C., C. Bertone, and U. Castiello. 2008. How the gaze of others influences object processing. *Trends in Cognitive Science* 12: 254–258.

Bird, A., and E. Tobin. 2012. Natural kinds. In *The stanford encyclopedia of philosophy* (Winter 2012 Edn.), ed. E.N. Zalta. http://plato.stanford.edu/archives/win2012/entries/natural-kinds/.

Butterfill, S., and N. Sebanz. 2011. Editorial: Joint action: What is shared? *Review of Philosophy and Psychology* 2: 137–146.

Crane, T. 1991. All the difference in the world. *The Philosophical Quarterly* 41: 1–25.

De Jaegher, Hanne, Ezequiel Di Paolo, and Shaun Gallagher. 2010. Can social interaction constitute social cognition? *Trends in Cognitive Sciences* 14: 441–447.

Epstein, B. 2012. *Review of Creations of the mind* (OUP), ed. S. Margolis and S. Lawrence. *Mind* 121: 200–204.

Fusaroli, R., B. Bahrami, K. Olsen, A. Roepstorff, G. Rees, C. Frith, and K. Tylén. 2012. Coming to terms: Quantifying the benefits of linguistic coordination. *Psychological Science* 23(8): 931–939.

Gallagher, Shaun. 2001. The practice of mind: Theory, simulation, or primary interaction? *Journal of Consciousness Studies* 8: 83–108.

Gallotti, M. 2012. A naturalistic argument for the irreducibility of collective intentionality. *Philosophy of the Social Sciences* 4: 3–30.

Gallotti, M., and C.D. Frith. 2013. Social cognition in the we-mode. *Trends in Cognitive Sciences* 17: 160–165.

Ghiselin, M.T. 1974. A radical solution to the species problem. *Systematic Zoology* 23: 536–544.

Guala, F. 2010. Infallibilism and human kinds. *Philosophy of the Social Sciences* 40: 244–264.

Hull, D. 1994. Historical entities and historical narratives. In *Minds, machines and evolution*, ed. C. Hookway. Cambridge: Cambridge University Press.

Hutchins, E. 1995. *Cognition in the wild*. Cambridge: MIT Press.

Hutto, D.D. 2008. The narrative practice hypothesis: Clarifications and implications. *Philosophical Explorations* 11: 175–192.

Knoblich, G., N. Sebanz, and S. Butterfill. 2011. Psychological research on joint action: Theory and data. In *The psychology of learning and motivation*, ed. B.H. Ross. San Diego: Elsevier publication.

Kripke, S. 1972/1980. Naming and necessity. In *Semantics of natural language*, ed. D. Davidson and G. Harman. Dordrecht: Reidel.
Mallon, R., E. Machery, S. Nichols, and S. Stich. 2009. Against arguments from reference. *Philosophy and Phenomenological Research* 79: 332–356.
Margolis, S., and S. Lawrence (eds.). 2007. *Creations of the mind: Theories of artifacts and their representation*. Oxford: Oxford University Press.
Menary, R. (ed.). 2010. *The extended mind*. Cambridge: MIT Press.
Michael, J., W. Christensen, and S. Overgaard. 2013. Mindreading as social expertise. *Synthese*. doi:10.1007/s11229-013-0295-z.
Millikan, R. 1984. *Language, thought and other biological categories*. Cambridge: MIT Press.
Obhi, S.S., and N. Sebanz (ed.). 2011. Moving together: Towards understanding the mechanisms of joint action. *Experimental Brain Research* 211: 329–336.
Putnam, H. 1975. The meaning of meaning. In *Language, mind, and knowledge*, ed. K. Gunderson. Minneapolis: University of Minnesota Press.
Reddy, V. 2012. A gaze at grips with me. In *Joint attention: new developments in psychology, philosophy of mind and social neuroscience*, ed. A. Seemans. Cambridge: MIT Press.
Samson, D., I.A. Apperly, J.J. Braithwaite, B.J. Andrews, and S.E. Bodley Scott. 2010. Seeing it their way: What other people see is calculated by low-level and early acting processes. *Journal of Experimental Psychology: Human Perception and Performance* 36: 1255–1266.
Schmitz, M., B. Kobow, and H.B. Schmid (eds.). 2013. *The background of social reality*. Dordrecht: Springer.
Searle, J.R. 1995. *The construction of social reality*. New York: Free Press.
Searle, J.R. 2007. Social ontology and the philosophy of society. In *Creations of the mind*, ed. S. Margolis and S. Lawrence. Oxford: Oxford University Press.
Searle, J.R. 2010. *Making the social world*. Oxford: Oxford University Press.
Sterelny, K., and P.E. Griffiths. 1999. *Sex and death: An introduction to the philosophy of biology*. Chicago: University of Chicago Press.
Thomasson, A.L. 2003. Realism and human kinds. *Philosophy and Phenomenological Research* 3: 580–609.
Thomasson, A.L. 2007. Artifacts and human concepts. In *Creations of the mind*, ed. S. Margolis and S. Lawrence. Oxford: Oxford University Press.
Tomasello, M., M. Carpenter, J. Call, T. Behne, and H. Moll. 2005. Understanding and sharing intentions: The origins of cultural cognition. *Behavioural and Brain Sciences* 28: 675–735.

Part I
Perspectives on Social Ontology

Chapter 2
Are There Social Objects?

John R. Searle

Abstract The fundamental unit of analysis in social ontology is not social objects but Social Facts, specifically Institutional Facts. In spite of the incredible variety of human civilization, all of the specific features of human institutional life are created by a single operation repeated over and over (representations that have the logical form of) the Status Function Declarations. Such representations create institutional reality by declaring Institutional Facts to exist. All Institutional Facts are Status Functions. Status Functions create Deontic Powers, and Deontic Powers provide desire-independent reasons for action. A consequence of this analysis is that the basic unit of social ontology is not the social object but the Institutional Fact. Because Institutional Facts have a propositional structure, they and their representations can function in human rationality in a way that objects cannot. Am I a social object? The question lacks a clear sense. But if you consider such facts as that I am a professor, a citizen of the United States, a property owner, and a licensed driver, all of these are constitutive of institutional reality, and they are all matters of Deontic Power relationships.

The whole subject of social ontology is relatively new in analytic philosophy, and for that reason, among others, we lack an adequate vocabulary and an agreed-on taxonomy for describing the phenomena that we hope to investigate. In my own work, I have found a certain approach to be immensely useful, and I want to present it first before criticizing what I take to be alternative and inconsistent approaches. My approach emphasizes the logical priority of facts over objects where institutional reality is concerned.

J.R. Searle (✉)
Department of Philosophy, University of California, Berkeley, CA, USA
e-mail: searle@berkeley.edu

M. Gallotti and J. Michael (eds.), *Perspectives on Social Ontology and Social Cognition*, Studies in the Philosophy of Sociality 4, DOI 10.1007/978-94-017-9147-2_2,

2.1 Status Functions and Institutional Facts

In analyzing society, the fundamental unit is not objects but facts. I will explain why in a few moments. The fundamental taxonomy is quite simple and I think reasonably well defined. A Social Fact is any fact involving collective intentionality of two or more animals. So the existence of money and the US government are Social Facts, and a bunch of puppies playing together with a tennis ball on a lawn is also a Social Fact. If the puppies have collective intentionality, that is, if there is any form of cooperation going on, then the process in which they are involved is a Social Fact or indeed a set of Social Facts. An important subset of Social Facts are those involving the creation and maintenance of what I call Status Functions, functions that can only exist because there is a collective acceptance on the part of sufficient numbers of the community that a status exists and with the status a function that can only be performed because there is such a collective acceptance of the status. Money, professors, political institutions, marriages, and governments are Status Functions. I am a professor at the University of California, Berkeley, and that position is a Status Function. All Status Functions are Institutional Facts. I originally evolved this terminology because I thought all Status Functions require human institutions for their existence. The institution consists of a set of constitutive rules, typically of the form "X counts as Y in context C." So, such and such counts as money, such and such counts as a professor, and so on. There is an awkwardness in this in that sometimes a Status Function can be created without a preexisting institution. For example, a group of children might just informally select somebody as the captain of the softball team. I am not sure if everybody would agree that we ought to call such facts Institutional Facts. In any case, I get a more elegant result if I include all of these things as Institutional Facts even if there was no institution prior to the creation of the fact. We get a rather simple and elegant set of derivations and equivalences, and here is how it goes:

1. All Institutional Facts are Social Facts, but not all Social Facts are Institutional Facts.
2. All Institutional Facts are Status Functions and all Status Functions are Institutional Facts. There is thus a complete equivalence between Status Functions and Institutional Facts.
3. Status Functions are created, consciously or unconsciously, by a certain class of linguistic representations, speech acts that have the form of declarations where you make something the case by representing it as being the case. This special subclass of declarations I call Status Function Declarations. All Institutional Facts (Status Functions) are both created in their initial existence and maintained in their continued existence by representations that have the logical form of Status Function Declarations.
4. The point of doing this is to create power, and the power relations are invariably what I call Deontic Powers: rights, duties, obligations, etc., and these are distinctive in that for anyone who accepts the relevant Status Functions, the Deontic Powers provide reasons for action that are independent of the preexisting desires of the agent in question. They create, in short, desire-independent reasons for action.

Not all Deontic Powers are institutional. People can have obligations quite independent of any institutional affiliation. For example, there are obligations that go with being a biological parent, quite apart from any institutional recognition. But, with very few exceptions, Institutional Facts create Deontic Powers. There is little point in creating the Institutional Fact if there is no deontology involved.

I think the exceptions reveal a power of the analysis. One can have an honorific status – one can, for example, become Miss Alameda County – without, officially, at least any new powers accruing. Furthermore, some things that we intuitively and pre-theoretically think of as institutions, such as the Christian calendar, do not as such create Institutional Facts. The fact that today is the 16th of October is not an Institutional Fact because it carries no deontology. Christmas Day, on the other hand, is an Institutional Fact because it has a deontology. I am, for example, entitled to a day off on Christmas Day.

2.2 The Priority of Facts over Objects

Why is the unit of analysis the fact rather than the object? There are a number of reasons for this and the following stand out. First, we have seen that the purpose of creating institutional reality is to create new powers. Property, government, money, universities, and summer vacations all enable us to do things that we would not be able to do without them. But how is it that we are given new power by institutional reality? And the answer is these are, without exception, Deontic Powers – rights, duties, obligations, etc. Now notice all of those have a propositional structure, and indeed the powers of institutional reality are always propositional. This means that the basic entities represented that give us the propositional structure must be what I call factitive; they must be features of the world that are propositional in structure. Institutional Facts satisfy that condition. Second, the reason that they have to be propositional in structure is that they have to function in human rationality. Human rationality does not operate with objects, it operates with propositional contents. Those propositional contents when true represent facts. So in reasoning what I am to do, I am confronted with such facts as that I am a professor, that I am a citizen of the United States, and that I am a licensed driver in the state of California. All of those factitive entities give me reasons for action of various kinds. So to summarize these two points: the entities created in institutional reality are factitive in structure and they have to be in order to create the powers that we are describing. And, secondly, their representations have to be able to function in human rationality, and those representations being propositional in structure represent entities in the world that have a propositional structure: factitive entities.

The deepest reason why the fundamental unit in social ontology, after collective intentionality, has to be the Institutional Fact and not the social object has to do with the role of institutions in human life and the role of rationality in human action and decision-making. Consider me as a person. Am I a social object? I do not even know how to answer the question under that description. But if you ask this question as: What about the fact that I am a professor in the University of California, I am a citizen of the United States, I am a tax payer in the state of California, and I am the owner of property in various places? All of these are facts and they function essentially in human rationality and therefore in human behavior. Why? Because rationality requires reasoning, and reasoning has to do with propositional entities. A famous example is "Socrates is a man, all men are mortal, and therefore Socrates is mortal." You cannot get that just out of inspecting Socrates, you have to have whole propositions. Now facts are propositional entities, they are what I call factitives; they have a propositional structure. A fact can function in human reasoning because the representation of the fact is in a propositional form. An object cannot do that. So in one sentence we can say: the priority of facts over objects in social ontology derives from the fact that facts have a factitive structure and therefore can function in human rationality in a way that objects as such cannot. It is only facts about objects which enable them to function in human rationality, and that is the whole point of having a social and institutional reality: it is to have a structure of ontology that functions essentially in motivating human behavior. "Objects" that figure in Institutional Facts are typically placeholders for patterns of activity. Think of corporations, money, and vacations.

Institutional Facts are the glue that holds human civilization together because they provide us with reasons for action that are independent of our inclinations. As far as I know, no nonhuman animals have Institutional Facts. They have desires and rational processes, but no Status Functions and no Institutional Facts. Why not? Well, to have those you have to have a language and you have to have a language with a certain power: the power to perform Status Function Declarations. Again, no nonhuman animal known to me has that.

Now, what is the notion of the social object in this taxonomy? There are social objects: as a professor I am also a human being and thus a material object. The $20 bill in my hand is an object; it is a piece of paper to which a Status Function has been assigned. But notice that in both cases it is the factitive status and not the "objective" status that matters for human institutional reality. So why do people want to talk about social objects? I think anybody interested in ontology at some point will be concerned with objects. It is no accident that Frege as part of his ontology of mathematics insisted that every number is a self-subsistent object, an independent object. The favorite model of an object is probably a material object, and the notion of a material object can be given at least a rough definition. Roughly speaking, a material object is a three-dimensional spatial entity that exists through the fourth dimension of time and has a solid surface. Such a concept is rough around the edges, but I think it is reasonably well defined. Why cannot we do a definition of a social object on analogy with a material object? I have never seen anybody seriously try to do it, but there is one huge disanalogy to start with. The examples that one can think of as social objects have an existence that is observer relative. So somebody is president or professor or something is a $20 bill, only relative to the attitudes that people take towards it and other things of that type, and those attitudes create new facts. Something is a material object regardless of what anybody thinks about it. But that is not true of those objects that figure essentially in Institutional Facts, such as the fact that someone is a president or the fact that something is money.

What does all this have to do with the investigation of social ontology in my various books and articles? *It reveals a fundamental misunderstanding of my project if people think that I am trying to define the notion of a social object or the notion of social category of objects.* Consider me, for example. Am I a social object? The only way we could approach this question would be to consider my role in various Social and Institutional Facts. Or perhaps to take a more promising example, consider a tennis ball. Is it a social object? As we have no well-defined technical notion of a social object and as we have no pre-theoretical concept of social objects, I do not know how to begin to answer the question. But now think of the same tennis ball served by my opponent in a tennis game and landing inside the lines of my service court. The fact that he made a good serve is an Institutional Fact and has consequences for the course of the game. The Institutional Fact that the ball was served functions essentially in the game. The ball considered by itself does not have this type of deontology.

Typically, a well-defined general term determines a set as its extension. So the definition I gave of "material object" will determine a set of material objects, and notice that something is a material object regardless of what anybody thinks about it, or if they think anything at all about it. But that is not true of those objects that figure essentially in Institutional Facts, such as the fact that I am a professor or the fact that this piece of paper is money. Anyone who thinks that the concept of a social object figures essentially in social ontology owes us not so much an inventory but a well-defined set of procedures for settling the question whether or not something is a social object, and I know of no such procedures. I think a serious difficulty with the project is that the notion of a set is extensional. Sets are defined by their members, and any two sets with the same members are the same set. But I am not sure that a definition of social object can be given that satisfies this condition. Consider the case of money. To make the account simpler, let us confine it to actual pieces of currency that have a physical existence as money. (Most money has no physical existence. We have only representations of money, not actual currency.) A piece of paper is money, that is, an item of currency, only if people regard it as money and behave appropriately. I have some "Confederate currency." There was clearly a time when this was money in the early days of the Confederacy. By 1865 it was losing its validity, that is, there was a section of the southern population that continued to regard it as money and use it and accept it as money, but there was another section of the population who no longer had that attitude. Now apply the Law of Excluded Middle. Was this piece of paper money or not at that time? Granted that it is no longer money today, was it then and there money? Notice that the theory of Institutional Facts has no problem answering this. Relative to one community it was money, relative to another community it was not. No puzzle or paradox is created. But if you think money is a social object, that is, currency is a social object, then this *object* has contradictory properties.

I think it may be harmless to talk about social objects and I have, myself, on occasion done so where I think the context made it clear what I am claiming. But it would be a serious mistake to think that a fundamental unit of analysis in social ontology is the notion of a social object. For the analysis of human society, the key notion is that of an Institutional Fact. Talk of objects will then naturally fit in or drop out of consideration as irrelevant.

2.3 A Conversation with John Searle: By Mattia Gallotti and John Michael

Editors

In laying out the foundations for a theory of social ontology, you make a fundamental distinction between Social Facts and Institutional Facts. Since you first suggested it in *The Construction of Social Reality*, many philosophers have taken this distinction as a starting point to develop their own approaches to social ontology. However, in focusing especially on the nature of Social Facts, many of these approaches are often formulated in terms that diverge from your initial characterization – referring to social "kinds," "categories," "objects," or "properties" of objects, instead of "facts." Has this change in the relevant terminology become a source of ambiguity or confusion in current studies of social ontology, particularly when accounts designed to counter your theory use different concepts to articulate their critiques? How could we interpret the concept of Social Facts in a way, if any, that could exploit connections with alternative characterizations?

JS

I think I answered this in "Are There Social Objects?" Anyone misses the point of my analysis if they think I am trying to analyze social objects. Social objects, trivially, occur in the analysis because anything that can be named by a noun phrase can be considered an object. But the fundamental theoretical notion is the notion of a fact, especially Institutional Facts.

Editors

While you postulate collective intentionality at the foundation of the institutional reality, several philosophers are unsure how to interpret the claim that a Social Fact is any fact involving the collective intentionality of two conscious animals. Concerns arise especially from analyses of facts other than Institutional Facts which, nevertheless, appear to be constituents of social reality and yet seem not to require collective intentionality for their formation. For example, in discussing the claim that Social Facts depend on collective attitudes for their creation, some people – following Ruth Millikan – are keen to emphasize that many Social Facts result from gradual processes, as people observe other people using objects in particular ways and copy those uses, adapting them to new purposes and to new contexts, such that some Social Facts seem to be established more through a functional history than through anyone or any group assigning particular Status Functions. So, what does it mean that a Social Fact is any fact involving the collective intentionality of two conscious animals?

JS

Suppose one primate begins to dig up insects with a stick. Suppose a second primate observes the first and imitates his behavior. He also digs with a stick. On my account this is not yet a case of collective intentionality, so not yet a Social Fact. "Social Fact" is a technical term, and it is open to anybody to use the term anyway he or she likes, or if somebody wants to call it a Social Fact that is fine by me, but I want a distinction between genuine cases of *collective* intentionality and cases that do not have collective intentionality. Suppose that our two primates get together with a very big stick and together use that stick to dig with – they *cooperate* – now it becomes a Social Fact because you have two agents acting in cooperation. This issue is a matter of arbitrarily defining a technical term, not a matter of making a substantive empirical claim.

The fact that many Institutional Facts gradually evolve over time is in no way an objection to the analysis. I assume, for example, that private property evolved simply out of the practice that people had of possessing and hanging onto certain things. The interesting question is: What is the logical structure of the evolution? Granted that it is typically unconscious, and granted that it is gradual, and granted that it extends overtime, I claim to have identified the logical structure of the resulting Institutional Fact. So the fact that there is a gradual unconscious evolution is in no way an objection.

Editors

A central claim of your theory of social ontology is that Institutional Facts require collective intentionality for their creation, so a theory of social ontology implies a theory of collective intentionality as its foundation. Is there a diversity of ways in which collective intentionality can put Institutional Facts into place? In the paradigm case, multiple individuals collectively intend that "X counts as Y" and do so freely and under conditions of common knowledge. In other cases, though, one person might establish an Institutional Fact by coercion – e.g., a tyrant decreeing that such and such is now a symbol with a particular meaning and function. In still other cases, intentional attitudes spread by contagion as it were, e.g., one person observes a second person expressing reverential awe towards an object and then infers that the object is sacred and subsequently expresses reverential awe towards it, whereupon a third person does the same, etc., until everyone is treating the object with awe. Do you think that in cases like these, Institutional Facts can be put into place without individuals performing acts that require taking a group perspective – as a "we"?

JS

There are several different kinds of cases that we are considering, and we need some principles for sorting them out. First of all, in my taxonomy it is not yet an Institutional Fact if it is not collectively accepted. The dictator can create an

Institutional Fact only to the extent that he gets members of the community to accept it. He may get acceptance by force and coercion, but there has to be some recognition on the part of others if it is to be an Institutional Fact.

The point about treating an object with "awe" is this: there is a crucial difference between doing this by oneself and doing it in cooperation with other people. If I regard the moon with awe and you regard the moon with awe, so far no collective intentionality and no Social Facts. If, however, we collectively become moon worshippers and treat the moon as a sacred object, then we have created a Social and, depending on how it is described, an Institutional Fact.

The key point in all of these cases is: Is there a collectively accepted deontology? One human observes another human worshipping the moon and imitates that behavior; there is not yet an Institutional Fact because there is no collective intentionality and no deontology.

Editors

On your view, Institutional Facts are established when multiple individuals collectively intend to assign Status Functions. For example, money is created when some group of people collectively intend to assign the function of money qua medium of exchange to slips of paper or gold or whatever. How do you analyze cases where the content of the collective intention does not match the Status Function? For example, we may all have the intention to treat one member of the group with deference and thereby accidentally make her or him into a leader/monarch without anyone having the intention of assigning the status of leader/monarch. In such a case, it seems that nobody has an intentional attitude the content of which is that a particular person object should have that particular function. So, do you think that the intentions that create Institutional Facts always contain (i.e., within their content) the constitutive rule which they put into place?

JS

People can inadvertently create someone as the leader of the tribe just by treating that person with more deference, respect, etc., and yet I want to say, unconsciously, they are creating an Institutional Fact. Why? Because of the way I have described it, a deontology emerges from their collective activity.

The key test is whether or not their activities create a new Institutional Fact and the key index of an Institutional Fact is: Is there a deontology that results? So if treating someone in a certain way assigns that person a certain status, even though the participants may not be fully conscious of assigning this different status, and if the resulting status affects behavior in a way that involves such things as obligations, rights, duties, and responsibilities, then the participants in question have created a new Institutional Fact.

Editors

Granted that a Social Fact is ontologically dependent on human minds, statements about them can also be epistemically objective. On one possible reading of this distinction and its role in *The Construction of Social Reality*, we can acquire knowledge of social kinds by pursuing objective and evidence-based scientific research along the lines of scientific research on natural kinds. But if people create Institutional Facts by collectively assigning Status Functions, how can it be that we do not already know everything there is to know about institutional reality? In what ways might our knowledge be incomplete and in need of supplementation by scientific investigation? Would you envision a situation in which people can be in error about which "objects" belong to which social-institutional kinds? If so, in what ways can this kind of error arise?

JS

A fascinating set of questions concerns facts about society that are discovered. So, for example, we discovered that we were in a recession where "recession" is defined as a decline in GDP for two or more consecutive quarters. The Institutional Facts in question are all cases of buying, selling, manufacturing, trading, speculating, etc. All of those can only exist if people think that that is what they are. In order for something to be private property, that is, bought and sold, it has to be thought of as private property, and the transaction has to be thought of as buying and selling. But something can be a recession even if no one thinks that is what it is. How is this possible? The answer is that such cases are systematic fallouts of collective intentionality. The collective behavior of a large society has systematic consequences, such as the decline in the gross domestic product.

Editors

A central aim of this volume is to explore ways in which social ontology and empirical research on social cognition (in particular on "theory of mind") can be mutually informative. For example, understanding the neural underpinnings of the capacity to think "as a group," if any, could help us dispel confusion about certain issues of social ontology like the relation between individual and collective intentionality. In general, it would be interesting to learn whether you think that social-cognitive research might discover facts that would inform or constrain our conceptions of social ontology, and vice versa. For example, given your view that Status Functions must be collectively accepted for an Institutional Fact to come into existence, do you think that learning about Institutional Facts during development, or reasoning about them in adulthood, might depend on the same psychological processes and brain areas that underpin theory-of-mind abilities?

JS

The most basic forms of Institutional Facts in such things as private property, marriage, family, and political power are natural outgrowths of more biologically primitive forms of social organization. Once you have pair bonding among human males and females, marriage is not a very big step; it simply institutionalizes the pre-institutional relation. Such is also the case with parenthood: "male parent" refers to a biological relation, and in our society, "fatherhood" adds an institutional component. Similarly with ownership of tools and dwellings: sheer possession evolves into ownership. I do not know if there is any well-defined neurobiological substrate for this evolution, but it would be interesting to find out.

Editors

Contemporary philosophical investigation has grown pluralistic and interdisciplinary. So, for example, there has been far more intermingling of analytic, naturalistic, and phenomenological approaches in recent years than seemed thinkable 20 years ago. This pluralism has clearly enriched and inspired philosophical research, but does this come at the cost of an overarching philosophical program or methodology? In more detail, does pluralism perhaps stand in the way of developing the kind of systematic "grand theory" of intentionality, consciousness, language, and sociality that you have so greatly contributed to articulate over more than 50 years of philosophical reflection?

JS

I think the right way to proceed in philosophy is simply for the philosopher to follow the questions that interest him or her. This is what I have always done, and I would recommend it to other people. Some very good philosophy is done by people who adopt a piecemeal approach. My own approach to philosophy has always been to try to develop the piecemeal answers to specific questions within larger theoretical frameworks. For me, the overall question is: How do we account for the human reality within what we know about the basic reality from physics, chemistry, and the other natural sciences? The steps in the development of that theory are to show, first of all, how consciousness and intentionality are biological phenomena naturally evolved by certain kinds of animals and, secondly, how some of them, specifically humans, developed language. What exactly is language and how is it structured? And third, how, once we have an account of language, we can give an account of human social reality that shows the role of language and collective intentionality in the creation, constitution, and maintenance of social reality. This is how I work in philosophy, but I am not insisting that other people should work this way.

Chapter 3
Deflating Socially Constructed Objects: What Thoughts Do to the World

Ruth Garrett Millikan

Abstract Intentions and conventions can "make a thing be what it is" in two different ways. Taken separately, neither has any magic in it at all. Neither produces objects of a kind that is in any way remarkable or that requires any special mode of understanding. Only by running these two ways together in our minds do we imagine "socially constructed" or "socially constituted" objects to be other than wholly mundane.

3.1 Some Preliminaries: Social Causes and Social Definitions

First, consider some ways in which just plain thoughts can make things "be what they are." If Johnny's parents truly believe that he is a genius and think this from his infancy, it is very likely to have a lasting effect on his personality. It will very likely affect who he turns out to be. Similarly if his parents think from his infancy that he is somewhat retarded, it will affect who Johnny turns out to be. Exactly *what* effects such thinkings will have will depend on how they are expressed and on Johnny's native disposition and native talents. For the moment, that is not my concern. I just want to begin by reminding us in a simple way that what one person thinks about another can be a pretty direct cause of what that other person comes to be like.

In some cases the kind of person that Johnny or Suzy is thought to be will have some tendency to make Johnny or Suzy become exactly that kind of person. It is likely, for example, that being thought of in our society as "a girl," hence as headed

R.G. Millikan (✉)
Philosophy Department, University of Connecticut, Storrs, CT, USA
e-mail: ruth.millikan@uconn.edu

M. Gallotti and J. Michael (eds.), *Perspectives on Social Ontology and Social Cognition*, Studies in the Philosophy of Sociality 4, DOI 10.1007/978-94-017-9147-2_3,

toward being "a woman," has a tendency to turn little girls into more stereotypical traditional western women than they otherwise would have been. Similarly, consider what it was, traditionally, to be born into a certain caste in India – to be a Brahmin (priest), or a Shudra (laborer), or an untouchable. These labelings, coupled with beliefs about the people so labeled, surely tended to make the beliefs come more true. The labelings, and consequent attitudes and treatment, definitely created persons of a certain kind. The creating was a causal creating, and not in any way mysterious. Women and Brahmins and untouchables have indeed been "socially constructed," if that means it was the attitudes and treatment by society that *caused* them have many of the traits they have had.

There is a second, different, but equally unmysterious way in which women or Brahmins or untouchables have been "socially constructed" or "made to be what they are" by society. The personality traits that these people came to have, intermingled in society's mind with the properties that society wrongly believed to be the causes of these traits (sex, parentage), caused them to be thought of as women, as Brahmins, as untouchables, hence to be called "women," "Brahmins" and "untouchables." Compare: what makes a dog into a dog? One answer is: fitting the rules governing application of the English word "dog."[1] Similarly for what makes a woman into a woman or a Brahmin into a Brahmin. Dogs and women and Brahmins are all "socially constructed" in the sense that the words "woman" and "dog" and "Brahmin" apply to them due only to social – in this case *linguistic* – convention. Similarly, what makes Peter into a bachelor, in this second sense, is that he is unmarried and a man. I will try, slowly, to show why this second, apparently trivial, sense in which things can be asocially constituted, just by being given a name, is important.

First Preliminary Summarized: There are two senses in which women, Brahmins, and untouchables might be said to be "socially constructed." Neither has any tendency to prove women or Brahmins ontologically special. To say that women and Brahmins and so forth are "socially constituted" or "socially constructed" would be confusing. Better, they are on the one hand *socially caused* and on the other they are *socially named*, and it is best not to run these two ideas together. That traditional women and Brahmins are members of their respective kinds is *not*, say, "merely relative to the intentionality of agents." Thinking may have made them members of kinds, but by *causing* them to be as they are, putting them under certain names, but not, of course, by fiat.

---

[1] I actually think there are no such rules, except being in the real kind named by the word "dog." On this, see (Millikan 2010; 2015 Chs. 2, 7).

The belief that having ideas of various "social objects" or "social kinds" might require having a theory of mind seems to result from the assumption that to think of a thing requires grasping its essential nature. Since it is true, of course, that what binds many such kinds together is the way in which people's intentions have causally molded them into kinds, it would follow that thinking of these kinds would involve thinking of people's intentions. I will expand some on this below, but the basic work needed is in the above references.

Is there anything special then that must be involved in *thinking* about women or about Brahmins? Is any special kind of understanding involved owing to the fact that these kinds are socially caused and socially named? Women and Brahmins are usually thought of, I imagine, as humans that have a characteristic kind of beginning and that grow up into a characteristic kind of adult. They are thought of – and indeed they actually are – *real* kinds, clottings of characteristic features generally found together, supporting a variety of rough inductive rules. What has caused these kinds to exit, what has molded them into kinds, clustering their various features together was not traditionally known by people. Certainly it is not generally thought about even now – any more than the various forces involved in evolution through natural selection that have molded rabbits into a coherent kind are generally known or thought about when thinking of rabbits.

Second Preliminary Summarized: Thinking about a socially caused and named kind does not require that you understand the origin of that kind as social but merely that you grasp its current character. Thinking of a socially caused kind, just like thinking of rabbits, is done in a perfectly ordinary way.

3.2 Artifacts as "Socially Constituted"

Another kind of thing that is sometimes said to be "socially constituted" and that sometimes has been thought also to require a special kind of understanding is artifacts. As a preliminary for this case, consider some ways in which people's *intentions* can make things be what they are.

If I intend to make a cake and, as a result, I do so, my intention will have been an important cause of there being a cake. More generally, in making a cake I intend to make something edible, and if what results is indeed edible, that will have been caused, in part, by my intentions that there be something edible. The cake and its edibleness will have been *caused* and in this sense "constructed" or "constituted" by my intention. That is a causal sense in which my intention has *made it be a cake* and also *made it be something edible*. Similarly, if I intend to make a bench for sitting on and, as a result, produce something nice for people to sit on, my intention will have been an important cause of the structure of the object I have produced. It will also have been an important cause of the fact that the bench is usable for sitting on. The bench and its goodness for sitting on will have been *caused* and in this sense "constructed" or "constituted" by my intention. That is one sense in which my intention has *made the bench be a bench* and also *made it be something good to sit on*. This sense is purely causal.

A second way in which my intentions, and this time also yours and other English speakers', have "made the cake into a cake" and "made the bench into a bench" concerns, again, the way we use words. We name many objects in accordance with the intentions behind their construction and, interestingly, we often do so regardless of how they actually turned out. Even if I have mistaken the salt for the sugar and made my cake accordingly, it will probably be called a "cake," though perhaps an "inedible cake." Even if my bench is too flimsy to sit on, it may be called a "bench" because of my intentions in making it. By contrast, simply intending to sit on a thing does not make it into a bench. Intending to sit on a box has no tendency, even verbally, to turn it into a bench. It is a thing's causal history, not present intentions for it, that may put it into an artifact function kind, making it, verbally, be what it is.

Again there is nothing here to make artifacts into other than ordinary objects. That it is a cake or a bench that I have made should not be said, for example, to be "*relative to* the intentionality of an agent." That would just be confusing. "Socially constituted" would have similar confusing effects. To be sure, the fact of something's being a cake or a bench is in part constituted by someone's *having had* an intention, but the "constituting" here is only verbal. It is like the way being a bachelor is partly constituted by being unmarried. Something's being a cake or a bench was also caused by an intention, but again "constituted by" would be confusing.

Third Preliminary Summarized: There are two senses in which cakes, benches, and other artifacts might, though very confusingly, be said to be "socially constructed" or, perhaps, "*relative to* the intentionality of an agent." Neither has any tendency to prove artifacts ontologically special. Cakes are just mixed up flour, sugar, and water; benches are just hunks of wood – with a history.

It does seem possible, however, that the *idea* of an artifact, unlike the idea of a woman or Brahmin, involves a new kind of *thought*. Indeed, we might suppose that entertaining the idea of an artifact would involve entertaining thoughts of people's prior intentions. Won't a person, say, a child, have to have the concept of intention, hence a "theory of mind," to have thoughts about cakes and benches?[2]

Many years ago, Ruth Krauss told us that children think that hammers are to hammer with and can openers to open cans with (and, amusingly, that "a tablespoon is to eat a table with"). They also think that *A Hole is to Dig* (the title of her beloved book), "a face is to make faces with," and "stairs are to sit on." J.J. Gibson tried hard to teach us that basic human as well as animal perception is perception for action, perception of affordances. In another context, I have argued that one huge gap between humans and other animals is exactly the we alone are capable, often, of separating our representations of pure matters of fact from entanglement with our goals, thinking of things other than affordances. We alone are capable, for example, of grasping and remembering *useless* facts (Millikan 2004 Chs. 18–19). But the grasping of affordances still remains a very large part of human perception and thought. Clearly, most of our routine actions do not go through a belief, desire, inference, intention then action loop. Perception guides action directly. The *everyday* way that artifact function-kinds are understood seems certain to be in terms of affordances. Far, however, from being any special new kind of cognition, this is the very oldest kind of all. Nor are affordances things that are "constructed" or "constituted" by the cognitive dispositions or capacities of the animals that perceive them. That an object or situation could afford something to an animal is a perfectly objective fact, nor it is one created by the animal. The animal did not create its own possibilities of action. The simplest idea of a functional artifact is merely as thing that is *for* this or that. No theory of mind is needed for that.

[2] Interesting, in this connection, is (Hughs 2008).

On the other hand, it is possible that children, *and adults*, also sometimes think vaguely of the artifacts themselves as having purposes, purposes lying *within* the artifact in a way analogous to the way people and other animals have purposes. When a tool fails to work, as when a can opener is too dull to open the can, certainly the child and often the adult think of this in a simple way as a failure simply of the can opener not, say, of its maker. The can opener is to open cans with but it cannot. This way of thinking has some similarities to personifying an object. To suppose that thinking this way would involve having a theory of mind, however, would be to mistake all understanding of purpose as having to involve a theory of mind. A more common way to understand purposes, however, as seen in infants and in many animals, is to understand purposiveness merely as goal directedness, as a tendency to effect a certain result despite changes or interference in circumstances. Similarly, Aristotle did not think of his final causes as involving anything's *intentions*.

3.3 Conventions

Many different things are called "conventions." Big Webster lists 13 meanings with a half dozen subtly different senses under each. What I would like to demystify here is not the meaning of the word "convention," but a certain thing about the workings of certain games on the one hand and public languages on the other that makes it natural to call both "conventional." I will begin by suggesting a broad and easy sense in which many things may be said to be "conventional," and I will try to show that conventional games and language forms are conventional in this sense. This will lead later to a discussion of "conventions" taken somewhat more broadly, conventions that govern various kinds of human institutions.

One kind of convention (in my present simple sense) is merely a pattern of behavior that is (1) handed down from one person, pair, or group of persons to others – the pattern is reproduced somehow – and (2) is such that if the pattern has a function, then it is not the only pattern that might have served that function about as well. That is, if this kind of convention has a function, there is a certain arbitrariness about the means by which it serves that function. If a different precedent had been set instead, a different pattern of behavior would probably have been handed down instead. Thus, it is conventional to put a wreath on the door at Christmas time, to dye eggs for Easter, to drink green beer on St. Patrick's day, and to dress baby boys in blue. In Japan it is conventional to eat with chopsticks, while in America, with a knife and fork. That these things are conventional does not mean that they are "conventions" in David Lewis's sense. First, it does not mean that there is some group in which these patterns are universally or nearly universally followed. Second, it does not mean that following these patterns solves coordination problems (although in many cases these patterns do solve coordination problems, thus accounting for their continued reproduction). Third, many things that are conventional in this sense are not prescribed or mandatory or obligatory in any way. Of course some things that are conventional, such as driving on the right in the United States, do solve coordination problems, are nearly universally followed, and are mandatory. But that is not what makes them be conventional in this simple sense.

3.4 How Moves in Conventional Games Are "Socially Constituted"

Playing chess and playing football are conventional activities in the above simple sense. To play chess is to follow certain rules in using a certain kind of board with a certain number of pieces of a certain number of distinct kinds, moving them according to certain rules, in an attempt to reach a certain kind of end configuration or position. Chess is a conventional game. The behavior that is the following of these rules using these pieces is handed down from one person to the next. The rules are not entirely arbitrary, of course. They would not be handed down as they are if they did not make an interesting game, but they are not at all like rules of skill. Which kind of pieces and which rules one uses for amusement is clearly an arbitrary matter, in the sense that there are other game pieces and rules that might have begun instead and been handed down instead. Other rules have of course been handed down for playing other games such as go or backgammon or football.

In the simple sense of "conventional" we are considering, a convention does not tell you what to do. It does not mandate behavior. For example, the conventions, the rules, of chess do not tell you what to do, but only what to do *if you wish to play chess*. They are "constitutive" only in the purely verbal sense; they *define* what is called "playing chess." That is all.

You can get these conventions wrong, of course. You can fail to reproduce the conventional chess patterns faithfully even though you are trying to. But the standard that has then been violated will have been set *only by your own intentions*. No social mandates will have been violated. True, in some circumstances, such as in tournaments, there will be external sanctions mandating that you follow the rules of chess, mandating that you should play chess rather than making up some other pattern of play. And if you have agreed to play chess with someone but then do not follow the rules, you will have broken an agreement, something there is a social mandate not to do. But there is no extra-contextual mandate that the chess pattern must always be reproduced whole, and not some of its parts separately. One can quit a chess game in the middle, or set up just an end game, or a just middle game, or change the rules in the middle, or play dolls with the pieces. It is just that this will not be reproducing the traditional pattern that has the name "chess."

What is it then for one person to have checkmated another or, taking John Searle's most famous example, to have made a touchdown in football and gotten six points?

It is for a person, or a team, to have been following certain conventional rules in a certain kind of activity and to have reached a certain point in that following. Checkmate "counts as" winning because, when following the chess conventions, that is the position on the board one was trying to attain. The convention – what is copied, reproduced – is in part trying to attain that position. And attaining what is conventionally tried for in a certain game is winning it. When following the conventional – the copied – pattern, the game stops after that. One may have reasons beyond winning to want to win, of course, but the convention goes only so far as to try for the position that is winning. Similarly, touchdowns are what you try for in football – or goal kicks or field goals. These are what add up, if one is repeating the pattern by following the traditional rules, to winning or losing in football. There is nothing ontologically peculiar about having checkmated someone or having made a touchdown and gotten six points. Nor is any peculiar mental capacity required to understand it.

Of course, the moves and outcomes of conventional games are not mere current physical happenings. To be conventional, the game must have a certain kind of history. It is not being played at all if the players are not *reproducing* certain patterns on the model of certain prior games – say, if the patterns occur by accident. The moves and outcomes of a conventional game *could not exist* without conventions, that is, unless there had been certain things *in their pasts*. That is a matter of definition. Also, the moves do not exist apart from the game. They are, by the meanings of the words for them ("checkmate," "touchdown"), smaller parts of larger handed-down conventional patterns.

Once again then, what has sometimes been called "social *constitution*" here is merely a matter (1) of having a *causal* social history, a history of social reproduction, and (2) that history being semantically required for application of a thing's name. Parts of the conventionally reproduced patterns of behavior called "games" are called "moves," and they also have more specific names such as "castling" and "putting the king in check" and "making a touchdown and getting six points." Nothing of a new ontological kind has entered the world here. Copying certain patterns on purpose and giving names to these patterns and to some of their parts – that is all that has occurred. I could do it all by myself if I wanted, inventing a game of solitaire and then naming its moves. Nothing social is even essential here. But that would not make my game conventional, of course.

Nor is there anything special involved in *thinking* of the game parts we call "moves." They are described with reference to "rules" the following of which produces the patterns. But these rules are not prescriptive rules. The patterns are indeed produced because the players intend to follow the rules, that being what it is for the players to be playing that game, these intentions *causing* the game to be played. But no one's intentions *constitute* the game or any of its parts, or any moves within it, in any richer sense. To think about game moves is just to think about past patterns and to think about copying them again, nothing more.

3.5 Conventions That Solve Coordination Problems

In the sense of "conventional" we are using, conventional activities involve reproduced patterns of activity that, if they have a function, have a somewhat arbitrary form in relation to that function. One kind of function that conventions can have is the function of solving coordination problems. Linguistic conventions are of this kind. This is true not just of linguistic conventions with the functions of conveying information or of directing activities, but also, of course, for those with the functions of performatives and of declarations.

A "coordination problem," as David Lewis understood it, is posed in a situation if several persons share a goal that can only be achieved by joint action, where what each person needs to do to help in achieving the goal depends on what the others will do, and where there is more than one combination of participant actions that would achieve the goal. Any particular solution to the coordination problem will then be somewhat arbitrary in relation to the result to be achieved. The solution to a coordination problem becomes "conventional," in the sense I am using, if that solution is often reproduced, that is, if new problems of the same kind are often solved in the same way because solved by copying earlier solutions.

No matter how the precedent for a coordination convention is originally set, I have argued (Millikan 1984 Chs. 3–4, 2004 Chs. 8–11; 2005 Chs. 1–3), if the coordination it effects is an obvious and important one, it will tend to proliferate, and it will tend to do so, contra Lewis, without anyone's having to think about anyone else's thoughts. Like other higher animals, people repeat behaviors that have been successful in achieving wanted results. Unlike most other animals, they tend also to copy successful behaviors of others. Behaviors that constitute solutions to coordination problems achieve results desired by all parties to the coordination; hence, these behaviors will tend to be reproduced when similar results are desired. No thoughts of other people's thoughts are required. The various parties in the coordination need not even recognize the problem as a coordination problem let alone think about one another's thoughts in order for the convention to proliferate.

Consider the conventions for correct social distance when conversing. These distances vary from culture to culture and are unconsciously reproduced by being learned as a skill. If you are at the wrong social distance, the one to whom you are speaking will move, so that to avoid slow circling about as you talk, you learn to stay at the conventional distance. Similarly, one might unconsciously learn to conform to the convention of driving on a given side of the road solely as a skill – as a means of avoiding oncoming traffic.

Exactly in this way, not only children but very smart primitives typically are unaware that the languages they speak are merely conventional. Specific language forms continue to be reproduced by speakers within a language community, mediated not by Gricean thoughts about others' intentions but primarily because, enough of the time, they prompt hearer responses that contribute to the fulfillment of speaker purposes in speaking. Similarly, hearers continue to respond in conventional ways, for example, by believing or by doing what they are told, because, often enough, the result is rewarding for them. Often enough, believing or doing what one is told leads to believing or doing what is useful or what will keep one out of trouble. No thoughts about one another's mental states are required to sustain these conventions.[3,4]

---

[3] These claims are clarified and supported in the references cited two paragraphs above.

[4] Similar things can be said about the use of money by ordinary people. It is typically used without any thought or understanding of the conventional nature of financial transactions.

Consider, for example, a speaker whose purposes in using the word "rabbit" can be achieved only when he effects communication about rabbits or manages to call attention to facts that concern rabbits. Such a speaker will eventually stop trying to use the word "rabbit" for these purposes if they are never achieved. Similarly, a hearer whose faculties turn his mind to rabbits whenever speakers use the word "rabbit" will soon unlearn this response if speakers never use the word "rabbit" in a way that carries information or intentions about rabbits. Again, consider those syntactic forms that get labeled "indicative" in various languages. These forms will generally have a number of alternative functions, but no form will be labeled "indicative" unless one of its central functions is to cause true beliefs having whatever propositional content the rest of the sentence determines. Production of false hearer beliefs may occasionally interest speakers but rarely serves the purposes of hearers. A hearer unable to interpret the indicative sentences he hears so as sometimes to extract genuine information from them would soon cease to form beliefs on their basis. And if hearers ceased ever using indicative sentences as guides in forming beliefs, speakers would stop trying to use them for purposes that required imparting beliefs. Further, if it were not sometimes in the interest of hearers to comply with imperatives (advice, instructions, directions, requests from friends, sanctioned orders, and so forth), hearers would soon cease to comply. And if hearers never complied with imperatives, speakers would soon cease to issue them and imperative syntactic forms would die out.

The social evolutionary mechanism at work here, resulting in a symbiotic relation between speakers and hearers, is exactly parallel to that which tailors the species-specific call of a bird and the response of its conspecifics to fit one another, or the nipple of the mother to fit the mouth of her infant, but with learning standing in for natural selection. Speakers (collectively) learn how to speak, and hearers learn how to respond in ways that serve purposes for both, each leaning on the settled dispositions of the others. This kind of co-tailoring requires only that there be functions served for both parties some critical proportion of the time. In the case of conventional language forms, it requires neither regular hearer compliance nor that speakers always speak with intentions that conform to the conventional uses of these forms. There can be lying, misuse, implicature, and so forth. Linguistic conventions, like other conventions in the simple sense used here, need not be regularly followed within any group of people. The function that stabilizes (or alternative functions that stabilize) the use of a linguistic form need not be regularly fulfilled. Stabilizing functions are not the same as either universal functions or average functions. Speakers within a language community are simply *adapted* to an environment in which hearers are responding, sufficiently often, to the forms speakers produce in ways that reinforce these speaker productions. Hearers are adapted to an environment in which speakers, sufficiently often, produce these language forms in circumstances such that making conventional responses to them aids hearers. Thus, the conventions of responding to these forms in given ways and of producing them for certain purposes are sustained.

Once again, notice that nothing here in the practice of ordinary language use is helpfully said to be "socially constituted." What we have are merely reproduced patterns involving a sequence of speaker intentional attitude, sentence produced, hearer comprehension, and hearer response. Each part is just another part of a conventional pattern. (Notice that this pattern includes part of what John Austin called the "perlocutionary" side of language use as well as the "illocutionary" side.)

3.6 Simple Illocutionary Acts

Three basic things are normally involved when one person speaks to another. There is the speaker's purpose, there is the conventional outcome of the language form used, and there is the hearer's actual response. All these three may line up, or any two may line up, or they may go three separate ways. The stabilizing function of a conventional linguistic form is a cooperative function in which speaker purpose and hearer response are lined up. The conventional outcome belonging to the form itself is production of that stabilizing hearer response. But sometimes a speaker's purpose in speaking is not to obtain that conventional outcome/response, and sometimes the hearer does not make that conventional response, and sometimes neither speaker nor hearer conforms to the conventional pattern.

Central cases standardly used to illustrate what Austin called "illocutionary acts," also central cases falling under many of our ordinary names for these acts such as "warning," "requesting," and so forth, are cases in which the speaker's intention and the conventional outcome match, although the actual outcome may not. A warning occurs, typically, when the person who says "I warn you" purposes to warn you, although you might not, of course, take warning. A request occurs, typically, when the person who says "I request that you…" purposes that you comply, although you might not do so. Traditional *discussions* of "illocutionary acts" tended to emphasize either speaker purposes or conventional outcomes *to the exclusion of the other*. Griceans emphasized speaker purposes; Austinians emphasized conventional outcomes. Strawson, in (1964), claimed that there were two separate kinds of illocutionary acts, some being Gricean, others conventional. But in fact, the most typical classical "illocutionary act" or "speech act" token is both. The speaker purposes what it is also a stabilizing function of the language form to accomplish.[5] Intention and stabilizing function agree. (Physically described language forms can have alternative stabilizing functions, of course. Speaker purposes very often concur with stabilizing functions that are more determinate than shows up on the face of the language.)

There is some vacillation then in the notion of an illocutionary act. Speech acts such as warning or requesting may be classed either according to speaker purpose or according to conventional outcome of the language form used, or both when they agree. But, interestingly, that vacillation does not matter for our purposes here. Both ways of classifying are by reference to history. The first looks to proximal

[5] For a full discussion, see my (2005 Ch. 8).

history in immediate psychological origin, the second to more remote history of function in the public language.[6] Thus, the way speech acts are named is exactly parallel to the way that functional artifacts are named. Speech act tokens have either a *causal* personal history of a certain sort or a *causal* social history of a certain sort, or both, this history being *semantically* required for application of their specific speech-act names. For example, saying "it is raining" in the context of the usual convention is classified as the same illocutionary act as saying "Es regnet." The speech act of asserting that it is raining can be achieved in many languages. What gets classified as the same speech act does not consist in the occurrence of any particular physical type. Compare chess, which might be played with variously shaped bottles on sand where squares have been appropriately marked out. But the fact that we name an illocutionary act by its the intention behind it or by its conventional outcome rather than its physical type does not affect its ontology. Like cakes and benches, speech acts are not "socially constituted" in any but our by now familiar ways. They are purposefully produced or reproduced by people, and they are named in accordance with history, either psychological or social, rather than shape.

3.7 Regulated Conventions: Performatives and Declarations

More credit needs to be given, however, to Strawson's claim that there are two kinds of speech acts, some conventional and others merely intentional. I have been using the term "convention" in a simple sense that is quite restricted. Besides conventional patterns of the kind I described above, there are social patterns that repeat but not by reproduction or not merely by reproduction. Instead they are prescribed by law or through other mechanisms, often associated with sanctions. Call these patterns and the moves within them "regulated." Examples are marriage ceremonies and other procedures prescribed in certain churches or states, naturalization ceremonies, meetings run in accordance with Robert's Rules, court proceedings of various kinds, voter registration procedures, and inauguration procedures. Where these patterns have a degree of arbitrariness to them, the patterns as a whole are naturally termed "conventional." We can call them "regulated" or "partially regulated" conventions. (Our earlier conventions I called "simple.")

There is no sharp line between simple and regulated conventions. Often patterns are partly simple with other portions being written into codes or laws. Marriage ceremonies, including the act of signing certain documents, are an example of this. Driving on the right in the USA is a coordination convention that belongs in both categories or between categories. One drives on the right following what others do for safety and also because it is the law.

[6] Each of these kinds of history independently lends what I have called a "proper function" to the item with that history. Linguistic forms in use always possess two sources of function, one corresponding to conventional meaning, the other to speaker purpose (Millikan 1984 Ch. 4, 2005 Ch. 8). This has the interesting result that a linguistic form in use sometimes possesses conflicting proper functions.

Moves within either regulated or simple conventional patterns often consist in people saying things. Saying "I bid six diamonds" is a move in bridge within a pattern that follows a simple convention. "The meeting is adjourned," said in the right context, is such a move in the context of a simple convention, but a convention that in some contexts is also mandated, hence regulated. There could also be cases, I suppose, in which this phrase was said directly following a consultation of Robert's Rules of Order rather than merely copied from earlier examples. The pattern of moves required to make a foreign-born person into a US citizen, including the necessary taking of oaths and so forth, is an example of a regulated pattern that contains sayings. The effects of having gone through this pattern are quite strictly regulated. More generally, all formal oaths seem to be moves in regulated conventions. "This road is legally closed" posted by the right authorities in the right place is a regulated move. A classic for speech act theory is "I now pronounce you man and wife."

The grammatical form used for conventional moves of this kind is typically declarative. But to constitute a move of this kind, the declarative sentence must of course be uttered in the right context, the context forming part of the pattern. You cannot bid six diamonds by saying "I bid six diamonds" if it is not bridge or if it is not your turn to play, or adjourn a meeting by saying "the meeting is adjourned" if you are not the chairman. Such requirements were labeled "felicity conditions" by Austin, but lacking them is in fact lacking part of the conventional move's *very shape*. What is reproduced or regulated as part of the pattern is not words but words in a context. Our names for such moves behave accordingly.

As in the case also of simple illocutionary acts, moves made within regulated conventional patterns are very often classed together and named in accordance with their conventional outcomes rather than in accordance with *either* their physical forms *or* their actual outcomes. Peter Strawson emphasized that there is a sense in which, for example, the chair's saying, at an appropriate time, that the meeting is adjourned "cannot fail to do so" (1964, p. 612). No matter what the members go on to do, there is a sense in which the meeting has indeed been adjourned, once the chair has spoken. Similarly, after the minister pronounces a pair man and wife, they are married, even if they do not act married and even if everyone else, including those responsible for enforcing the law, fails to treat them as it is conventional, or as it is regulated, to do. But that is only because for the meeting "to have been adjourned" simply is for a conventional move to have been made, the *conventional* outcome of which would be that no more debate occurs, no more motions are considered, and so forth. Similarly, after the minister or justice of the peace has said, at the appropriate time in the appropriate context, "I now pronounce you man and wife," the couple addressed cannot fail to be married *for the unmagical reason* that to be married simply is, verbally, for conventional moves to have been made the conventional outcome of which would be that they behaved in certain manners toward one another, were treated by the law in a certain manner, and so forth. But real outcomes are not always the outcomes that are conventional or regulated.

Making such a move "consists" (semantically) in purposefully doing something of a kind that would *conventionally* have a certain outcome in people's behavior. That is what bidding six diamonds or marrying a couple *consists* in. It "constructs" or "constitutes" so bidding or marrying in the sense, only, that it is what makes these acts fall under the verbs "bidding" and "marrying." Once again, social construction turns out to be merely causal on the one hand and merely semantic on the other.

References

Hughs, J. 2008. An artifact is to use; an introduction to instrumental functions. *Synthese* 168(1): 179–199.

Millikan, R.G. 1984. *Language, thought and other biological categories*. Cambridge, MA: The MIT Press.

Millikan, R.G. 2004. *Varieties of meaning, the Jean Nicod Lectures 2002*. Cambridge, MA: The MIT Press.

Millikan, R.G. 2005. *Language: A biological model*. Oxford: Oxford University Press.

Millikan, R.G. 2010. On knowing the meaning; with a coda on Swampman. *Mind* 119(473): 43–81.

Millikan, R.G. 2015. *Unicepts, language and natural information*. Oxford: Oxford University Press.

Strawson, P.F. 1964. Intention and convention in speech acts. *The Philosophical Review* 73(4): 439–460.

Chapter 4
How Many Kinds of Glue Hold the Social World Together?

Brian Epstein

Abstract In recent years, theorists have debated how we introduce new social objects and kinds into the world. Searle, for instance, proposes that they are introduced by collective acceptance of a constitutive rule; Millikan and Elder that they are the products of reproduction processes; Thomasson that they result from creator intentions and subsequent intentional reproduction; and so on. In this chapter, I argue against the idea that there is a single generic method or set of requirements for doing so. Instead, there is a variety of what I call "anchoring schemas," or methods by which new social kinds are generated. Not only are social kinds a diverse lot, but the metaphysical explanation for their being the kinds they are is diverse as well. I explain the idea of anchoring and present examples of social kinds that are similar to one another but that are anchored in different ways. I also respond to Millikan's argument that there is only one kind of "glue" that is "sticky enough" for holding together kinds. I argue that no anchoring schema will work in all environments. It is a contingent matter which schemas are successful for anchoring new social kinds, and an anchoring schema need only be "sticky enough" for practical purposes in a given environment.

Among the most useful skills we have, as humans, is our ability to anchor new social kinds. We do this routinely. The furniture of today's world includes brands like Nike, Budweiser, and Blackberry; financial instruments like variable annuities, CDOs, and swaptions; technologies like screwdrivers, smartphones, and web services; dances like the Lindy Hop, jitterbug, and krump; textiles like gabardine, herringbone, and bouclé; subcultures like hipster, gopnik, and cybergoth; jobs like professor, President, barista, and climatologist; and so on. All of these are social creations, populating the world more richly and densely than it once was.

B. Epstein (✉)
Tufts University, Medford, MA, USA
e-mail: brian.epstein@tufts.edu

M. Gallotti and J. Michael (eds.), *Perspectives on Social Ontology and Social Cognition*, Studies in the Philosophy of Sociality 4, DOI 10.1007/978-94-017-9147-2_4,

In this chapter, I will not concern myself with whether we genuinely introduce new social kinds into the world. I will take it for granted that we do, although this is a more loaded assumption than it might seem to be. My concern will be with *how* we do so. In particular, I argue against the idea that there is a single generic method or algorithm or set of requirements for anchoring new social kinds. Instead, there is a variety of "anchoring schemas," or methods by which new social kinds are generated. Not only are social kinds a diverse lot, but the metaphysical explanation for their being the kinds they are is diverse as well. My aim in this chapter is to explain what this claim means and put forward an intuitive case for it.

4.1 What Is Anchoring? Dividing Social Ontology into Two Fields

Although it is seldom recognized, social ontology divides into two separate fields of inquiry. First is what I will call the "grounding project." This is the inquiry into the grounds for the existence of a social object (such as a screwdriver or a hipster), the grounds for an object to have a social property (such as *being a screwdriver* or *being a hipster*), or to be a member of a social kind (such as *screwdriver* or *hipster*).[1] This project is close to the one Frege initiated in *The Foundations of Arithmetic* of 1884. Following Frege, we might distinguish two different kinds of conditions associated with a property or kind: its instantiation conditions and its identity conditions. The instantiation conditions are the conditions a given object needs to meet in order to have the property, or to be a member of the kind.[2] The identity conditions are the conditions under which two objects having that property are identical. If, for instance, an object x satisfies the instantiation conditions for *screwdriver,* then it is a screwdriver. If both x and y are screwdrivers, and moreover satisfy the identity conditions for *screwdriver,* then they are the same screwdriver. The aim of the grounding project in social ontology is to give these sorts of conditions.[3] For something to be a screwdriver, is it sufficient for it to be used to turn screws? Does it have to have a certain shape? Does it have to have been manufactured with a certain

[1] Searle 1995, 2010 has popularized "institutional facts" as the central subject of social ontology. In his usage, however, the term is misleading. Many entities he discusses, such as dollars, boundaries, governments, etc., are social objects or kinds, not facts. And it is not clear that many of these involve institutions, in any of the standard senses of the notion.

[2] It is tedious to keep say "properties or kinds" or "having a given property or being a member of a given kind," so I will mostly just speak of either properties or kinds, depending on which is most convenient. But the points about one can, in general, be extended to points about the other. Also, to be precise, Frege's analytic project was largely directed to terms and concepts, not properties. But roughly parallel distinctions apply.

[3] Strictly speaking, the identity conditions of a property are included among its instantiation conditions (see Noonan 2009). Elsewhere, I have argued that despite this, we can nonetheless distinguish identity conditions from instantiation conditions (Epstein 2012b). Here I will mostly just speak of instantiation conditions, for brevity.

functional intention in mind? All these are questions in the Frege-style inquiry. They ask what it takes, what the conditions are, to ground the fact that something is a screwdriver.

The second inquiry I will call the "anchoring project." Though it has an equally long pedigree as the grounding project, it is a little less familiar. Suppose that a given social property or kind has such-and-such instantiation conditions and such-and-such identity conditions. The anchoring project asks why are *these* the property or kind's instantiation and identity conditions? Or, to put the question slightly differently, why is *this* the property or kind that we have introduced or created? What have we done—or what facts are there in the world—that put a given property or kind, having these instantiation and identity conditions, in place? As I will term it, what facts *anchor* the property or kind?[4]

A traditional approach to the anchoring project—for quite a few social properties and kinds, at least—comes from Hume: they are introduced by convention.[5] For instance, Hume argues that the property *being an owner* is conventional. Many communities, for instance, once had the convention that the first person to occupy a piece of virgin territory is the owner of that property. In Hume's view, for a convention to be in place, within a community, is for members of the community to share certain beliefs about what will be to their mutual benefit. Thus, Hume's answer to the question *What makes it the case that first occupants of a piece of land are its owners?* is that we share various beliefs about how various practices involving first occupancy will be of mutual benefit. Those shared beliefs—the things that in Hume's view put in place a convention—are not the same as the conditions for someone to be an owner. For someone to be an owner of this sort is to be the first occupier of virgin territory. The shared beliefs about the benefits of the practice do not make any particular person an owner. Rather, the shared beliefs *put in place* or *anchor* the conditions for being an owner.

John Searle puts forward a somewhat different theory of anchoring, in his works on institutional facts.[6] In Searle's view, properties like *being an owner* or *being a dollar* are anchored in certain collective attitudes we take, as a community. These collective attitudes are not just shared beliefs. According to Searle, for the members of a community to collectively accept something, or collectively recognize something, is for each of the community members to have a "we-accept" or "we-recognize" attitude toward it. Thus, according to Searle, what makes the first person to occupy

---

[4] It is my view that the anchors of a social kind are entirely distinct from the kind's instantiation conditions. Whatever puts the conditions in place for *being an owner*, or for *being a screwdriver*, or for *being a hipster* is not itself among those instantiation conditions. This is a controversial stance. Some intuitive reasons for this claim come out in the next sections, but my principal aim is to clarify the notions of anchoring and anchoring schemas. The rest of the paper does not depend on a rigid distinction between anchors and grounds: work on anchoring schemas is reasonably neutral on the question of whether the anchors of a social kind are among its instantiation conditions. For detailed treatment of this point, see Epstein (forthcoming).

[5] This tradition is actually a good bit older but is most familiar from Hume.

[6] Searle 1995, 2010.

a piece of territory its owner is this: we collectively accept that people who are first occupiers have the status and powers accorded to owners. The conditions for being an owner are anchored in collective acceptance.

Both Hume and Searle have unitary theories of how social properties and kinds are anchored. They both give a single account or schema for anchoring. In Hume's view, there is something special about convention, and in Searle's, something special about collective acceptance or recognition. But is there only one anchoring schema? What would it even mean for there to be more than one? To make sense of this, consider an analogous notion, widely discussed in a different field: the idea of *word-introduction procedures* in the philosophy of language.

4.1.1 Descriptive Semantics Versus Foundational Semantics

In recent years, philosophers of language have distinguished two different fields within semantics.[7] One is "descriptive semantics." This is the inquiry into what the meanings of words and sentences are. Some people hold, for instance, that the meaning of a proper name such as 'Plato' is just its referent, the person Plato. Others hold that the meaning of 'Plato' should be analyzed along the lines of "The person who wrote the Symposium, taught Aristotle, etc."[8] Both of these theories of the meaning of a proper name are theories in the field of descriptive semantics. Also in descriptive semantics are theories of how the meanings of complex expressions are composed out of the meanings of words in combination with one another.

The second field is "foundational semantics." This is the inquiry into what makes it the case that words have the meanings they do. For proper names, for instance, many people endorse a "baptism-transmission" theory.[9] This theory holds that the name 'Plato' has the meaning it does in virtue of its initial attachment to the person Plato a couple of thousand years ago and the subsequent causal transmission of that name from person to person. A different theory holds that 'Plato' has the meaning it does in virtue of our current beliefs and communication practices.

The distinction between descriptive semantics and foundational semantics parallels the distinction I am advancing, between the grounding and anchoring projects in social ontology. Both descriptive semantics and foundational semantics are inquiries into the metaphysics of language. Descriptive semantics is the inquiry into certain key (perhaps essential) properties of words—namely, their semantic properties.[10] Likewise, foundational semantics is not just an inquiry into historical happenstance, why a word happened to acquire those semantic properties. Instead, it is the inquiry into the facts that "put in place" the semantic facts. It looks for the metaphysical explanation for a word to have the meaning it does.

---

[7] See Stalnaker 1997.

[8] See Kripke 1972/1980.

[9] Kripke, *op cit.*

[10] On the question of the essential properties of words, see Kaplan 1990 and Simchen 2012.

To be clear, although there are parallels between descriptive semantics and the grounding inquiry, we should take care to note that they are not the same thing. They cannot be the same, because there are many social properties we do not have words for. (There are, for instance, many properties that social scientists discover in their work.) Moreover, investigating the meaning of a word like 'screwdriver' is not the same thing as investigating the instantiation conditions of the social kind *screwdriver.* (For instance, a widely held theory of meaning takes the word 'screwdriver' simply to "refer directly" to that social kind. That is the entire descriptive semantics of the word 'screwdriver' and says nothing about the instantiation conditions of the kind *screwdriver.*) Equally, foundational semantics is not the same thing as the anchoring inquiry. Foundational semantics gives a metaphysical account of what puts in place a word, while the anchoring inquiry gives a metaphysical account of what facts put in place a social property.

Nevertheless, there are revealing parallels between the pairs of inquiries. In both domains—semantics and social ontology—we study a kind of tool. Words are linguistic tools, and social kinds are social tools. Yet these are not just ordinary tools, but tools of a special sort: they are what we might call *universal tools.* Words are tools for expressing propositions, for saying things about actual and possible situations. (Words do other things as well, of course.[11] But expressing ways the world is, was, or will be, or how it might be, is a key function words have.) Words are tools we apply to a *universe* of different situations—all the different possible ways the world might be, at any time, past, present, or future. They are not just tools for describing a restricted set of situations. A sentence like "A cat is on a mat" can be evaluated in any situation, any time, any world, even ones where English is not spoken.

Similarly, social properties and kinds are universal tools as well. They serve a variety of functions: we reference them when we recognize things, classify things in various situations, find and correct departures from norms, draw inductive inferences, and accomplish other practical matters. They too are applicable across a universe of different situations: we can look at any object whatever, in any situation, and assess whether that object is a member of the kind *teacher, tire, hem,* or *hipster.* That does not mean that social properties and kinds are not anchored in local contexts in the actual world. The kind *hipster,* for instance, is anchored by a range of idiosyncratic facts about our current society. But its potential instantiation is not limited to that current situation.

Because these fields investigate universal tools, both semantics and social ontology need to make a sharp distinction between two kinds of contexts: (1) the contexts in which the tools are employed and (2) the contexts in which the tools are set up, or put in place. The reason for sharply separating these kinds of contexts is more easily seen in semantics. As I mentioned, when we evaluate the truth or falsity of a sentence like "A cat is on a mat," we might be interested in evaluating a situation ten thousand years ago, before English existed, or a million years ago, before any language was spoken. Or we might be interested in evaluating it in a world where there are no

[11] See Austin 1962.

people at all. The descriptive semantics of the sentence "A cat is on a mat" is all that matters in evaluating the truth or falsity of that sentence, and the descriptive semantics is independent of the foundational facts that make that sentence mean what it does in English. When we evaluate the truth or falsity of "A cat is on a mat," we only need to look around the world for cats and mats, not for facts about what makes words have their meanings.

In semantics, that is, we distinguish the "contexts of evaluation" from the "contexts of assignment." Contexts of evaluation are the ones in which we evaluate expressions according to a fixed descriptive semantics. When we evaluate different situations in which the sentence "A cat is on a mat" may be true or false, we are considering contexts of evaluation. In *evaluating* the sentence, the foundational facts are irrelevant. When we browse around among contexts of evaluation, we take the descriptive semantics to be fixed as it is, even in the historical and possible situations where English does not exist. In ignoring the facts of foundational semantics, we allow the tool of linguistic expressions to be universally applicable.

Of course, there are also facts about the world that put those semantic facts in place. To investigate this—that is, to do foundational semantics—we shift from contexts of evaluation to contexts of assignment. When we browse around contexts of assignment, we are not considering the facts that might make a sentence like "A cat is on a mat" true or false. Rather, we are browsing around the facts that make the word 'cat' have the meaning it does, the word 'on' have the meaning it does, and so on. In contexts of assignment, that is, we are not concerned about the evaluation of sentences. Instead, we consider the facts that put the descriptive semantics in place.

In social ontology, we likewise need to sharply separate two different contexts. Social properties and kinds are universal tools: they can be instantiated in any situation whatever. We can look back at ancient societies and evaluate whether there are classes or castes, aristocrats or serfs. We can visit remote cultures and inquire as to whether they have various forms of dance or song. We might look for baristas in the Ottoman Empire or in seventeenth-century England and variable annuities among the ancient Egyptians. We might find that the Egyptians do not have variable annuities, but only proto-annuities. Or we might find that there is, in their context, an entity satisfying the instantiation conditions of *being a variable annuity.*

In evaluating whether a social property is instantiated in a given situation, we take those situations to be *contexts of instantiation.* A property like *being President,* or *being the jitterbug,* or *being a cybergoth* applies to an object just in case it satisfies the relevant instantiation conditions. To evaluate whether an object has one or another of these properties, the anchors of those instantiation conditions are irrelevant.

However, we can also investigate the facts that anchor social properties and kinds, that is, the facts in virtue of which those properties have the instantiation conditions they do. Like the investigation into foundational semantics, in this second inquiry we shift to a different context. Instead of browsing through contexts of instantiation, we browse through contexts of anchoring. In thinking about different contexts of anchoring, we are thinking about different ways various social properties can be anchored. In those contexts, we are not concerned with applying social properties—that is, about whether a given object satisfies the instantiation conditions for a given social property. Rather, we might investigate which rules various people collectively accept, or which beliefs they have about mutual benefit. In considering contexts of anchoring, that is, we are concerned with the facts in virtue of which a social property is set up to be the particular universal tool it is, to be applied in any range of contexts of instantiation.

4.1.2 Foundational Schemas and Anchoring Schemas

Foundational semantics investigates the facts that put words in place. One central part of this inquiry is the question of what procedures can be used for introducing words. (Another part of the inquiry is about how words are transmitted from person to person.) Much of the emphasis of foundational semantics has been on proper names. Different theorists have different accounts about what it takes to fix the reference of a proper name. One school argues that there is a single way for a proper name to be fixed in a language: the person introducing it needs to have a certain kind of acquaintance with the named object. A different school takes a broader view: reference fixing requires only unique identification of the referent, not acquaintance with it. Again, these are both metaphysical theories, explaining what grounds the fact that a proper name has the reference it does.

It is also possible that there is more than one schema for fixing the reference of a proper name.[12] When we expand the inquiry beyond proper names, this is even more plausible: different words have their meanings in virtue of different kinds of facts. Some words may be defined, some words may be introduced by designating a sample by pointing at it, and some may be introduced by designating a sample by describing it. It may be that words of different types are introduced by different schemas. For instance, proper names might be introduced with one schema and certain predicates with another. Or it may be that two different introduction schemas can be used to introduce words of several different types. It is the job of foundational semantics to characterize these schemas. These schemas are general methods or functions that describe which types of facts in the context of assignment metaphysically explain why words of a given type have the descriptive semantics they do.

A theory of anchoring, analogously, investigates the facts, in contexts of anchoring, which put social properties and kinds in place. Its aim is to characterize anchoring schemas. These are general methods or functions that describe which types of facts in the context of anchoring metaphysically explain why social kinds of a given types have the instantiation conditions they do. Hume's and Searle's respective theories propose different anchoring schemas, just as the acquaintance theorists and the latitudinarians propose different word-introduction schemas.

---

[12] See Epstein 2008.

4.2 Multiple Anchoring Schemas

Is there just one overarching schema for anchoring social properties and kinds, or are there many? It is possible to trivialize this question. Suppose there are three different schemas. We could just combine them into one single schema, which is the disjunction of the three. Equally, if there is just one schema, we could always break it up into sub-cases, turning one unified schema into several schemas. Either of these, however, is just to play games. Putting aside tricks, this is a substantive question at the heart of social ontology: is the diverse furniture of the social world all explained in one way, by one generalized operation of our individual minds, or our collective minds, or our practices? Is the social world in its entirety a kind of projection of powers, by our minds, onto real substrates?[13] Is it patterns of natural phenomena to which we assign labels?[14] Or is there more than one sort of account for social properties in general?

Consider the following three cases. All three draw on a key characteristic of many social kinds that hardly shows up in Searle's account: many kinds are what they are because of the properties of actual tokens.[15] To explain why some kind K is the kind it is, we must look to actual objects in the world and the properties they have in common. We cannot only look to how we think about some set of objects, or how we cognize them. Instead, properties of sets of tokens of K, and the relations among them, are part of the "glue" holding together K as a kind.[16] The following three cases are not meant to be particularly unusual or distinctive. They are easily described cases of different sorts of social kinds, having histories that closely resemble one another.

Case 1: The Aldino typeface

In the late fifteenth century, Manutius Aldus commissioned Francesco Griffo, the Venetian punch cutter, to design a slanted typeface. It was attractive and highly legible, and its overlapping forms made efficient use of space on the page. Aldus named the new typeface 'Aldino.' Griffo's design was so successful that Aldus had the forms reproduced numerous times. He printed many volumes in the Aldino typeface.

Case 2: Pocket books

Aldus was also responsible for another innovation: the pocket book. In 1501, he began to print editions of Greek and Latin classics in small books

---

[13] This is the sort of view Searle puts forward.

[14] As in Dennett 1991.

[15] Richard Boyd and Ruth Millikan highlight this in an exchange on "historical kinds" (Boyd 1999; Millikan 1999). See also Elder 2004.

[16] Ruth Millikan and Richard Boyd introduced this image in their exchange (Boyd and Millikan, *op cit.*). They also speak of the "ontological ground for the unity of a kind." That terminology is not ideal, however, especially in light of the extensive recent literature on grounding, which uses the term 'ground' in a somewhat different way. Their respective theories in their exchange are, in part, theories of anchoring schemas. Theories, that is, about the sorts of things in the world—the histories, the causal mechanisms, and the qualitative regularities—that set up the conditions for a disparate set of objects to be members of a kind.

with vellum covers. The first of these "libri portatiles" was an edition of the works of Virgil. Aldus went on to apply this format to dozens of books.

Case 3: Italics

Other printers took up the style of the Aldino typeface. Later versions refined and modified the slanted script typeface, and slanted script letterforms became widespread throughout Italy. Later on, this widespread letterform style was given the name 'italic'.

Each of these stories involves families of reproduced tokens—families that are not so different from one another. But in each case, a different sort of social kind is anchored. For each of these kinds, we can pursue both the grounding and the anchoring project. Both are rather complicated to work out in detail, but it is not too difficult to sketch plausible answers so long as we are content to leave them rough.

Consider the conditions a thing must satisfy in order to be an instance of the Aldino typeface. Like many kinds, members of Aldino can be any of a number of different sorts of entities. A particular set of marks on a page might be an instance of the Aldino typeface, or else a font description on a particular computer or a set of metal type in a drawer might be. But to be an instance of Aldino is not just to have a particular pattern of letterforms. Instead, Aldino is plausibly a historical kind. For something to be an instance of that kind requires that it be a historical descendent of Griffo's original punches. If an identical letterform somehow occurred in nature, accidentally occurring, not a product of reproduction but just happenstance, it would not be an instance of Aldino. Likewise, if someone came up with an identical letterform from scratch, entirely causally disconnected from the history of reproduction of Griffo's punches, it also would not be an instance of Aldino.[17] There are also qualitative conditions for something to be an instance of Aldino. Certain variations in letterforms are tolerated, but significant deviation from Griffo's forms suffices to preclude a set of marks, a font description, or a set of punches from being an instance.[18]

The instantiation conditions for *pocket book* are somewhat different, despite the fact that Aldus reproduced the format much as he did the Aldino typeface. For an object to be an instance of a pocket book more likely involves a generic function rather than being tied to one single historical family. Among the conditions for something to be a pocket book is plausibly that it has the function of being easily carried around in a pocket. We might understand this condition as a causal-role function, or else perhaps as a "Proper function": the function of being easily carried around in a pocket is part of the explanation for its having been produced.[19] In either case, it has different sorts of instantiation conditions than Aldino does. For something to be an instance of Aldino requires that it be a member of a particular historical family, while for something to be an instance of *pocket book* does not. It is also plausible that there are qualitative characteristics an object must have, in order to be a pocket book, not just functional ones. A scroll that can be easily carried around in a pocket is not a pocket book.

---

[17] See Millikan 1984, Ch. 16.

[18] See Elder, *op cit.*

[19] Millikan 1984.

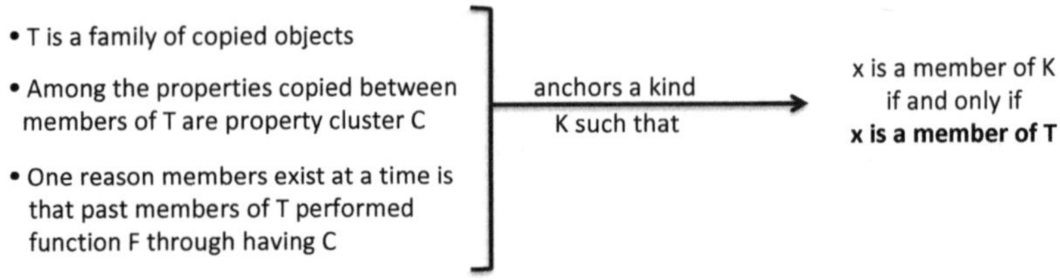

Fig. 4.1 Schema with dominant ancestry/teleofunction

The instantiation conditions for *italic,* in contrast, are purely qualitative. Today italics function more commonly for emphasis than for compactness, but whatever their function is, it has no bearing on whether a letterform is italic. All it takes for a letterform to be italic is for it to be written in a slanted script style. Despite the similarity of its historical origins to Aldino, the conditions for a typeface to be italic are akin to those for a typeface to be "oblique." An oblique typeface is a slanted typeface, and an italic typeface is a slanted script typeface. (It is a peculiar quirk of the literature on artifacts and social kinds that current theories focus almost exclusively on functions and so do not accommodate purely qualitative kinds, despite the fact that there is a good deal of evidence that many artifact kinds have purely qualitative instantiation conditions.[20])

Here we have three kinds with similar reproductive histories, and yet with three different sorts of instantiation conditions. Each of these kinds, in being anchored as it is, makes very different use of the tokens, their relation to one another, and other features of the environment. They are not held together by the same glue. Aldino is plausibly a historical kind in the sense of Millikan 1984, 1999. Its dominant glue is the functional explanation for the proliferation of that particular family. Figure 4.1 gives a rough depiction of a schema of this sort.[21]

In this figure, the anchoring facts are listed on the left side, and the instantiation conditions of the kind are on the right. The figure represents a schema for anchoring a kind whose membership conditions are just that one is a member of a particular "reproductively established family." The family of copied objects is "glued together" by the fact that the reason for their being copied as they are—and hence for being reproduced and hence members of T in the first place—is that C performs F.

Pocket books are similar, except that they have been invented and reinvented many times, filling a fairly obvious "ecological niche." The niche they fill is that people want to be able to easily carry their reading around with them. But as I mentioned, it is plausible that the kind *pocket book* is not restricted to one particular historically reproduced family. It applies as much to today's

[20] See Epstein 2012a.

[21] For a clear presentation of Millikan's picture, see Godfrey-Smith 2004. I take some of the notation in this figure from that paper.

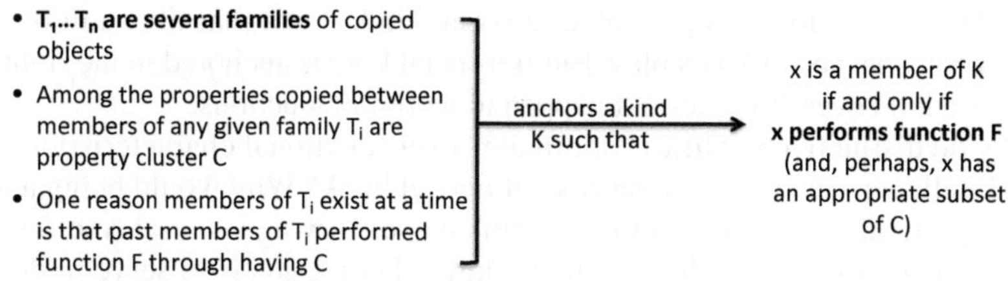

Fig. 4.2 Schema with dominant generic function

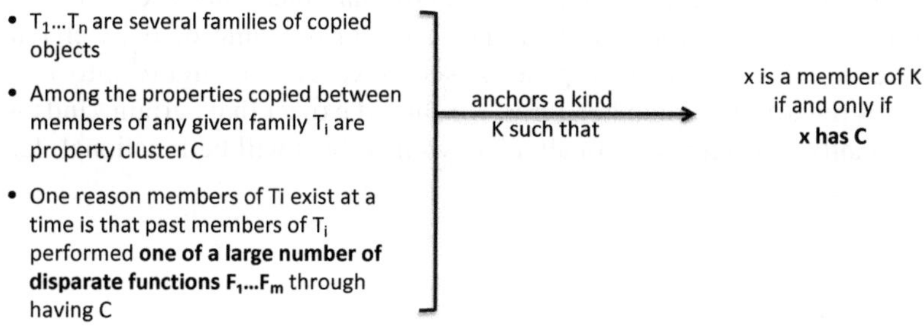

Fig. 4.3 Qualitative dominance

Penguin paperbacks as it does to Aldus's *libri portatiles,* regardless of the historical connectedness of these families. Figure 4.2, then, is a plausible anchoring schema for *pocket book*.

The schema for anchoring *italic* also draws heavily on the existence of billions of easily recognized tokens, easily recognizable because of the simple qualitative contrast between their features and those of the billions of tokens of other letterforms that do not have those features (e.g., Roman characters). But *italic* is different from *pocket book*, in that there is no easily identified function at all, nor do we have a particular stake in associating a token with its actual ancestors, as opposed to its doppelgangers. Thus, *italic* is plausibly anchored with a schema such as (Fig. 4.3).

These are only three of potentially a great number of anchoring schemas. There may be many ways to "glue together" a kind with qualitative instantiation conditions, or a functional kind. The aim of these examples is only to illustrate a few sorts of glue. Moreover, even if these three kinds have distinct "glues," still that does not entail that they have three different practical uses, as kinds. It may be, for instance, that all three kinds are useful for drawing inductions in a subfield of social science.[22] Kinds anchored in several different ways may all be effective in that role. There may be several schemas, all of which are successful in practice, for anchoring kinds that serve in inductions. It is important to notice that serving in inductions is not a

[22] Boyd and Millikan, *op. cit.* This is the role that many philosophers have insisted that social kinds play. My own inclination is that social kinds serve more diverse purposes, but for present purposes, it is fine to take this more limited perspective.

plausible *criterion* for gluing together a social kind. It is a plausible aim of social kinds or role that social kinds play. But if a social kind is anchored in the right way, then it is a kind even if it does not happen to work in inductions.[23]

Why do distinctive qualities "dominate" over functional characteristics, in the case of italic, or vice versa, in the case of pocket book? Why would being a member of a particular historical family dominate over serving a causal role function, or vice versa? Sticking to the idea that a key role of kinds is to serve in drawing inductive inferences in the social sciences, it is easy to see how this can happen. When a large set of tokens is qualitatively distinct but functionally diverse, we respond more consistently to qualities than to functions. And when it is functionally unified, that functional unity is not only an outcome of our behavior but influences it. If a practical purpose of social kinds is to figure into inductive inferences regarding human behavior, we should expect that certain kinds will be predominantly or even purely qualitative, while others will be functional, familial, or otherwise.

4.3 How Can These Glues Be Sticky Enough?

Ruth Millikan has criticized certain liberal approaches to kinds, in particular ones that resemble the "dominant generic function" case I described above. Papineau 1992 and Macdonald 1992, for instance, present approaches to biological kinds that are less tied to particular historical families than is Millikan's. (Theirs is an approach to biological kinds, but similar arguments can be applied to the social case.) They argue that a functional kind can have multiple realizations in different reproduced families, when all the families are reproduced under similar selection pressures. For instance, there may be one generic selection pressure leading to different sorts of eye, or leading to different sorts of swimming traits. In such cases, eyes and swimmers may be biological kinds.

Millikan, for her part, does not deny that organisms under similar selection pressures can develop strikingly similar characteristics. However, she denies that that is sufficient to group these different realizations into a kind. In particular, she denies that such a "kind" would be sufficient to ground inductions:

> Our question is not how a variety of different objects might come to exhibit the same functional property, but whether these objects would then form a proper natural kind over which inductions to further functional properties would be grounded. That a variety of objects all exhibit the same functionalist property for the same reason would not seem, by itself, to imply that they are alike in any other respects.[24]

---

[23] This is a (correct) feature of most all views. If, for instance, a kind is a Searle-style institution, or a Millikan-style teleofunctional kind, or a Boyd-style "homeostatic property cluster" kind, inductions over it may of course still fail.

[24] Millikan 1999, p. 59.

One might think, Millikan points out, that realizations of a function in different families form a kind because they are selected to respond to the same pressures in a given ecological or evolutionary niche. But she objects:

> This idea suffers from a misunderstanding of the role of an evolutionary niche. An evolutionary niche is not something that a species finds itself in and must then respond to, but something it creates for itself as it evolves by random mutation... Pairs of unrelated species in similar niches often do display some analogous characteristics, presumably for good reason, but occasional illuminating comparisons across species are not laws about the causal powers of niches.[25]

Millikan's argument is this. Consider members of two different families, both of which reproduce under similar selection pressures. That is not enough to ensure that the members in question have *additional* functional properties in common. In a single family, common properties will be copied because they realize the function. We can rely on this in order to be able to draw further inductions. But we cannot do the same when the families are different. This, then, is an example of an argument that some putative anchoring schema is not "sticky enough." It argues that the schemas proposed by Papineau and by Macdonald, as with the one I suggested in Fig. 4.2, are insufficient to generate kinds over which we can draw inductive generalizations.

Millikan is surely right that we have to be careful about inferring similar characteristics from similar selection pressures. Her conclusion, however, is too general. Though we need to be careful, the fact that various families of organisms all solve a similar functional problem may indeed ground various sorts of unity. The fact that members of different species can swim, for instance, influences the ecosystem of predators that evolve to pursue swimmers, as opposed to nonswimmers. The presence of those predators, in turn, introduces new functional requirements on the entire class of swimmers. This establishes a link among functional properties, within that ecosystem: diverse families of swimmers are selected to exhibit new sets of functional properties in common. This, of course, is a simple example. But the linkages among functional properties arise even more easily in the social case, where we often care less about how objects perform their functions than we are about the fact that they do. So we pattern our behaviors accordingly: that is, according to what we care about or respond to. The fact that we respond to certain functional characteristics feeds back, in the social case, into objects having those functional characteristics also having other properties in common, functional and otherwise. Millikan is right that members of a kind like *pocket book* influence the ecological niches within which they are developed. But those feedback loops can serve to unify the niches across families as easily as they can divide them. Having descriptive properties in common does the same thing, in the social realm. Where there are billions of objects having some easily recognizable feature in common, that alone can ground cascades of social patterns.

That is only a quick response to Millikan's particular argument that this one sort of anchoring schema is not "sticky enough" to generate kinds. The real problem, however, is not with her particular argument, but with any argument of this form.

[25] Millikan 1999, p. 60.

It is too much to ask of *any* anchoring schema that it *guarantees* that kinds generated according to it will succeed at their intended role. No anchoring schema, for instance, will guarantee that kinds so generated will underwrite successful inductive inferences. If the circumstances are infelicitous, inductions will fail even over members of a Millikan-style reproductively established family.

It cannot be known a priori that even Millikan's schema is successful at anchoring kinds, supposing it is. Instead, its success depends on contingencies of the circumstances. How sticky an anchoring glue is depends on how congenial the environment is to that sort of glue. A glue that will fail in hot climates may be excellent in cold ones. Similarly for an anchoring schema: being related in a given way may underwrite inductions in one "climate" and fail in another. This is as true of Millikan's schema as it is of any other. The ecosystems in our world happen to be regular enough that Millikan's schema generally works, to generate kinds that figure into inductive inferences. But that is a contingent matter. As a contingent matter, other anchoring schemas work as well. An anchoring schema need only be "sticky enough" to put in place tools that are practical.[26]

The contingency, practicality, and multiplicity of anchoring schemas do not mean the end of the anchoring inquiry, nor do they devalue that inquiry. We do not understand the nature of the social world if we do not understand anchoring, any more than we understand the nature of language without understanding what makes words have the meanings they do. In fact, these observations about anchoring schemas are only the first step in reconstructing a social ontology free of commitment to one secret sauce that makes the social world exist. Slogans like "for something to be a social object, it must be thought of as a social object," or "for something to be a social object, it must be created with some functional intention in mind," are widely repeated. But they are frankly incredible, given the immense diversity of the social world and the scanty understanding we have of it. An inquiry into the anchoring of the social world, I suggest, might better begin with broad investigation of diverse cases of social kinds, and investigation into the purposes social kinds may play. With these, we have a better hope of finding the various practical schemas by which social objects, properties, and kinds are set up, such that they—as a practical matter—tend to fill their roles and purposes.

References

Austin, J.L. 1962. *How to do things with words*. Oxford: Clarendon.

Boyd, R. 1999. Kinds, complexity and multiple realization: Comments on Millikan's "historical kinds and the special sciences". *Philosophical Studies* 95(1–2): 67–98.

Dennett, D. 1991. Real patterns. *Journal of Philosophy* 88(1): 27–51.

Elder, C. 2004. *Real natures and familiar objects*. Cambridge, MA: MIT Press.

Epstein, B. 2008. The realpolitik of reference. *Pacific Philosophical Quarterly* 89: 1–20.

[26] A similar point applies to reference-fixing procedures, I argue in Epstein 2008.

Epstein, B. 2012a. Review of *Creations of the mind,* ed. Margolis and Laurence. *Mind* 121(481): 200–204.
Epstein, B. 2012b. Sortals and criteria of identity. *Analysis* 72(3): 474–478.
Epstein, B. Forthcoming. *The ant trap: Rebuilding the foundations of the social sciences.* New York: Oxford University Press.
Godfrey-Smith, P. 2004. A modern history theory of functions. *Noûs* 28: 344–362.
Kaplan, D. 1990. Words. *Proceedings of the Aristotelian Society* 64: 93–119.
Kripke, S. 1972/1980. *Naming and necessity*. Cambridge: Harvard University Press.
Macdonald, G. 1992. Reduction and evolutionary biology. In *Reduction, explanation, and realism*, ed. D. Charles and K. Lennon, 69–96. Oxford: Oxford University Press.
Millikan, R.G. 1984. *Language, thought, and other biological categories: New foundations for realism*. Cambridge: MIT Press.
Millikan, R.G. 1999. Historical kinds and the "special sciences". *Philosophical Studies* 95: 45–65.
Noonan, H. 2009. What is a one-level criterion of identity? *Analysis* 69: 274–277.
Papineau, D. 1992. Irreducibility and teleology. In *Reduction, explanation, and realism*, ed. D. Charles and K. Lennon, 45–68. Oxford: Oxford University Press.
Searle, J.R. 1995. *The construction of social reality*. New York: Free Press.
Searle, J.R. 2010. *Making the social world: The structure of human civilization*. Oxford: Oxford University Press.
Simchen, O. 2012. Necessity in reference. In *Reference and referring*, ed. W. Kabasenche, M. O'Rourke, and M. Slater, 209–234. Cambridge: MIT Press.
Stalnaker, R. 1997. Reference and necessity. In *A companion to the philosophy of language*, ed. B. Hale and C. Wright, 534–554. Oxford: Blackwell.

Chapter 5
On the Nature of Social Kinds

Francesco Guala

Abstract According to the so-called *difference thesis*, unlike natural kinds, some social kinds depend ontologically on our attitudes toward them. The difference thesis puts realism into question. It implies that these kinds can only be invented, not discovered, and that we cannot be wrong about them. In this chapter, I will challenge the difference thesis, arguing that dependence on collective propositional attitudes directed toward the kind itself is neither necessary nor sufficient for an institutional kind to exist. I will argue that it is unnecessary and insufficient even for the core cases – like money – that are usually cited in support of the thesis. If I am right, then realism holds across the board. Institutional kinds are not radically different from natural kinds: their properties ought to be discovered, and people can be massively wrong about them. Folk concepts and institutional kinds may diverge considerably, and social science is the best source of knowledge we have concerning the structure of social reality.

5.1 Kinds

A kind, according to Aristotle, is what makes an individual entity be what it is. I am what I am in virtue of belonging to the kind "human being" and of having essential properties like the capacity to think and talk to other members of my species. These properties according to Aristotle are given by nature – not by us. Scientific knowledge is knowledge of these essential properties. Science aims at discovering the nature of things.

This chapter was written while I was supported by an MIUR grant "Rientro dei Cervelli". Muhammad Ali Khalidi, Enrico Terrone, Raimo Tuomela, and two anonymous referees provided several comments that improved the presentation of the argument. Special thanks go to Mattia Gallotti for his stubborn determination to make me put these views on paper and for several discussions that have helped to clarify my ideas on social ontology over the years. As usual, I am fully responsible for all the mistakes that remain.

F. Guala (✉)
University of Milan, Milan, Italy
e-mail: francesco.guala@unimi.it

M. Gallotti and J. Michael (eds.), *Perspectives on Social Ontology and Social Cognition*, Studies in the Philosophy of Sociality 4, DOI 10.1007/978-94-017-9147-2_5,

This Aristotelian conception of kinds is held only by a minority of contemporary philosophers. The term "kind" however is still widely in use, both in metaphysics and in the philosophy of science. The language of kinds is associated with the idea that the world comes already structured before we look at it. There are natural ways of classifying things, classifications that are independent of our theories.

Some philosophers identify real kinds with the categories of our most advanced scientific theories. These "scientific" kinds, unlike other classifications, support robust and reliable inductive inferences.[1] Other philosophers in contrast emphasize essential properties and the idea that natural kinds provide a fundamental, timeless classification of the entities that populate the universe. These philosophers associate natural kindhood with objective, universal order, emphasizing their metaphysical rather than pragmatic function.[2] But beyond these disagreements most natural kind theorists share a realist orientation. The language of "kinds" is used in opposition with the language of "classes", "sets", classifications that are human-made, invented, and possibly conventional.

Obviously many categories that we use have little to do with natural kinds. I am a philosophy professor, a Juventus fan, and an investor in safe government bonds, for example. Some of these categories are scientifically relevant and are used for explanation and prediction. And yet none of these kinds is "natural": there would be no Juventus fans or cautious investors in a world where concepts like "football fan" or "owner of government bond" did not exist. This has been considered by many philosophers as deeply problematic: these *social* or *human kinds* seem to be dependent on human classificatory practices.[3]

There are different ways to construe this problem. The following thesis, I think, captures the concerns of many social theorists:

Difference thesis: unlike natural kinds, social kinds depend crucially on our attitudes toward them.

The "attitudes" here are to be understood as *propositional attitudes* held by the members of a social group, such as collective beliefs, acceptance, or recognition.[4] In a recent paper, Muhammad Ali Khalidi (2013) proposes a useful distinction between two types of attitudes: (1) attitudes directed toward the individuals that belong to a social kind and (2) attitudes directed toward the kind itself. For example, if we all believe that Mick Jagger is the leader of the Rolling Stones, then he is the band's leader (type 1 attitude, directed toward an individual token). But we may also accept

[1] The use of "scientific" instead of "natural kind" is advocated by Hacking (1991). See also Boyd (1991) and Dupré (1993).

[2] See, for example, Ellis (2001) and LaPorte (2004). For a survey of natural kind theories, cf. Bird and Tobin (2012).

[3] See, for example, Barnes (1983), Ruben (1989), Searle (1995), Hacking (1995), and Bloor (1997) – but the issue is older and the list could be longer. From now on, I will use the terms "human" and "social kind" interchangeably.

[4] There is a lively discussion in the philosophy of social action concerning the nature of collective attitudes (intentions, desires, beliefs), with some scholars defending reductionist accounts and others arguing for the irreducibility of collective intentions (see, e.g. Tollefsen 2004). In this chapter, I shall remain neutral on this issue and use the term "collective" in a generic fashion.

some conditions that define what being a bandleader amounts to, in general; for instance, we may believe that if one of the members writes all the songs of the band, then he or she is the leader. In this case, the attitude is directed toward the kind itself. As another example, consider the case of money: we consider a paper bill as money if and only if it has been issued by the Central Bank. The kind money is constituted by the attitude, and the attitude is directed toward the kind, by specifying conditions for individual tokens to belong to that kind.

Some philosophers have noticed that there are social kinds that do not fit into any of these two cases.[5] Paradigmatic examples are categories like "discriminated minority" and "inflated currency". No attitude toward either tokens or kinds is necessary for them to exist. The reason is that they are *unintended consequences* of underlying mechanisms that work quite independently of anyone having any attitude toward the tokens or the kinds. Thus inflation and racism do not require any explicit collective acceptance or beliefs in order to exist. People can be totally unaware of being racists or, conversely, discriminated against. In fact, they do not even need to have a concept or a term for racism in their vocabulary. In these cases, there does not seem to be any major difference between social and natural kinds: although the existence of these kinds presupposes the existence of human activities, no classificatory practice or categorization is required.

Still, there is general agreement that *some* social kinds are crucially dependent on collective attitudes – the attitudes are constitutive of their kindhood, so to speak. This is sufficient for the difference thesis to hold for a highly relevant portion of social reality: all that is required is that *some* social kinds are genuinely different from natural kinds. Cases that are routinely mentioned in support of the difference thesis include money, private property, prime ministers, professors, football clubs, and government bonds. For all these social entities, collective attitudes are said to be crucial. Following an established terminology introduced by John Searle (1995), I will refer to these attitude-dependent kinds as *institutional* kinds.

The existence of institutional kinds has important philosophical and practical consequences, for the difference thesis puts realism into question. It implies that some kinds can only be invented, not discovered. It suggests that we cannot be wrong about institutional kinds: whatever fits the conditions that we take to be essential for being money *must be* money.[6] In general, it suggests that the social sciences play a rather different role and have a different status from the natural sciences. Their role is not to discover but to describe and organize, perhaps occasionally even create a body of knowledge that belongs to our folk conception of reality.

These are bold claims that should not be taken lightly. In fact, I think that they should not be taken at all: in this chapter I will challenge the difference thesis, arguing that *dependence on collective propositional attitudes directed toward the kind itself is neither necessary nor sufficient for an institutional kind to exist*. I will argue that it is unnecessary and insufficient even for the core cases – like money – that are

[5] See Searle (1995), Thomasson (2003), and Khalidi (2013).

[6] For an explicit defence of these claims, see Ruben (1989) and Thomasson (2003). But many other philosophers of social science have held similar positions – see, for example, Hayek (1943: 8) and Bloor (1997: 35).

usually cited in support of the thesis. If I am right, then realism holds across the board. Institutional kinds are not radically different from natural kinds: their properties ought to be discovered, and people can be massively wrong about them. Folk concepts and institutional kinds may diverge considerably, and social science is the best source of knowledge we have concerning the structure of social reality.

My challenge to the difference thesis will proceed as follows: in the next section the claim that social reality depends on propositional attitudes will be analysed in two separate parts, stating respectively that these attitudes are necessary and that they are sufficient for a token to belong to an institutional kind. In Sect. 5.3, I shall reiterate the well-known point that the conditions that people accept for membership in a kind are often completely mistaken. But I shall also argue that this should lead us to abandon the difference thesis, contrary to what some philosophers have said. In Sect. 5.4, I will explain why collective attitudes are unnecessary for kindhood. I will do so using the example of money, although the point applies more generally: institutional kinds are constituted by systems of actions and beliefs in equilibrium, and the conditions that philosophers identify for kind membership are just coordination devices that facilitate the convergence of such actions and beliefs. In Sect. 5.5, I will elaborate this point to refute the sufficiency part of the thesis. Section 5.6 will wrap everything up with some reflections and conclusions.

5.2 The Formula

What sort of claim am I going to challenge, exactly? In the previous section, following Khalidi (2013), I have distinguished two versions of the difference thesis. The first one says that unlike natural kinds institutional kinds are constituted by propositional attitudes directed toward their individual members.[7] Formally, the claim can be represented as follows:

$$\mathrm{X\,is\,K} \leftrightarrow \mathrm{CA}\left(\mathrm{X\,is\,K}\right).$$

In this formula, X is a token entity that is a member of kind K. CA is a collective attitude like belief, acceptance, or recognition.

The second version of the difference thesis states that social kinds are constituted by attitudes toward the kinds themselves or, more precisely, toward the conditions (properties) that make each individual X a member of K:[8]

$$\mathrm{X\,is\,K} \leftrightarrow \left[\mathrm{CA}\left(\mathrm{X\,is\,K\,if\,C}\right) \& \mathrm{C}\right].$$

[7] For ease of presentation, I will not keep saying "unlike natural kinds", except when it is relevant.

[8] The attitude in principle could be directed directly toward the properties that constitute the kind – for example, CA(K has P). In practice, social kinds are usually constituted by physical tokens (pieces of paper or metal, for instance) that satisfy certain special conditions. Hence the formula CA(X is K if C). This version is shaped on Searle's (1995) formula for constitutive rules: "X counts as Y in C" – the main difference is that C is a condition of satisfaction rather than a domain condition as in Searle's formula.

The notation is the same as before, except that now the attitude involves crucially a set of conditions C.[9] The first formula arguably depends on the second one, because implicitly or explicitly the community members must apply criteria to decide which tokens are to be accepted as members of K and which ones are not. By stating the conditions C, the second formula simply makes the criteria explicit. As an example, take the paradigmatic case of money: a particular piece of paper is money if and only if we accept that in order to count as money a paper bill must be issued by the Central Bank, and this bill has been issued by the Central Bank. To simplify the discussion in the course of this chapter, I will refer primarily to the second version of this formula. This should have no significant consequences since everything that I will say will be applicable to the other version as well.

Notice that the difference thesis does not merely say that institutional kinds depend on collective beliefs or attitudes. The claim is much more specific: the attitude in the formula must be directed toward K, by stating conditions of kindhood, that is, by specifying the properties that make X belong to K.[10] This is important because the simple dependence thesis (the claim that social kinds depend on collective beliefs) distinguishes social from natural kinds in a trivial way only: to say that propositional attitudes figure among the properties or mechanisms that constitute social kinds does not challenge realism. Social science deals with phenomena that depend on mental states, just as biology deals with phenomena that depend on chemical substances. This is rather trivial and philosophically insignificant in itself. A conventionalist or constructionist account makes a much more interesting and contentious claim: it says that institutional kinds are constituted by beliefs *about the kinds themselves*.

For analytical purposes, it will be useful to break the formula in two parts (Guala 2010: 248–9). The first part states that collective acceptance is *necessary* for social kindhood:

$$\mathrm{X\,is\,K} \rightarrow \left[\mathrm{CA}\left(\mathrm{X\,is\,K\,if\,C}\right) \,\&\, \mathrm{C}\right].$$

The second part states that collective acceptance is jointly *sufficient*, with the realization of C, to make X an institutional entity of type K:

$$\left[\mathrm{CA}\left(\mathrm{X\,is\,K\,if\,C}\right) \,\&\, \mathrm{C}\right] \rightarrow \mathrm{X\,is\,K}.$$

In the sections that follow, I will challenge them both, starting from the necessity statement.

[9] Notice that to accept the conditions is not sufficient, in itself, to guarantee that X is K: it must also be the case that the Cs are instantiated.

[10] This is similar to the distinction between the "Object-General" and the "Object-Specific Thesis" drawn by Edouard Machery in his chapter.

5.3 Necessity

As we have seen, there are clear examples of social kinds that do not require collective attitudes (inflation, unemployment). So is this part of the argument redundant? No, because I want to argue for a stronger claim here. I want to argue that collective attitudes are unnecessary even for those cases – institutional kinds – that are usually considered paradigmatic for the difference thesis. The point is not merely that there are exceptions, but rather that there are no "core" cases at all.

I will proceed in two steps: first, I will argue that we can all be wrong about the nature of *any* institutional kind. This suggests that our collective attitudes are strictly speaking irrelevant for the existence of kinds. In fact – and this is my second step – I will argue that the conditions C that are usually taken to be necessary for kindhood are actually redundant and can be dispensed with. For this reason, what people believe or accept regarding K is not constitutive of institutional reality.

The first point is far from new. It is a philosophical and sociological platitude that people are often unaware of the true conditions of existence of institutional kinds. In fact, they sometimes hold massively incorrect beliefs about them. People may believe that the king is divinely ordained or that money is anchored with a commodity base (e.g. the bullion stored in the safe of the Central Bank). According to John Searle, for example,

> the process of creation of institutional facts may proceed without the participants being conscious that it is happening according to this form.... In the very evolution of the institution [of, say, money] the participants need not be consciously aware of the form of the collective intentionality by which they are imposing functions on objects. In the course of consciously buying, selling, exchanging, etc., they may simply evolve institutional facts. Furthermore, in extreme cases they may accept the imposition of function only because of some related theory, which may not even be true. They may believe that it is money only if it is "backed by gold" or that it is marriage only if it is sanctified by God or that so and so is the king only because he is divinely authorized. (Searle 1995: 47–48)

Searle's caution is motivated in part by a desire to hedge the acceptance theory from cheap counterexamples. Clearly many institutional facts are not consciously accepted as such – at least by most of us, most of the time – so the very notion of collective attitude must be formulated in such a way as to account for this fact. Collective acceptance must be turned into a weaker concept.

One solution is to interpret "acceptance" broadly, to include any kind of implicit agreement with a rule. Since any pattern or practice can be described by a rule, there is always a rule that can be said to be implicitly "accepted" or "recognized" by the members of the relevant community. But now the thesis sounds suspiciously tautological, and the explanatory weight of the propositional attitudes becomes dubious. One could say that two gorillas are husband and wife, for instance, because their behaviour fits the rule "X and Y are married if they groom each other". But no propositional attitude toward the kind "marriage" plays any substantial role in the explanation of gorilla behaviour, and supporters of the difference thesis surely should not be happy with a cheap victory of this sort.[11]

5.4 Coordination

To say that collective attitudes and conditions of acceptance do not play an essential role in the constitution of institutional kinds is not to say that they are useless or that they never play any role in the maintenance of the kinds themselves. Such a statement would be exaggerated and ungenerous to those philosophers who have correctly identified collective attitudes as an important cogwheel in the creation and maintenance of social reality. But what is their role exactly?

The role of collective attitudes – when they do play a role – is causal. Accepting a set of conditions C facilitates the formation of mutually consistent beliefs about the behaviour of a large number of individuals seeking coordination. Another way to put it is to say that the conditions we impose for the membership of institutional kinds are essentially *coordination devices*.

Why do we accept worthless paper bills in exchange for valuable goods or services? I accept euro bills as payment because I am confident that I will be able to use them later to purchase other goods. The people who will take my bills will do so for the same reason: they will take them as payment because they will believe that others will take them, and so forth. Of course in principle different entities could fulfil the function of medium of exchange; but the process works a lot more smoothly if we all accept the same things and we all share the same beliefs concerning what will be accepted in the future.

A primary role of the Central Bank is to ensure coordination among traders by enforcing a monopoly on the issuing of money. The bank prints bills that will be used by everyone, because everyone believes that the others believe – and so forth – that they will continue to be used as media of trade. If an entity X (a paper bill) fulfils the condition C (being issued by the Central Bank), then it counts as money. But this means only that being issued by the Central Bank makes us very confident that the bill will be accepted in the future.

The whole thing looks suspiciously magical. Why should C matter? What is so special with a piece of paper that carries the stamp of the Central Bank? In fact there is more to say about money, a lot of properties or conditions that philosophers usually fail to mention but that are absolutely crucial to understand the nature of this

[11] Thomasson (2003) endorses a "non-cognitivist" interpretation of collective attitudes similar to the one sketched in the text and uses it to defend infallibilism about social kinds. I have criticized the infallibilism of Thomasson and others (e.g. Ruben 1989) in Guala (2010).

institution. But to know what these properties are, we must turn to social science and, in particular, to economics.[12]

The conditions C merely have a facilitating role. To function properly, a medium of exchange must fulfil other conditions that are *not* included in C. The key one as we have seen is that everyone must believe that others will want to hold the paper bills in the future. But this belief should better not hang up in the air: people must have good reasons (incentives) to hold currency. The state plays an important role at this point: it can guarantee a certain level of demand for the currency in the future, via taxation. If the state will only accept paper bills issued by the Central Bank as payment, then we can be confident that in the future people will have to hold at least some official currency for tax purposes. This is true of course only to the extent that the state is strong and stable and will have the means to collect taxes. So, unsurprisingly, the strength of a currency is strictly linked with the political strength of the state.

The state collects paper bills via taxation and puts them back into the economy by paying salaries to the employees of the public sector. If they meddle with the latter part of the cycle, as we know, governments and central banks can devalue the currency, creating inflation. In extreme cases of hyperinflation, a currency may even become worthless paper. This is because in order to function properly a currency must be a reliable *store of value.* Standard economics textbooks remind us that the store of value condition is a fundamental presupposition for a currency to work as a medium of exchange.[13] And this will be true only if the quantity of currency is relatively stable. So it seems that fulfilling conditions C is neither necessary nor sufficient. A cigarette can be money even though clearly it has not been issued by the Central Bank, and a bill that has been issued by the Central Bank may fail to work as medium of exchange.

5.5 Sufficiency

We now have the conceptual tools to debunk the second plank of the collective attitude formula. Notice that the store of value property – and other properties that back it up, like the stability of the quantity of money – is not included in C. But then being issued by the Central Bank is not what makes a token bill a member of the kind "money". The conditions C merely coordinate our beliefs that individual paper bills fulfilling certain conditions will be accepted as means of payment in the future. And even this coordination function can only be performed under certain happy

[12] Philosophers sometimes state bluntly that economics currently lacks a theory of money – which is plainly false and unnecessarily offensive. Smit et al. (2011) explain in non-technical terms what money is, from the point of view of economic theory, and how the economic account relates to philosophical accounts based on collective attitudes.

[13] See, for example, Dornbusch and Fischer (1994: 374).

conditions. Money is constituted by a system of actions and beliefs about actions in equilibrium, not by arbitrary conventions concerning the issuing of paper bills.

Of course people may still collectively decide to *call* the bills that are issued by the Central Bank "money" even though the equilibrium has collapsed. Imagine a currency that has been completely devalued: is it still money? In a superficial sense it is. Perhaps when people see a bill, they say "it's money", even though they do not actually use it for trade. Suppose that they prefer to use cigarettes as a medium of exchange. When asked what is that thing they hold in their pockets, they say "this is a cigarette", not "this is money". But for all interesting purposes, the cigarettes are money and the bill is just paper.

The point is that one thing is to be recognized as money in a system of folk classification; quite another is to *be* money. The former does not imply the latter, contrary to what the sufficiency thesis suggests. Folk classificatory practices are in principle quite irrelevant. What matters is not what type of attitude people have toward a certain class of entities (the conditions they *think* the entities ought to satisfy in order to belong to that class), but what they do with them in the course of social interaction. The relevant attitudes, in other words, are directed toward the attitudes of other people.

In a recent paper, Guala and Hindriks (2013) have argued that general terms like "money", "private property", "professor", etc., simply summarize bundles of actions or strategies that are associated with each term. These actions are equilibrium solutions of complex games of social interaction. One such action, for example, is described by a rule saying that "if the bill has been issued by the Central Bank, then you should accept it as payment". Another is that "if you have a land registry certificate in your name, then you can resell your house" and so forth. In simple coordination problems, a single rule will suffice ("if you are in Britain, then drive on the left"). But when the actions are numerous and complex, it is useful to cluster and subsume under the umbrella of a single theoretical term: a new concept (money, private property, professorship) is introduced for economy of thought.[14] For example:

1. If a house is registered in your name at the Land Registry office, then it is your property.

The concept "property" in turn implies a large set of actions (things that you can do with your property).

2. If a house is your property, then you can sell it, refurbish it, rent it out, destroy it, etc.

The "etc." at the end of the list is important: one reason why we use the term "property" is that it summarizes all the things that you can and cannot do with a house that is registered in your name. When the list is finite and short, as in the case of traffic, there is no need to introduce a new term. (That is why we do not have a

[14] The idea of treating constitutive formulae as rules for the introduction of theoretical terms was originally developed by Hindriks (2009). In Guala and Hindriks (2013), we integrate this idea with game-theoretic notions of equilibrium and correlation device.

special term for the institution of driving on the left-hand side of the road.) But in general it is possible to formulate a set of rules without using the theoretical term. In the case of property, we can eliminate the theoretical term like this:

3. If a house is registered in your name at the Land Registry office, then you can sell it, refurbish it, rent it out, destroy it, etc.

Other social terms like money are also dispensable:

1′. If a bill has been issued by the Central Bank, then it is money.
2′. If it is money, then it can be used to purchase commodities, it can be deposited in a bank account, it can be lent to a friend, etc.

Eliminating "money" we obtain:

3′. If a bill has been issued by the Central Bank, then it can be used to purchase commodities, it can be deposited in a bank account, it can be lent to a friend, etc.

So to the extent that theoretical terms like "property", "money", or "professor" refer to something real, they refer to profiles of actions. The real content is not in the C conditions ("issued by the Central Bank"): it is in the strategies ("accept it as payment") that are associated with the theoretical term ("money"). The kind money ultimately is nothing but this set of actions and the related set of expectations. The C conditions are useful in so far as they simplify our decisions: they are *coordination devices* that help us identify quickly and without lengthy inspection an appropriate set of actions in the given circumstances. (Should I accept a piece of paper as payment? Yes, because it has been issued by the Central Bank.) But to focus on the C conditions as what makes something a member of K is a perceptual mistake. It mistakes the coordination device for the system of actions and expectations that a social institution is.[15]

In some cases, of course, people can dispense with a coordination device. If they endorse a correct theory of the kind in question – of the properties and mechanisms that make X a member of K – then knowledge of these properties will be sufficient for kindhood. But this is hardly a relief for the difference thesis, because the collective attitude toward the kind itself becomes redundant. To realize why this is the case, let us consider a simplified theory of money. Suppose that moneyhood depends exclusively on the power of the state to levy taxes. Suppose that knowledge of this power is sufficient to convince every citizen that the bills issued by the Central Bank will continue to be requested by others in the future. If everybody believes that the use of a certain currency (X) will be enforced by the state, then X is money:

$$CA\left[\text{X will be used to pay taxes}\right] \to \text{X is money.}$$

The formula only says that people have a certain attitude toward future uses of X. It does not say that they ought to collectively accept a theory of what constitutes

[15] Mallon (2003) discusses the role that social kinds play as devices to stabilize behaviour ("coordination devices", in the language that I have used in this chapter).

money. Of course they might endorse such a theory, in which case the formula could be expanded as follows:

$$CA\begin{bmatrix}\text{(X is money if and only if X will be used to pay taxes)}\\ \text{and (X will be used to pay taxes)}\end{bmatrix} \rightarrow \text{X is money.}$$

The expanded formula is implied by the former, compact one. But notice that the first proposition between brackets (X is money if and only if X will be needed to pay taxes) is redundant: the rest of the formula already states the conditions for X to be money: X is money if people believe that it will be used to pay taxes. The compact formula does not support the difference thesis, however, because it does not involve any attitude toward the kind itself. It does not challenge realism, and it does not distinguish institutional from natural kinds along any philosophically interesting dimension. Endorsing a theory of money certainly helps in a number of ways, but it is not sufficient to constitute money.

5.6 A Farewell to the Difference Thesis

I have argued that holding propositional attitudes (of collective acceptance, belief, or recognition) toward an institutional kind is neither necessary nor sufficient for the existence of the kind itself. It is unnecessary, because people may ignore the true instantiation conditions (what really makes X belong to K) and therefore may be wrong about the nature of the kind. It is insufficient, because being aware of the true conditions does not guarantee that the token really is an instance of K. There are other properties that constitute institutional kindhood, and such properties do not involve collective attitudes toward the kind itself. The conditions C typically play a coordination role that – albeit useful and important in a number of cases – has scarce ontological relevance.

If the arguments I have presented are sound, then it follows that the differences between institutional and natural kinds are less important than many philosophers have thought. The characteristic properties of institutional kinds ought to be discovered, just as in the natural realm. Membership in an institutional kind, moreover, is not a purely conventional matter. Conventions do play a role, but only in the choice of the devices that coordinate actions and beliefs. The choice of these devices may be arbitrary, within certain limits, but it is not essential for the constitution of institutional kinds.

The truly important properties – those that turn a token piece of paper into money, for example – are not conventional at all: they involve facts like people's beliefs about the likelihood that others will accept paper bills in exchange for goods and services. These beliefs in turn depend on hard facts like the number of bills circulating in the economy or mechanisms and dispositions like the enforcement power of the state. Collective attitudes toward the kind itself are neither necessary nor sufficient for the constitution of money.

There is a weaker, trivial sense in which conventionalism holds at a purely linguistic level. We cannot be wrong in *calling* X money, if X fulfils all the conditions C that we accept as sufficient for the sort of things that the folk call "money". Our choice of language, or how we classify things for the purposes of everyday dealings and communications, is indeed a conventional matter. But what *is* money – the nature of K and membership in K – is not conventional at all. Fulfilling the conditions C that we take to be essential for moneyhood does not turn X into an instance of money, because other conditions must be fulfilled. And, conversely, many things that do not fulfil the collectively accepted conditions may indeed be money.

Let us bid farewell to the difference thesis, then, without any regrets, because what counts as an institutional kind is independent of our propositional attitudes toward the kind itself.

References

Barnes, S.B. 1983. Social life as bootstrapped induction. *Sociology* 17: 524–545.

Bird, A. and Tobin, E. 2012. Natural kinds. In *The Stanford Encyclopedia of Philosophy*, ed. E.N. Zalta, http://plato.stanford.edu/archives/win2012/entries/natural-kinds/.

Bloor, D. 1997. *Wittgenstein, rules, and institutions*. London: Routledge.

Boyd, R. 1991. Realism, anti-foundationalism, and the enthusiasm for natural kinds. *Philosophical Studies* 61: 127–148.

Dornbusch, R., and S. Fischer. 1994. *Macroeconomics*, 6th ed. New York: McGraw-Hill.

Dupré, J. 1993. *The disorder of things*. Harvard: Harvard University Press.

Ellis, B. 2001. *Scientific essentialism*. Cambridge: Cambridge University Press.

Guala, F. 2010. Infallibilism and human kinds. *Philosophy of the Social Sciences* 40: 244–264.

Guala, F. and Hindriks, F. 2013. *A unified social ontology*. DEMM working paper 2013–2020. Milan: University of Milan.

Hacking, I. 1991. A tradition of natural kinds. *Philosophical Studies* 61: 109–126.

Hacking, I. 1995. The looping effect of human kinds. In *Causal cognition: A multidisciplinary debate*, ed. A. Premack, 351–383. Oxford: Clarendon.

Hayek, F.A. 1943. The facts of the social sciences. *Ethics* 54: 1–13.

Hindriks, F. 2009. Constitutive rules, language, and ontology. *Erkenntnis* 71: 253–275.

Khalidi, M.A. 2013. Three kinds of social kinds. *Philosophy and Phenomenological Research*. doi:10.1111/phpr.12020, online first.

LaPorte, J. 2004. *Natural kinds and conceptual change*. Cambridge: Cambridge University Press.

Mallon, R. 2003. Social construction, social roles, and stability. In *Socializing metaphysics*, ed. F.F. Schmitt. Lanham: Rowman and Littlefield.

Ruben, D. 1989. Realism in the social sciences. In *Dismantling truth*, ed. H. Lawson and L. Appignanesi, 58–75. London: Weidenfeld and Nicolson.

Searle, J. 1995. *The construction of social reality*. London: Penguin.

Smit, J.P., F. Buekens, and S. du Plessis. 2011. What is money? An alternative to Searle's institutional facts. *Economics and Philosophy* 27: 1–22.

Thomasson, A. 2003. Realism and human kinds. *Philosophy and Phenomenological Research* 68: 580–609.

Tollefsen, D. 2004. Collective intentionality. In *Internet Encyclopedia of Philosophy*, ed. J. Fieser and B. Dowden. http://www.iep.utm.edu/coll-int/.

Chapter 6
Normativity of the Background: A Contextualist Account of Social Facts

Enrico Terrone and Daniela Tagliafico

Abstract The ontology of society built by John Searle consists of two parts. The first concerns the definition of a social fact as the establishment of a status function by means of collective intentionality and declarative speech acts. The second concerns "the Background," that is, a set of capacities supporting the whole apparatus of status functions, intentionality, and speech acts. Yet in Searle's discourse, the Background comes after the fact, when the social reality is already constructed. By contrast, this chapter argues that in order to explain what a social fact is, the Background should take part in the formula that summarizes the establishment of the status function. The Background is to be characterized in terms of social practices establishing implicit norms that precede and ground the explicit rules instituted by intentionality and language. Therefore, the original formula for the constitution of social facts, namely, "X counts as Y in C," should be rephrased as "'X-in-C counts as Y"—and C should be related to the Background. Finally, this chapter argues that this formulation can address the problematic case of "freestanding Y terms," that is, status functions lacking physical bearers. The solution lies in conceiving of X no longer as a mere object but as a causal-historical process that embodies a status function Y in virtue of its being sustained by the Background within a context of social practices.

Both in *The Construction of Social Reality* (1995) and in *Making the Social World* (2010), the ontology of society built by John Searle consists of a theory in the foreground and a theory in the background. The theory in the foreground (Chap. 1–6 in 1995, Chap. 1–5 in 2010) concerns the definition of a social fact as the establishment of a status function by means of collective intentionality and declarative speech acts. In the 1995 version, Searle summarizes such a theory in the

E. Terrone (✉) • D. Tagliafico
University of Turin, Torino, Italy
e-mail: enriterr@gmail.com

M. Gallotti and J. Michael (eds.), *Perspectives on Social Ontology and Social Cognition*, Studies in the Philosophy of Sociality 4, DOI 10.1007/978-94-017-9147-2_6,

formula: "the concrete entity X counts as bearer of the status function Y in the context C," while in 2010 the formula is simply: "let there be the status function Y in the context C." Conversely, the theory in the background of Searle's social ontology (Chap. 6 in 1995, Chap. 7 in 2010) concerns what he calls "the Background," that is, a set of capacities supporting the whole apparatus of status functions, intentionality, and speech acts.

In both essays the Background comes after the fact, when the social reality is already constructed and the social world made. The Background only completes a figure that has previously been drawn independently of it. By contrast, in this chapter we will argue that in order to explain what a social fact is and how it is constituted, the notion of the Background has to be introduced first and it has to take part in the formula that summarizes the establishment of the status function. For this purpose, we will analyze the notion of a Background by focusing on its different characterizations and roles in the 1995 and the 2010 versions of Searle's social ontology. We will show that in 1995 the Background is appropriately characterized but its role is problematic, whereas in 2010 the role is better focused but the characterization is problematic.

We will argue that the main role of the Background is to enable the normative dimensions of collective intentionality, language, and social facts. Therefore, the Background neither can be described as a mere neurophysiological mechanism of rule reflection, as in Searle's 1995 account (it would lose its normative role), nor can be characterized as having a shared intentional content, as in Searle's 2010 account (its foundation of collective intentionality would be circular). Following Wittgenstein (1953) and Brandom (1994), we will propose to characterize the Background in terms of social practices establishing implicit norms that ground explicit rules instituted by intentionality and language. But if the Background can establish norms, then it does not simply support the construction of social reality; it directly constitutes social facts. Therefore, the general formula for the constitution of social facts has to be rephrased in the following terms: "X-in-C counts as Y."[1] Here, the context C is not a mere backdrop of the relation between the concrete entity X and the status function Y. Rather, C is what makes X count as Y, and it does that by means of the normativity of the Background.

Finally, we will argue that the formula "X-in-C counts as Y" can address the issue that primarily motivated Searle's shift from the 1995 formula to the 2010 one: the case of "freestanding Y terms" raised by Smith (2003). The formula "X-in-C counts as Y" addresses this issue by conceiving of X no longer as a mere object but as a causal-historical process that embodies a status function Y in virtue of its being sustained by the Background within a context of social practices.

[1] Searle uses the symbol "Y" to indicate both the status function and its bearer (cf. 1995, p. 46). In this sense, one could equally say "X-in-C counts as Y = the leader" or "X-in-C counts as bearer of Y = leadership." Instead, if one intends Y as strictly referring to the status function, then the general formula should be more explicitly rephrased: "X-in-C counts as bearer of Y."

6.1 The Role of the Background in *The Construction of Social Reality*

In the wake of his previous accounts (1983 and 1992), in 1995 Searle conceives of the Background as a set of capacities that offer a non-intentional foundation for intentionality: "Intentional states function only given a set of Background capacities that do not themselves consist in intentional phenomena [...] It is important to see that when we talk about the Background we are talking about a certain category of neurophysiological causation" (1995: 129). Intentional states are essentially underdetermined and their contents need an interpretation. Only the Background can interpret these contents so as to definitively determine their conditions of satisfaction. Since the Background is essentially non-intentional, its interpreting of intentional contents is not an intentional act like ordinary interpretations, but rather some sort of mechanism.

The main task of the Background in social reality is to make rule following broader and more efficient. This task requires an already established institutional system of rules that ensures normativity.[2] The Background allows institutional rules to be followed by those members of the society who do not have a representation of these rules in their mind. Rules are first institutionally established and then "reflected" (Searle 1995: 142) by the members of the society by means of their Background capacities. But how, exactly, does such a "reflection" take place? In what sense are some Background capacities "sensitive to the rule structure" (Searle 1995: 145)?

In the 1995 book, these questions remain unanswered. We only know that the Background depends upon the rules it must reflect, and Searle's social ontology is thus exposed to Wittgenstein's skeptical paradox: "no course of action could be determined by a rule, because every course of action can be made out to accord with the rule" (1953: §201).[3] In other words, when a certain rule R1 must be applied, it may be applied either correctly or incorrectly. But how can we, as agents, correctly apply R1? And how can we, as observers, assess the correctness of an application of R1? We need a meta-rule R2 (what Wittgenstein calls "a rule of interpretation") that relates R1 to its correct applications. Yet R2 has to be applied in turn; therefore, we need a meta-rule R3 telling us how to apply R2, and so on. The final result is an infinite regress.

---

[2] "There is a socially created normative component in the institutional structure, and this is accounted for *only* by the fact that the institutional structure is a structure of rules" (Searle 1995: 146, our emphasis). Schmitz summarizes Searle's point as "the assumption that normativity could not be socially created except by creating an institutional rule structure" (2013: 115).

[3] In developing this paradox, Kripke argues that it threatens the whole apparatus of rules, meanings, concepts, functions, and so forth, since there is no way to solve "the problem of how our finite minds can give rules that are supposed to apply to an infinity of cases" (1982: 54), nor can we appeal to more fundamental rules, because "the skeptical move can be repeated at the more 'basic' level also" (1982: 17).

Let us consider as an example the constitutive rule R1 establishing that a certain kind of object issued by the Bureau of Engraving and Printing under the authority of the US Treasury counts as money (cf. Searle 1995: 45–46). First, we need a meta-rule R2 that establishes how to correctly apply R1. Searle characterizes this need as:

> a puzzle about how we can define 'money,' if part of the definition is 'being thought of, or regarded as, or believed to be money.' I asked: does this not lead to a circularity or infinite regress in any attempt to define the word, or even to give an explanation of the concept of money? But the resolution of the paradox is quite simple. The word 'money' marks one node in a whole network of practices, the practices of owning, buying, selling, earning, paying for services, paying off debts, etc. (1995: 52)

From this perspective, we can conceive of the meta-rule R2 as specifying that the rule R1 (which establishes that an object satisfying certain conditions counts as money) can be correctly applied to "owning, buying, selling, earning, paying for services, paying off debts, etc." But, unlike what Searle argues, the infinite regress is not stopped, because we need in turn a meta-rule R3 that specifies what are the cases of "owning, buying, selling, earning, paying for services, paying off debts, etc." which the meta-rule R2 can be correctly applied to. Once we will have established R3, we will need a meta-rule R4 specifying how to correctly apply R3, and so on.

6.2 The Background and the Skeptical Paradox

Searle (2002) explicitly addresses Wittgenstein's skeptical paradox by arguing that the Background can stop the infinite regress by providing a basic non-intentional application that does not require rules of application in turn: "It is just a fact about our practices, about the way we were brought up to behave, that we count certain sorts of things as correctly applying a rule and others not [...] It is always possible to offer alternative interpretations of any intentional content. But what fixes the interpretation in actual practice, in real life, is what I have elsewhere called 'the Background'" (Searle 2002: 264).

In addressing the skeptical paradox, Searle thus relates social practices ("the way we were brought up to behave") to the Background.[4] Yet our practices and the way we were brought up to behave are—at least partly—*in the world*, whereas the Background, as a set of capacities constituted by a certain category of neurophysiological causation, is definitely *in the head*. How can a neurophysiological mechanism in the head exactly match a practice in the world? Searle implicitly answers to this question by maintaining that the

[4] In his analysis of Searle's social ontology, Runde points out this connection by observing that "the Background is shaped, in some cases decisively so, by the particular context and culture in which we grow up" (2002: 17). According to Viskovatoff, Searle introduces the notion of a Background "because intentionality cannot produce itself, but is made possible by non-intentional rule-following, so he needs a concept like that of practices" (2002: 70); in this sense, the Background works as "a device to graft the idea of social practices [...] into an individualist, internalist theory of intentionality" (2003: 71).

Background "is sensitive" to the practices taking place in the world and "reflects" them by means of the appropriate mechanisms of neurophysiological causation. Since the Background is essentially a causal system, its "being sensitive" and its "reflecting social practices" must be causal processes. So the Background is just the neurophysiological mechanism whereby social practices bear upon intentionality—the "Trojan horse" of social practices in the domain of intentionality. The "internal Background" is the way in which our brain implements the "external Background" constituted by social practices. Speaking of the Background as internal to the head, as Searle does, seems to be just shorthand for the Background as a system of social practices.

Some of the Background practices are indeed derived by intentionally established rules, as Searle claims in his 1995 book. Yet intentionality in turn needs the Background in order to establish rules. To avoid circularity, there must be some non-intentional, intrinsically normative social practice that, by constituting the Background, enables intentionality to establish new rules, which the Background itself will eventually reflect afterward. In order to fully face the skeptical paradox, the Background has to ground not only rule following but also rule establishing. Without the Background fixing the interpretation, the "legislators" cannot grasp and share the content of the rule they are explicitly establishing. Therefore, they would have no means of really establishing the rule.[5]

A Searlian reply could consist of appealing to the distinction between a superficial "local Background" that reflects social practices and a biological "deep Background" that is hardwired in human minds (1983: 143–144). The biological "deep Background" would ground the establishing of the rules, which would afterward be "reflected" by the social local Background. Yet, it is hard to explain how a complex, interactive process such as the establishing of a rule could rely on an exclusively biological—and not at all social—Background. Neurophysiological mechanisms alone are not sufficient for establishing a rule, that is, for establishing whether something that occurs has to be taken as correct or incorrect, since there are no correct or incorrect occurrences in the causal domain of biology: all that occurs is always biologically appropriate simply by occurring.[6] In order to underpin the establishing of a rule, the Background must be something more than a mere physiological facilitator of intentionality.

In this sense, a foundation of normativity that makes reference only to the biological "deep Background" must face objections that are rooted in Hume's "is-ought problem" and in Moore's "naturalistic fallacy." Searle (1964) argues that we can overcome the naturalistic fallacy and derive an "ought" from an "is" by means of the illocutionary force of speech acts. Yet speech acts in turn require normative

[5] In Brandom's terms, "the conclusion of the regress argument is that there is a need for a *pragmatist* conception of norms—a notion of primitive correctnesses of performance *implicit* in *practice* that precede and are presupposed by their *explicit* formulation in *rules* and *principles*" (1984: 21).

[6] A similar point is made by Stahl: "Someone who fails to follow a rule does not just deviate from a descriptive regularity which we supposed her behaviour to exhibit, but we can also say that she acts *incorrectly* (Searle 1995: 146). This normative aspect of action cannot be integrated into a story of mere causation" (2013: 129–130).

practices. You cannot perform a speech act in a merely biological world. In order to perform a speech act, you already need a basic layer of social agreement.[7] Hard-wired biological skills are arguably necessary for somebody to take part in such basic practices, but the naturalistic fallacy shows that the normativity of these very practices cannot be explained only in terms of the built-in capacities of the practitioners.[8] Neither can such a normativity be explained in terms of speech acts, since they in turn rely upon this basic normative layer. In order to characterize this layer, we need to refer not only to neurophysiological mechanisms but also to basic pragmatic devices, for example, expectations and sanctions, whereby normativity emerges from social interactions of individuals endowed with peculiar biological capacities. From this perspective, it is the Background itself, ultimately understood as an inextricable intertwining of basic practices and neurophysiological mechanisms, that allows us to derive an "ought" from an "is."[9]

6.3 The Role of the Background in *Making the Social World*

In the 2010 version of Searle's social ontology, the Background seems to play a direct role not only in rule following but also in rule establishing. As intentionality can construct social facts, so does the Background. On the one hand, Searle now claims that the Background can constitute power relations and norms of behavior, and since power relations and norms of behavior are what status functions are made of, it follows that the Background can create social facts on its own.[10] On the other hand, Searle introduces an "intentionality constraint" according to which

[7] As Gebauer puts it, "in illocutionary speech acts, the self acts as a person who is socially created and institutionally anchored in a social context" (2000: 74).

[8] As pointed out by Tomasello and his collaborators, a psychological skill like "joint attention" with its underlying neurophysiological "infrastructure" can play a key role in rule following. But joint attention in turn needs some contextual normative support: "Suppose that an adult points to an opaque bucket for the infant. If he does this out of the blue, the infant cannot know whether he is pointing to direct her attention to the container's color, its material, its contents, or any other of myriad possibilities. However, if they are playing a hiding-finding game together, and *in this context* the adult points to the bucket, the infant will very likely infer that he is pointing to inform her of the location of the hidden object. Fourteen month-old infants make just such an inference in this situation […], but chimpanzees and other apes do not" (Tomasello and Carpenter 2007: 122, our emphasis).

[9] A similar point is made by Schmitz: "This is a basic kind of normativity and it does not depend on the presence of rules. It is not essential that adults who know the rules give the feedback as in Searle's baseball example. It is sufficient that players react normatively to one another. Their emotional reactions are primitive forms of directives and evaluations. In this way, common (shared, collective) background dispositions, common skills, habits, and tendencies are established." (2013: 117–118).

[10] "Some (not all) of the Background practices and presuppositions can constitute sets of power relations […] The Background and Network, as I have defined them, contain, among other things, a set of norms of behavior" (Searle 2010: 156).

any exercise of power must have an intentional content.[11] To sum up, the Background works as an exercise of power, all exercises of power have intentional content; therefore, the Background has intentional content. That is why—we believe—Searle concludes that "in the case of Background power, like the criminal law, we have a standing power and a standing intentional content" (2010: 158). Yet that seems to be quite a puzzling move: how can the Background, originally characterized as the non-intentional foundation of intentionality, now have "a standing intentional content"?

There is no explicit answer in Searle's text, just an implicit one that we can try to make explicit. In 2010, though not in 1995, Searle distinguishes between the Background and the Network: they both support intentionality, but the Network is intentional, whereas the Background is not. The Network is constituted by all the "surrounding" intentional states that contribute to the conditions of satisfaction of a given intentional content, whereas the Background is constituted by capacities that definitively determine these conditions of satisfaction so as to enable intentionality to work. For example, the Network of the intentional content "if the traffic light is red, you have to stop" includes beliefs about the functioning of traffic lights, cars, and brakes, whereas the corresponding Background is an underlying blind mechanism that allows us to directly move from the conscious vision of a red light and its unconscious surrounding beliefs to the action of braking.

Following Searle's declaration that he "will use 'Background' as short for both Network and Background" (2010: 155), we can make sense of the claim that the Background satisfies "the intentionality constraint" by considering the term "Background" as referring not only to the Background, strictly understood, but also to the Network. Yet this solution contradicts Searle's most sophisticated account of the Background, contained in *The Rediscovery of the Mind* (1992), which underlies both the 1995 social ontology and the 2002 discussion of the skeptical paradox. In that text, Searle recalls that in his earlier view, he was thinking of the mind as containing an inventory of mental states but also admits that he was mistaken:

> I now think the real mistake was to suppose that there is an inventory of mental states, some conscious, some unconscious. Both language and culture tend to force this picture on us. We think of memory as a storehouse of propositions and images, as a kind of big library or filing cabinet of representations. But we should think of memory rather as a *mechanism* for generating current performance, including conscious thoughts and actions, based on past experience. The thesis of the Background has to be rewritten to get rid of the presupposition of the mind as a collection, an inventory, of mental phenomena, because *the only occurrent reality of the mental as mental is consciousness*.
>
> The belief in an occurrent reality that consists of unconscious mental states, and that is distinct from Background capacities, is an illusion based largely on the grammar of our language. Even when Jones is asleep, we say that he believes Bush is president and that he knows the rules of French grammar. So we think lying in there in his brain, sleeping too, are his belief that Bush is president and his knowledge of French. But in fact all his brain contains is a set of neuronal structures, whose workings at present are largely unknown, that enable him to think and act, when he gets around to it. (Searle 1992: 187, our emphasis)

[11] "The concept of power is logically tied to the concept of the intentional exercise of power [...] No intentionality, no exercise of power. [...] Let us call this 'the intentionality constraint'" (Searle 2010: 151).

In this amended account, there are no more unconscious intentional states (i.e., the Network) surrounding the currently conscious one. There is only conscious intentionality supported by a non-intentional mechanism (i.e., the Background). That is why—we believe—in his 1995 and 2002 texts, Searle no longer needs to call the Network into question; he has explained it away by reducing it to the Background.[12]

Still, in Searle's 2010 social ontology, the Network is back in action. In order to make the Background conform to the "intentionality constraint," Searle implicitly comes back to what in 1992 he characterized as his mistaken earlier view. A quite puzzling clause of the "intentionality constraint" is symptomatic of such an implicit regression: "The intentional exercise of power may have unintended consequences and *the intention may be unconscious*, but all the same all exercises of power have intentional contents" (Searle 2010: 151, our emphasis). The Background is thus endowed with an unconscious intentional content that Searle specifies in the following terms:

> Where the social Background and Network norms function as power mechanisms, they function as *standing Directives*. They tell each member of the society what is and what is not acceptable behavior. What exactly is their intentional content? Well, because we are talking about the Background, we are not talking about something members of society are consciously thinking. [...] The certainty of sanctions can constitute an unconscious exercise of power when the intentional content is implicit. The intentional *content* in its most general *form* is: 'Conform!' (2010: 158, our emphasis)

Yet "Conform!" does not seem to be a shared intentional *content*, which tells each member of the society what is and what is not acceptable behavior. Otherwise, it would be reduced to a rule of behavior that in turn requires a rule of application, and we would be brought back to Wittgenstein's skeptical paradox without the possibility of stopping the infinite regress by means of the Background, because this time the content of the Background is precisely what is at stake. Rather, "Conform!" seems to be—as Searle himself writes—a *form* whereby social practices enable us to share intentional contents thereby establishing rules of behavior. The Background as a power mechanism cannot have a shared intentional content, if one wants to avoid circularity, since such a power mechanism is precisely what enables us to share intentional contents.

At this point, Searle's theory faces the two horns of a dilemma: either (1) give up the intentionality constraint (i.e., "no intentionality, no exercise of power") and accept that the Background can exercise power even without a shared intentional content or (2) give up the possibility that the Background directly exercises power and accept that it can only reflect intentionally instituted rules. Choosing horn (2) amounts to coming back to the account of the Background proposed by Searle in his 1995 construction of the social reality, with the consequent exposure to the skeptical paradox and to the infinite regress. By contrast,

[12] In Searle's words: "the Network is that part of the Background that we describe in terms of its capacity to cause conscious intentionality" (1992: 188). As Marcoulatos points out, starting from *The Rediscovery of the Mind* "the idea of unconscious intentionality [...] is abandoned [...] Consequently, the Network is largely absorbed into the Background, which is defined, as before, in neurophysiological terms" (2003: 69).

choosing horn (1) involves a truly renewed account of the social world, in which the normativity of the Background underpins shared intentional contents. If all of this is right, Searle's 2010 claim that the Background can directly exercise power can be reconciled with his 1992 (and 1995) view according to which the Background is absolutely non-intentional. For this purpose, the formula of the creation of social facts must be rephrased so as to show that the Background, understood as a power mechanism, can create social facts on its own without the need of a shared intentional content.

6.4 Rules and Norms

In *The Construction of Social Reality*, constitutive rules have the form: "X counts as Y in C." The term X basically designates a material entity or a series thereof, while Y designates a status function, that is, a set of commitments and entitlements corresponding to power relations and patterns of behavior. Collective intentionality, by means of the speech acts that disclose it, connects the object X to the status function Y. For instance, "X = a piece of metal satisfying certain conditions" counts as "Y = money" in virtue of the collective intentionality of a given community. But what about the context C?

Searle says very little about it. At first sight, C seems to simply designate the scope of the connection between X and Y. According to this interpretation, the formula claims that "X counts as Y in C." A piece of metal counts as money only in those nations that recognize it as such; for instance, "X = Sestertius" counts as "Y = money" in "C = ancient Rome," but it has no power to buy in "C* = the contemporary United States." Interestingly, however, if we link C with X thereby producing the formula "X-in-C counts as Y," C becomes something more than the scope of the connection between the object X and the status function Y. The context C can now be related to the Background constituting such a connection. That being the case, if the declaration "Sestertius counts as money" was done in the contemporary United States, it would not produce exactly the same status function Y as in ancient Rome, but a new status function Y*. To use the same word, namely, money, to refer to both cases is just a matter of lexical parsimony, but the distributions of powers that are individuated by Y and Y* in principle are different. In spite of some relevant similarities, Y and Y* are determined by two different contexts of normative practices: ancient Rome, on the one hand, and the contemporary United States on the other hand. For example, in ancient Rome Sestertii's owners were entitled to buy human beings as slaves, whereas owning Sestertii in contemporary United States would not involve, at least in principle, such an entitlement.

To sum up, the former interpretation—"X counts as Y in C"—means that the object X is paired with the function Y and that this pairing accidentally takes place in the context C (but it could be placed in any other context). By contrast, the latter interpretation—"X-in-C counts as Y"—means that the object X is paired with the function Y *in virtue of* its belonging to the very context C. The difference between

"X counts as Y in C" and "X-in-C counts as Y" concerns the role of C with respect to X and Y. In the former interpretation, the link between X and Y can be established independently of any C, and only secondly applied to some C. Instead, in the latter interpretation there is no way to relate X to Y without relying on a particular C. This interpretation does not reduce the context C to a mere geographical backdrop of the relation between X and Y, but conceives of it as involving the Background that makes X count as Y.

Searle has never explicitly related the context C to the Background, but at least one of his examples encourages this move. In his *Responses to Critics of The Construction of Social Reality*, he observes: "in a group of children someone may just emerge as the acknowledged leader of the group without any official recognition or authorization. The leader is just another person until the emergence of the status-function. There is no prior institutional fact in virtue of which he or she is the leader, rather the emergence of their status as leader is the institutional fact in question" (1997: 457). Here, it is not that "X = a certain child" counts as "Y = the leader" in virtue of a declaration (or some "official recognition or authorization"), but he or she *emerges* as "Y = the leader" because of his or her being X-in-C, that is, because of the intrinsic normativity of the group of children as a basic social practice.[13] In a different context C*, a different group of children would in principle attribute to "X = a certain child" a slightly different set of powers Y*. And again, it is only for reasons of lexical parsimony that we call both Y and Y* "leadership," but the set of powers that constitutes the status function is negotiated within the context and cannot be individuated in an absolute way, independently of a given context.

Something similar happens in this thought experiment proposed by Brandom:

> A prelinguistic community could express its practical grasp of a norm of conduct by beating with sticks any of its members who are perceived as transgressing that norm. In these terms it is possible to explain for instance what it is for there to be a practical norm in force according to which in order to be entitled to enter a particular hut one is obliged to display a leaf from a certain sort of tree. The communal response of beating anyone who attempts to enter without such a token gives leaves of the proper kind the normative significance, for the community members, of a license. In this way members of the community can show, by what they do, what they take to be appropriate and inappropriate conduct. (1994: 34)

Here, "X = a certain kind of leaf" counts as "Y = a license" not in virtue of an explicit rule, grasped by collective intentionality, but rather—and once again—in virtue of its being an X-in-C, an object embedded in a practice. In a different context C*, the same kind of leaf X could have similar associated powers Y*, but we could never have the certainty that these powers are exactly the same as those associated

[13] Despite their apparent abstractness and explicitness, even the constitutive rules of chess, in order to acquire meaning, need to be grounded in a context of competitive game playing, that is, a normative practice embodying the notions of victory and defeat. As explained by Roversi, "the concept of checkmate is connected to those of attack and of king, and the concept of king is in turn connected to that of castling; but apart from noticing these connections, someone observing the system from a close-up view will not be able to appreciate how these connections established by constitutive rules can create meaning. This can be understood only when institutional elements are viewed *in the context of an already meaningful practice*" (2010: 233, our emphasis).

with the status function Y in the context C. If the context C* is different from—and unrelated to—the context C, there is no way of establishing that the same status function Y is instantiated in both C and C* in spite of the fact that our lexical parsimony leads us to use the same word ("license") in both cases. For example, it might be the case that Y, as an X-in-C, means "you can enter and stay as long as you want" whereas Y*, as an X-in-C*, means "you can enter and stay until the end of the day."

In the "X-in-C counts as Y" formula, the status function Y no longer needs to be grasped and shared by the community members: rather it emerges from the Background by imposing power relations and norms of behavior even if the members of the community cannot exactly represent all of these in their mind. From this perspective, collective intentionality and language are no longer the foundations of social facts, but only the most explicit means whereby the Background can constitute social facts.

The difference between the role of intentionality and the more basic role of the Background in the creation of social facts corresponds to the difference highlighted by Brandom (1994: 21–30) between *rules* and more basic *norms*. Explicit specifications by means of *rules* can just make *norms* that are implicit in the Background partially explicit. Unlike what Searle claims, it is not the Background that reflects rules, but rather rules that reflect the normativity of the Background. Yet rules just provide us with partial approximate representations of the normativity of the Background. The normative core of the Background remains beyond the reach of rules.[14]

Both rules and norms differ from causal physical laws since physical laws only describe *what happens* whereas rules and norms state *what ought to happen*. Both rules and norms take place in the "logical space of reasons" rather than in the physical space of brute facts and causes. Still, rules differ from norms since norms implicitly determine customs, whereas rules partially make explicit and codify the normative dimension implicit in human practices. In this sense, rules emerge from norms, but there is a basic layer of norms that could never be fully codified in rules and nevertheless bears upon the working of all rules.[15]

Since explicit rules rely on implicit norms embodied in practices, a social fact is not a connection between a concrete entity X and an abstract deontic structure Y, but rather the emerging of such a deontic structure from a normative practice. There is no way to

[14]As Zaibert and Smith put it: "there are provinces in the kingdom of normativity that have nothing to do with conventional rules. Surely some of these provinces affect the structure of social ontology" (2007: 174).

[15]Wittgenstein calls this basic layer "the bedrock": "'How am I able to obey a rule?'—if this is not a question about causes, then it is about the justification for my following the rule in the way I do. If I have exhausted the justifications I have reached the bedrock, and my spade is turned, then I am inclined to say: 'This is simply what I do'" (Wittgenstein 1953: §217). Searle's Background in some sense replicates Wittgenstein's bedrock. Yet "Wittgenstein's problem is to steer a course between a Scylla and a Charybdis" (McDowell 1984: 342), that is, between explicit rules and brute causal laws. Instead, Searle's account of the Background—as we have shown—is often stuck between the Scylla of intentionality and the Charybdis of biology. Only if we conceive of the Background basically in terms of practices we can try to steer such a course.

wholly disentangle the status function from the normative practice, to wholly make it explicit as a rule. By observing from the outside the abovementioned community in which "X=a certain kind of leaf" counts as "Y=a license," we could try to make the notion of license partially explicit ("having an entitlement to enter the hut") and eventually try to import it into our community by means of an explicit declared rule stating that "X=a certain leaf" counts as "Y=a license." Yet Wittgenstein's skeptical argument shows that this rule cannot exactly replicate the original norm, but only approximately emulate it. Without a shared practice, there is no way to guarantee that what a license has been, is, and will be for that community exactly corresponds to what a license henceforth will be for our community. Between their rule "X-in-C counts as Y" and our rule "X*-in-C* counts as Y*," there will always be a margin of difference: X and X* can coincide (they can be the same kind of leaf), but C and C* relate to two different historical communities so as also Y and Y* in principle will be different status functions.

By acknowledging the dependence of social facts on implicit norms, we can overcome a problematic presupposition of Searle's ontology that Marcoulatos outlines in the following terms:

> Searle's concept of *imposition of function* presupposes two levels of existence: a primary one where things exist as (meaning/function/value-wise) neutral material entities, and a superimposed one where their particular meanings and functions are assigned subjectively or intersubjectively [...]. There are two ontologically distinct orders of existence, which are never truly integrated (2003: 79).

The formula "X-in-C counts as Y" integrates these two ontologically distinct orders of existence by transforming the superimposed function into something that historically emerges from the natural human world. The context, as involving the Background, provides us with a basic layer of implicit norms from which the status functions can emerge rather than be superimposed.

6.5 The Case of Freestanding Y Terms

The formula "X-in-C counts as Y" allows us to address the main issue that determined the change in Searle's formula from 1995 to 2010. This problem concerns what Barry Smith calls "freestanding Y terms": in social facts like corporations or electronic money, the status function Y is not *embodied in* a single object X, but only *represented by* some inscriptions, which do not count as the function Y but rather instantiate it, as the inscriptions on a piece of paper instantiate a poem. According to Smith, Searle's theory can provide only a partial account of the social reality for the following reason:

> Such a theory is analogous to an ontology of works of art that is able to yield an account of, for example, *paintings* and *sculptures* (the lump of bronze *counts as* a statue) but not *symphonies* or *poems*. For a symphony (as contrasted with the performance of a symphony) is not a token physical entity at all, rather—like a debt or a corporation—it is a special type of abstract formation (an abstract formation with a beginning, and perhaps an ending, in time). (2003: 23)

In order to face Smith's objection, Searle admits that the formula "X counts as Y in C" is just one form—not the only one—in which we articulate the most general logical form of the creation of institutional reality, that is: "We (or I) make it the case that a Y status function exists in C" (cf. 2010: 101). The price to pay for this new formula seems to be quite high, to the extent that social facts reveal themselves to be abstract formations. In this sense, Searle weakens his naturalism whereby only physical reality ultimately exists and ends by implicitly endorsing what Marcoulatos (2003: 79) calls "a sort of sociological idealism: in essence, social reality is grasped as structures of representations." The status function Y turns out to be an abstract structure graspable by collective intentionality that instantiates Y in a context C.

In discussing the role of the Background with respect to language, Recanati (2003) argues that Searle's semantics wavers between a Fregean account, whereby an utterance instantiates a proposition in a context, and a contextualist account, whereby only an utterance in a context counts as a proposition. Likewise, Smith's freestanding Y terms show that Searle's social ontology is unstable between a Platonist account, whereby status functions are self-standing abstract structures that can be instantiated in concrete contexts, and a naturalistic account, whereby there are no genuine status functions without a context (just like, according to contextualism, there is no genuine meaning without a context). Searle's 2010 formula seems to implicitly resolve such an instability in favor of the Platonist account. Although Searle does not intend to give up his original naturalistic commitment, it is hard to see how naturalism can be reconciled with the formula "We (or I) make it the case that a Y status function exists in C," in which the freestanding Y term must be, as pointed out by Smith, an abstract formation. That is why Smith in his paper *Document Acts* (Forthcoming) brands as inconsistent Searle's attempt to argue for the formula "We (or I) make it the case that a Y status function exists in C" without giving up naturalism. Still, the formula "X-in-C counts as Y" can provide us with a way to build a naturalistic account of freestanding Y terms. Of course, we cannot account for corporations or electronic money exactly as we accounted for coins or presidents, since in the former cases there is no material object X embodying the status function Y. Nevertheless, in the case of freestanding Y terms, we can still treat X as a *process*, that is, a causal-historical chain that can involve representations and inscriptions (cf. Sperber 2006) and that is sustained by expectations, interactions, and sanctions (cf. Brandom 1994). This chain does not require that the status function be an abstract type that is grasped by collective intentionality. Instead, the chain itself creates the "type," embodies it, and uses it as a transmitting mechanism that sustains and stabilizes its historical development.[16]

[16] Searle claims that, in the case of institutional entities, "codification specifies the features a token must have in order to be an instance of the type" (1995: 53). Yet, prior to any attempt to explicitly codify the features that are normative for the tokens, the status function as a type is historically constituted by the tokens themselves, which hold and possibly proliferate with the support of normative practices. Millikan (2004) stresses the importance of having a certain history in order to be a certain social fact. This history involves the iteration of a given pattern of behavior that individuates the social fact. Yet our account differs from Millikan's (just as from Sperber's) with regard to the role that normativity plays in such a historical process. We do not

Smith compares freestanding Y terms to symphonies, but some philosophers of art (e.g., Rohrbaugh 2003; Davies 2012) show that we can conceive of musical works not as abstract structures, but rather as "historical individuals" that are brought into existence by an act of invention and kept into existence by normative practices and transmitting mechanisms. Likewise, social facts that are individuated by freestanding Y terms can be conceived of as historical individuals whose existence relies on normative practices and transmitting mechanisms that constitute and iterate them. "X-in-C counts as Y" is thus the most general form of the creation of institutional reality, subsuming both the case in which X is the singular concrete *embodiment* of the status function Y and the case of the so-called freestanding Y terms in which, instead of a single X, there are multiple concurrent *representations* of a given social entity. In the former case, X is a token *embodying* the status function Y in virtue of its being related to the Background. In the latter case, X is a process relying upon the Background and connecting a series of tokens which *represent* the status function. For example, the American Constitution is not an abstract deontic structure Y grasped by the legislators and instantiated in a signed parchment X. It is the signed parchment itself that, as the outcome of an act in the appropriate historical context, gives rise to a causal-historical chain that—as an X-in-C—embodies the deontic structure Y.[17]

To conceive of the status function as a created type rather than as an abstract structure of power relations leads us to focus on the historicity of social entities. Every community has its own legal system, just like it has its own language, in virtue of having its own history. Legal systems cannot be easily exported from one country to another since social entities are not Platonic types but rather created types—better to say, historical individuals. A given status function Y cannot be arbitrarily instantiated by a multiplicity of unrelated tokens; rather, it can only emerge from the pairing of the object (or process) X with a specific context C. This is not to say that social entities are absolutely singular. Social entities can be iterated; they can have multiple instances. But such a repetition can only take place in a specific context, by means of distinctive practices. For example, we can have multiple instances of the American Constitution, like we can have multiple instances of Mahler's *Third Symphony*. Yet, in order to preserve not only the "letter" of the Constitution but also its "spirit," that is, its deontic meaning and its normative force, all these instances have to belong to the same causal-historical chain and the transition from link to link in the chain has to be governed by distinctive practices.

Indeed, there are two kinds of normativity at play in social ontology, and therefore two kinds of repeatability. On one hand, the status function Y establishes what

---

believe that normativity can be simply explained in terms of basic biological purposes of achieving the wanted results (cf. also Millikan 1990). There is something more in normativity: a social constraint that is irreducible to individual adaptive purposes and that gives us, in Searle's words, "desire-independent reasons for action."

[17] In this sense, we can vindicate the claim that a document can truly constitute a social entity (cf. Ferraris 2012), rather than simply representing it. The document can constitute a social entity by inaugurating the causal-historical chain that composes the process X from which the status function Y emerges.

is correct to do and what somebody is committed or entitled to do (call it "Y-normativity"), and every time that person exercises this power, the social fact is repeated (call it "Y-repeatability"). On the other hand, there is a standard of correctness establishing which entities X are appropriate to instantiate the status function Y (call it "X-normativity"), and every time a new X is produced, the instantiation of the social fact is repeated (call it "X-repeatability"). For example, the five-dollar bill involves a Y-normativity stating what is *correct* to do with such a bill but also an X-normativity stating which features (both intrinsic and relational) a piece of paper must have in order to be a *correct instance* of a five-dollar bill. Y-normativity allows the social entity to exercise its distinctive power in a variety of situations, whereas X-normativity allows the social entity to be instituted, preserved, and possibly repeated in a variety of situations.

More specifically, practices concerning X-normativity establish whether, at a given time t:

(I) there can be just one entity X correctly embodying a given status function Y at t (e.g., the US President); (II) there can be a certain number of different entities X_1, X_2,... all correctly embodying the same status function Y at t and therefore constituting different social entities with the same status function (e.g., undergraduate students in philosophy or five-dollar bills); or (III) there can be multiple instances I_1, I_2,... all correctly belonging to the process X and therefore all correctly representing at t only one social entity possessing the status function Y that is embodied in the process X (e.g., the American Constitution and its multiple copies). Normative practices govern the construction of the chain of instances that constitutes a social entity by establishing the circumstances in which new instances should be linked to the chain. For example, unlike what happens in (II) and (III), in (I) a new instance can be linked to the chain of US Presidents only when the last President is no longer in charge.[18]

---

[18] Thomasson takes into account what we have called X-normativity by distinguishing three kinds of rules allowing for the creation of social entities: "Singular Rules: 1. (Of a) We collectively accept: Sa (where "S" names a social feature) [...] Universal Rules: 2. For all x, we collectively accept that (if x meets all conditions in C, then Sx) [...] Existential Rules: 3. We collectively accept that (if all conditions C obtain, then there is some x such that Sx)" (2003: 280–283). In principle, Thomasson conceives of rules in a sharply pragmatic way: "Although the 'rules' of the game (Walton's 'principles of generation' and Searle's 'constitutive rules') must be at least implicitly understood and accepted in order to do their work, they may or may not be explicitly stipulated. They may simply be embodied in background knowledge and practices—as we, say, become competent players of children's games, appreciators of art, or members of society—and need not be something the participants explicitly have in mind or can verbally articulate" (2003: 279). Yet in formulating her three basic rules for social ontology, Thomasson overlooks such an original proposal. She tries, indeed, to reduce the context in Searle's formula ("X counts as Y in C") to a set of conditions C that should guarantee the link between the object X and the function Y. But those conditions work in turn as explicit *rules*, so as we are led back to Wittgenstein's skeptical paradox, that is, to the problem of rules that need to be supported by other rules, with the consequent infinite regress. In order to stop the regress, we need to reintroduce the context and conceive of it no longer in terms of explicit conditions but rather in terms of implicit practices. That is why we need a context also in the case of Singular Rules, although Thomasson does not consider this possibility.

6.6 Conclusion

Both in his 1995 and in his 2010 accounts of social ontology, Searle argues that social facts are created by collective intentionality by means of constitutive rules that are expressed by declarative speech acts. On the other hand, he also claims that collective intentionality, in creating social facts, is supported by the Background. In this chapter, we have tried to specify the role that the Background plays in the creation of social facts. We have argued that the Background cannot be reduced to a neurophysiological mechanism in the brain (as Searle suggests in his 1995 *The Construction of Social Reality*) since Wittgenstein's skeptical paradox reveals that the intentional establishment of rules in turn needs a normative foundation, which involves not only built-in biological skills but also pragmatic interactions. Nor can the normativity of the Background be explained in terms of an "intentionality constraint" according to which the Background is required to have an intentional content (as Searle suggests in his 2010 *Making the Social World*) since the Background is a precondition of shared intentional contents. So the Background is neither wholly physiological (otherwise it would lack normativity) nor intentional (otherwise its foundation of collective intentionality would be circular). Instead, we can conceive of the Background in terms of those basic social practices that are capable of instituting implicit norms that underlie explicit rules established by collective intentionality and speech acts.

This pragmatic account of the Background has led us to rephrase the formula of the creation of social facts in the following terms: "X-in-C counts as Y." According to such a formula, there is no longer a collective intentional act that grasps a deontic structure Y and—either necessarily (according to Searle 1995) or possibly (according to Searle 2010)—associates it with a particular X in a context C. Instead, there is a social practice in a context C that allows a particular X (either an object or a process) to embody a status function Y. A social entity is no longer a mere placeholder for an abstract status function, but a historical outcome that constitutes and embodies a status function in virtue of its belonging to a context—in virtue of its being embedded in the normative practices that constitute the Background. In this sense, the "X-in-C counts as Y" formula vindicates Searle's social ontology against Gebauer's claim that "ontology is not a suitable philosophical discipline for the description of society" (2000: 76). According to Gebauer, indeed, due to its very nature, ontology is missing the feature that essentially constitutes the social, namely, historicity. Yet the problem, on closer inspection, is not ontology but a too narrow account of it. By conceiving of the Background in terms of normative practices, social ontology can effectively take history into account.

Acknowledgments We are especially grateful to Francesco Guala, Diego Marconi, the editors, and the anonymous referees for their helpful comments on earlier versions of this chapter.

References

Brandom, Robert. 1994. *Making it explicit: Reasoning, representing, and discursive commitment.* Cambridge: Harvard University Press.

Davies, David. 2012. Enigmatic variations. *The Monist* 95: 643–662.

Ferraris, Maurizio. 2012. *Documentality: Why it is necessary to leave traces.* New York: Fordham University Press.

Gebauer, Gunter. 2000. Habitus, intentionality, and social rules: A controversy between Searle and Bourdieu. *Substance* 29(3): 68–83.

Kripke, Saul A. 1982. *Wittgenstein on rules and private language.* Cambridge: Harvard University Press.

Marcoulatos, Iordanis. 2003. John Searle and Pierre Bourdieu: Divergent perspectives on intentionality and social ontology. *Human Studies* 26: 67–96.

McDowell, John. 1984. Wittgenstein on following a rule. *Synthese* 3(58): 325–363.

Millikan, Ruth Garrett. 1990. Truth rules, hoverflies, and the Kripke-Wittgenstein paradox. *The Philosophical Review* 99(3): 323–353.

Millikan, Ruth Garrett. 2004. *Varieties of meaning: The Jean Nicod lectures 2002.* Cambridge, MA: MIT Press.

Recanati, François. 2003. The limits of expressibility. In *John Searle*, ed. Barry Smith, 189–213. Cambridge: Cambridge University Press.

Rohrbaugh, Guy. 2003. Artworks as historical individuals. *European Journal of Philosophy* 11: 177–205.

Roversi, Corrado. 2010. Constitutive rules in context. *Archiv für Rechts- und Sozialphilosophie* 96(2): 223–238.

Runde, Jochen. 2002. Filling in the background. *Journal of Economic Methodology* 9: 11–30.

Schmitz, Michael. 2013. Social rules and the social background. In *The background of social reality*, ed. Michael Schmitz, Beatrice Kobow, and Hans Bernhard Schmid, 107–125. Berlin: Springer.

Searle, John R. 1964. How to derive "ought" from "is". *The Philosophical Review* 73: 43–58.

Searle, John R. 1983. *Intentionality. An essay in the philosophy of mind.* Cambridge: Cambridge University Press.

Searle, John R. 1992. *The rediscovery of the mind.* Cambridge: MIT Press.

Searle, John R. 1995. *The construction of social reality.* New York: Free Press.

Searle, John R. 1997. Responses to critics of *the construction of social reality. Philosophy and Phenomenological Research* 57: 449–458.

Searle, John R. 2002. *Consciousness and language.* Cambridge: Cambridge University Press.

Searle, John R. 2010. *Making the social world: The structure of human civilization.* Oxford: Oxford University Press.

Smith, Barry. 2003. John Searle: From speech acts to social reality. In *John Searle*, ed. Barry Smith, 1–33. Cambridge: Cambridge University Press.

Smith, Barry. Forthcoming. Document acts. In *Institutions, emotions, and group agents. contributions to social ontology*, ed. Anita Konzelmann-Ziv and Hans Bernhard Schmid. Dordrecht: Springer.

Sperber, Dan. 2006. Why a deep understanding of cultural evolution is incompatible with shallow psychology. In *Roots of human sociality: Culture, cognition, and interaction*, ed. Nick J. Enfield and Stephen C. Levinson, 431–450. London: Berg.

Stahl, Titus. 2013. Sharing the background. Searle, Wittgenstein and Heidegger about the background of rule-governed behaviour. In *The background of social reality*, ed. Michael Schmitz, Beatrice Kobow, and Hans Bernhard Schmid, 127–146. Dordrecht: Springer.

Thomasson, Amie L. 2003. Foundations for a social ontology. *Protosociology* 18–19: 269–290.

Tomasello, Michael, and Malinda Carpenter. 2007. Shared intentionality. *Developmental Science* 10: 121–125.

Viskovatoff, Alex. 2002. Searle's background: Comments on Runde and Faulkner. *Journal of Economic Methodology* 9: 65–80.

Viskovatoff, Alex. 2003. Searle, rationality, and social reality. *American Journal of Economics and Sociology* 62: 7–44.

Wittgenstein, Ludwig. 1953. *Philosophical investigations*. Oxford: Blackwell.

Zaibert, Leo, and Barry Smith. 2007. The varieties of normativity: An essay on social ontology. In *Intentional acts and institutional facts: Essays on John Searle's social ontology*, ed. Savas L. Tsohatzidis, 157–173. Dordrecht: Springer.

Chapter 7
Social Ontology and the Objection from Reification

Edouard Machery

Abstract In contrast to atoms, chemical substances, and species, money, touchdowns, and marriages would not exist, were it not for human beings. But, how does the existence of these social entities depend on human beings? According to Searle, the existence of social entities depends on people's collective recognition that something possesses a particular function, and this recognition brings these social entities to life. The goal of this chapter is to assess this influential proposal. I argue that an important and well-established finding about how people conceive of their social world—which sociologists and psychologists call "reification"—is incompatible with Searle's proposal about the mode of existence of social entities.

No doubt, money, touchdowns, and marriages are real: How much money people have exerts a large influence on their life satisfaction (Sacks et al. ms), touchdowns can produce bliss in the denizens of a whole city (they do in Pittsburgh), and married couples pay less tax than unmarried couples. But the mode of existence of money, touchdowns, marriages, and similar entities differs strikingly from that of atoms, cells, chemical reactions, fields, rocks, planets, and plants: In contrast to the latter, the former, which I will call "social entities," would not exist, were it not for human beings: Were it not for us, there would be no money, touchdowns, marriages, and perhaps even no gender or races.

How does the existence of these social entities depend on human beings? John Searle (1995, 2010) has put forward one of the most influential answers to this question. As a first approximation, according to Searle, the existence of social entities depends on people's collective recognition (a collective mental state) that something possesses a particular function (roughly, a capacity to do things), and this recognition brings these social entities to life, so to speak (more on this below). Money is real and has the causal powers it has, because people collectively recognize that you can do some things, and not others, with money, and this collective recognition brings money to life.

E. Machery (✉)
University of Pittsburgh, Pittsburgh, PA, USA
e-mail: machery@pitt.edu

M. Gallotti and J. Michael (eds.), *Perspectives on Social Ontology and Social Cognition*, Studies in the Philosophy of Sociality 4, DOI 10.1007/978-94-017-9147-2_7,

The goal of this chapter is to assess this influential proposal. I will argue that an important and well-established finding about how people conceive of their social world—which sociologists and psychologists call "reification"—is incompatible with Searle's proposal about the mode of existence of social entities as well as with similar views.

Here is how I will proceed. In Sect. 7.1, I will present Searle's proposal about social ontology in more detail. In Sect. 7.2, I will describe reification, and I will provide evidence for the reality of this social and psychological phenomenon. In Sect. 7.3, I will explain why this phenomenon is incompatible with Searle's proposal as well as with similar views. In Sect. 7.4, I will examine six different ways a proponent of Searle's views about social ontology could attempt to accommodate reification, and I will argue that they all fail.

7.1 Searle on Social Ontology

In this chapter, I will interpret "social entity" broadly: Social entities include physical objects whose signification is determined by social convention (e.g., stop signs), events (e.g., signing a contract or scoring a touchdown), social practices (e.g., bowing as a form of greeting), social norms (e.g., wearing a tie at work or not eating with one's hands), and social kinds (e.g., physicians, gender, or races).

While the existence of social entities such as stop signs, etiquette norms, gender, contracts, and so on obviously depends on human beings, it is less clear what exactly it is about human beings their existence depends on. Human cognition is a natural candidate. Searle, for instance, writes (2010, ix, my emphasis) that "we make statements about social facts that are completely objective—for example, Barack Obama is president of the United States, the piece of paper in my hand is a twenty-dollar bill (…). And yet, though these are objective statements, the facts corresponding to them are all created *by human subjective attitudes*."

There are at least two different ways of spelling out the claim that the existence of social entities depends on cognition. First, the Object-General Thesis proposes that social entities in general would not exist if people did not have a particular kind of cognition. Theorists fill in the placeholder "a particular kind of cognition" in various ways. Tomasello has recently emphasized the role of collective intentionality, in particular shared intentions and goals (Tomasello et al. 2005). Mindreading is another natural candidate for filling in this placeholder. In any case, the Object-General Thesis does not assert that for any particular social entity to exist, people have to cognize *this* entity in a particular way or have to have particular attitudes toward *it*. So, the existence of money does not depend on people having particular attitudes directed toward money specifically.

In contrast to the Object-General Thesis, the Object-Specific Thesis asserts that the existence of any social entity depends on people cognizing *it* in a particular manner or having particular attitudes toward *it*. So, on this view, money exists only if people cognize it in a particular manner.

Searle (1995, 2010) has proposed a particular version of the Object-Specific Thesis by identifying the required attitude toward money, marriage, etc., with the collective recognition that these social entities have a particular significance, which Searle calls a "status function"—namely, a function that an entity possesses by virtue of having a particular social status. Collective recognition occurs when each individual constituting a particular collective (a society, a team, a company, etc.) recognizes, or acknowledges, the social status of a particular object and its attendant function (see, particularly, Searle 2010, Chap. 5). While other collective mental states such as collective intention or we-intention during cooperation are possessed by individuals (they are in each individual's head), they are irreducible to noncollective mental states such as intentions about my own actions ("I-intentions"). By contrast, collective recognition can be reduced to people's individual recognitions. Social entities are created, qua social entities, by this collective recognition. Collective recognition has such a power because they are related to declarations—a speech act that "makes something the case by declaring it to be the case," 2010, 69 (see also Chap. 5)—and because social entities have the mode of existence of the facts created by declarations. For instance, the speech act, "The conference is open," is a declaration that actually opens a conference, and social entities have the same mode of existence as the beginning of a conference, whose existence depends on a declaration. So, according to Searle, money exists because we collectively recognize that money has a specific function and thereby create money qua money.[1] Searle summarizes this hypothesis as follows at the beginning of his recent book, *Making the Social World* (2010, 7):

> The distinctive feature of human social reality, the way in which it differs from other forms of animal reality known to me, is that humans have the capacity to impose functions on objects and people where the objects and the people cannot perform the functions solely in virtue of their physical structure. The performance of the function requires that there be a collectively recognized status that the person or object has, and it is only in virtue of that status that the person or object can perform the function in question. Examples are pretty much everywhere: a piece of private property, the president of the United States, a twenty-dollar bill, and a professor in a university are all people or objects that are able to perform certain functions in virtue of the fact that they have a collectively recognized status that enables them to perform those functions in a way they could not do without the collective recognition of the status.

In the remainder of this chapter, I will focus mostly on the Object-Specific Thesis, coming back to the Object-General Thesis in the last section.

7.2 Reification

Reification occurs when a social entity is taken to be a natural one. That is, the social nature of the entity, including its mind-dependent mode of existence, is not recognized. So, money is reified if people do not grasp the social and mind-dependent

[1] Searle's (2010) views differ somewhat from his (1995) views. I will ignore this complication here. The objection from reification applies to both views.

mode of existence of money. Reification is a common phenomenon. People seem disposed to reify various types of social phenomena, including norms (e.g., etiquette norms), social roles and socially determined behaviors (e.g., gender-specific behaviors), social kinds (e.g., races), and objects endowed with a social significance (e.g., money; see Lea and Webley 2006).[2]

Let us consider the reification of social roles and social kinds first. A wealth of psychological research suggests that people tend to be psychological essentialists in the social domain as they are in the biological domain. Psychological essentialism is the disposition to assume that members of kinds (e.g., dogs) share an essence that determines the properties kind members characteristically have or are taken to characteristically have (Medin and Ortony 1989; Gelman 2003). This psychological proclivity is particularly important in the biological domain—indeed, it may arise from this domain and be then extended to other domains, including the social domain.

In the social domain, psychological essentialists assume that members of social kinds (women, Arabs, African Americans, etc.) share an essence that determines what kind they belong to and produces the properties they are taken to characteristically have. Socially determined behaviors are thus seen as being caused by this essence instead of being the products of social norms and forces. Thus, if people are essentialist about social kinds, they reify membership in these kinds as well as the social properties that are taken to be characteristic of these kinds (what social theorists call "social roles").

A common experimental design to study people's essentialist proclivity is the Switch-at-Birth task. In this task, participants are told about a baby (or a newborn animal) that is taken from her (its) birth family and is raised in an adoptive family. They are then asked whether, when growing up, the child (animal) will belong to the kind of her (its) genetic parents or in that of her (its) adoptive parents and whether she (it) will have the characteristic properties of the former or of the latter. This task has been used both in the biological and social domains.

Experiments involving the Switch-at-Birth task suggest that in many cultures lay people often conceive of national, ethnic, and racial identities in an essentialist manner (e.g., Hirschfeld 1996; Gil-White 2001; Machery and Faucher 2005a, b). For instance, Gil-White (2001) reports that in Mongolia Kazakhs and Mongols often judge that an adopted child would have the ethnic identity of her birth parents, and not of her adoptive parents, and that she would have the behaviors that are allegedly characteristic of the identity of her genetic parents (including magic!).

The disposition to essentialize, and thus reify, national, ethnic, and racial identities seems to develop spontaneously in children throughout the world, but for at least some identities, it is overridden in some cultures at a later stage of life. Using the Switch-at-Birth task, Astuti et al. (2004) examined the ascription of ethnic identity among the Vezos of Madagascar. They found that, according to children, ethnic identity was inherited at birth from one's genetic parents instead of being a social

[2] I am not claiming that people reify all social entities. Nor I am claiming that everybody reifies. Commonsense and empirical findings would belie these two claims.

property. In contrast, Vezo adults viewed social identity as a social property: For them, anybody who lived as Vezos do was a Vezo.[3]

Historical evidence also suggests that the disposition to essentialize national, ethnic, and racial identities is not a culturally local phenomenon. Voltaire (1756) wrote that "when they do not mix with natives, races do not change, in whatever countries they are transplanted. The mucous membrane of Negroes [sic], which, as we know, is black and is the cause of their color, is a clear proof that there is in each species of men, as in plants, a principle that distinguishes them. Nature has subordinated to this principle different degrees of intelligence as well as the character of nations, which changes so rarely. This is why Negroes are the slaves of other men."

Essentialization is not limited to national, ethnic, and racial identities. For instance, it also extends to other social kinds and roles, such as gender, and to the behaviors that are taken to be characteristic of men and women (Prentice and Miller 2006).

The essentialization of social kinds and social roles is not the only form of reification. Social norms get reified too: People tend to ignore the social origins of many social norms (e.g., etiquette norms), treating them instead as mind-independent, natural norms. Much sociological research supports this claim. Gabennesch (1990, 2047) refers to the "evidence that children and adults 'reify' social formations by apprehending them as something other than social products."

The reification of social norms may seem at odds with the extensive literature on the so-called moral-conventional distinction. According to Turiel and his colleagues (e.g., Nucci and Turiel 1978; Smetana 1981), all over the world, from a very early age on, people distinguish two kinds of norms along four dimensions: How bad a norm violation is, whether a norm ceases to apply when whoever is in a position of authority or power declares that it does not apply anymore, whether a norm applies universally or only locally, and how a norm is justified. A first kind of norm—which Turiel and colleagues call "moral norms"—is characterized by the following cluster of properties: Violating them is very wrong; they are authority independent and hold universally; their existence is justified by appealing to the harm or injustice caused by norm violations or by appealing to the rights of the victims of norm violations. In contrast, a second kind of norms—"conventional norms"—has the following properties: Violating them is not very wrong; they are authority dependent and hold only locally; their existence is not justified by appealing to harm, injustice, or rights.

If people do distinguish these two types of norms, then they should have a clear understanding of the social origins and mode of existence of social norms like etiquette norms. They should view social norms, such as the norms requiring to wear a tie at work or to drive on the right side of the road, as local and authority dependent, thus as being of social origins. They should not reify them, contrary to the hypothesis entertained in this chapter.

So, do people really genuinely reify social norms? Recent research has cast doubt on the strength of the evidence for Turiel's hypothesis (for further discussion,

[3] Other experimental paradigms also lead to the conclusion that national, ethnic, and racial identities are commonly essentialized (e.g., Rhodes and Gelman 2009; Birnbaum et al. 2010).

see Machery 2012). In a classic article, Haidt et al. (1993) have shown that people judge that some norms that do not cause harm or result in any injustice hold universally. Participants were presented with several vignettes, including the following one:

> A family's dog killed by a car in front of their house. They had heard that dog's meat was delicious, so they cut up the dog's body and cooked it and ate it for dinner.

Participants of low socioeconomic status in both Brazil and the USA judged that the action was universally wrong. More recently, Kelly et al. (2007) have shown that people judge that some norms prohibiting harm hold only locally. They compared participants' judgments about the wrongness of corporal punishment (whipping a sailor who disobeys an order) now and in the past (on modern boats versus on boats in the past). Many participants disapproved of corporal punishment for a current norm violation, but not for a past norm violation. In summary, it does not seem to be the case that norms divide into two kinds along the lines hypothesized by Turiel and colleagues, and their theory does not undermine the claim that people often reify social norms.

Objects endowed with social meaning can be reified too, at least to some extent. For instance, Lea and Webley (2006) review the evidence suggesting that money—an obviously social object—is treated by the brain in the same way as natural stimuli (food, liquids, etc.). People tend to desire money in the same way that they desire these stimuli, and accumulating money produces the same type of pleasure as acquiring natural stimuli.

The upshot of this discussion should be clear. In many cultures, many people fail to recognize the social nature of many social phenomena and treat them as if they were natural phenomena. That is, in many cultures, many people reify many social phenomena.

7.3 Reification and Searle's Version of the Object-Specific Thesis

As we saw, according to Searle, a social entity like a touchdown exists because people collectively recognize that this entity has a particular status function. Now, recognition of the social status and attendant function of an entity can only occur if people grasp its social mode of existence. Remember that for Searle recognitions—the attitudes the existence of social entities depends on—are similar to declarations. A conference organizer can declare a conference to be open or over (as is done in Mexico, for instance) because the beginning and the end of a conference are the kind of thing whose existence is created by this kind of speech act. By contrast, it would make no sense to declare that striking a match causes a fire or that water is constituted by H_2O since causal relations and material constitution are not the kind of thing created by this kind of speech act: It is just meaningless to say, "I declare water to be made of H_2O." Thus, when people think of an entity as being natural, they cannot make a declaration about its existence. Relatedly, entities believed to be natural, including reified social entities, are not proper targets of recognitions.

We thus end up with three propositions that are together inconsistent:

1. There are social entities.
2. People reify social entities.
3. For any social entity *x*, *x* exists if and only if people collectively recognize its status function.

Proposition 3 expresses Searle's version of the Object-Specific Thesis. This inconsistent triad of propositions can be illustrated by considering races:

1′ Races are real.
2′ People reify races.
3′ Races exist if and only if people collectively recognize their social status and the attendant social roles.

Let us suppose with social constructionists about race that races are real and that they are social constructs (1′; see Omi and Winant 1994; Mills 1998; Haslanger 2000; Taylor 2000). Does their existence, qua social entities, depend on people collectively recognizing their social status and the attendant social roles (expectations about how Blacks, Latinos, etc., should and do behave), as Searle's version of the Object-Specific Thesis (3′) would suggest? As we have seen in Sect. 7.2, people reify races (2′): They tend to think of races as natural, biological kinds, and they often adopt an essentialist attitude toward them. But, if people think that races are natural, biological kinds, they cannot collectively recognize, in the relevant sense, the social status of races nor their attendant social roles. Thus, 1′, 2′, and 3′ cannot all be true, and at least one of these propositions must be rejected.

Either 1 or 2 or 3 must be rejected. Because 1 is not controversial and because 2 is supported by the kind of evidence reviewed in Sect. 7.2, 3–Searle's version of the Object-Specific Thesis–should be rejected. Reification is inconsistent with the hypothesis that the mode of existence of social entities depends on collective recognition. Searle's claim about the ontology of social entities is erroneous.

In addition, the objection from reification plausibly generalizes to other versions of the Object-Dependent Thesis, though perhaps not to all. Many versions of the Object-Dependent Thesis probably assume that social entities have a distinct status in cognition as they are the targets of a distinct kind of attitudes. But they are unlikely to be so distinguished when they are reified.

7.4 Objections and Replies

Searle is aware of the phenomenon of reification (2010, 107–108, 118–119), but he does not see any tension between this phenomenon and his views about social ontology. What is going on? Can reification be easily accommodated in Searle's framework? In this final section, I discuss six possible responses to the claim that reification is inconsistent with Searle's version of the Object-Specific Thesis.

7.4.1 Conceptual Claim and Empirical Evidence

One could first respond on behalf of Searle that his version of the Object-Specific Thesis is a conceptual claim (consistent with some comments by Searle 2010, 48–49, 66): It is a claim about the content of the concept of a social entity that is established by conceptual analysis (whatever this amounts to). Since conceptual claims are not empirical, they cannot be falsified by empirical facts. As a consequence, reification, an empirical phenomenon, could not falsify the view under consideration.

This response is problematic. First, it is dubious that the claim that the existence of social entities depends on collective recognition is conceptual. And this, for three reasons. Unlike many conceptual claims, for example, the claim that an uncle is a brother of a parent, it is not obvious or intuitive. But, perhaps, conceptual claims need not be obvious. Unlike many conceptual claims, such as the claims that bachelors are unmarried and that red is a color (assuming that these are analytically true), it is not analytically true. But, perhaps, we need to distinguish analytic from conceptual claims (however the distinction is drawn). Finally, unlike many conceptual claims, such as the claim that knowledge is not to be identified with justified true belief, it is not defended or justified by considering possible cases and possible counterexamples. Its epistemology differs from that of plausible conceptual claims.

Second, assuming that Searle's version of the Object-Specific Thesis is a conceptual claim, it may not be a correct claim about the content of the concept of a social entity. The empirical fact of reification should perhaps lead us to conclude that Searle has mischaracterized the concept of a social entity.

Third, assuming that Searle's version of the Object-Specific Thesis is a correct conceptual claim and assuming that reification occurs, then we would have to conclude that there are no social entities: Money, marriages, touchdowns, gender, and so on are not social entities. But we would still need to understand in what way, or in virtue of what, money, marriages, touchdowns, gender, etc., exist, and it would still be the case that their existence does not depend on people collectively recognizing such entities.

It would do no good to replace the response that Searle's version of the Object-Specific Thesis is a conceptual claim with the response that it is an a priori claim. Variants of the three points just made could easily be developed against this new formulation.

7.4.2 A Weaker Version of Searle's Object-Specific Thesis

The research on psychological essentialism about social kinds and social roles and on the reification of social norms shows that not everybody reifies social objects. There is often at least a minority, and sometimes even a majority, of people who do not follow this tendency and who understand the social origins and mode of existence of social entities. So, to address the objection from reification, one could weaken Searle's version of the Object-Specific Thesis as follows:

> A social entity *x* exists if and only if *some* people collectively recognize its status function.

This weakened version replaces the claim that people in general need to recognize collectively the status function of a social entity with the claim that *some* people (adults, experts, etc.) need to do so. A proponent of Searle's social ontology could even rightly insist that something like this formulation has to be the right way of expressing Searle's proposal and that the correct version of the Object-Specific Thesis cannot be that every human being thinks of social entities in a particular way (say, that every human being harbors the relevant collective recognition). Surely, the existence of touchdowns cannot depend on the way babies, children, people with severe cognitive disabilities, etc., think of them.

This objection should be resisted on at least two grounds. First, to be taken seriously, the thesis would need to be spelled out in much more detail. How many individuals are required for the reality of social entities? Who should these be? Second, it is not the case that for all social entities some people clearly understand their social origins and mode of existence. Race provides a clear counterexample to this view. For a very long time, every adult thought of races as natural, biological kinds, and no one thought of them as social kinds. But people's beliefs notwithstanding races were social kinds then; they did not become social when people started to understand their social nature.

7.4.3 Fundamental and Derived Social Entities

A different way of amending Searle's version of the Object-Specific Thesis consists in distinguishing two kinds of social entities: fundamental and derived social entities. The latter are somehow produced by the former; their existence depends on the existence of the former. This distinction in hand, one could amend Searle's views as follows:

A social entity *x* exists if and only if either:

1. *x* is a fundamental social entity and people (or perhaps some people) collectively recognize that *x* has a particular status function or,
2. *x* is a product of a fundamental social entity (*x* is then a derived social entity).

One could then respond to the objection from reification as follows. The fact that some social entities are reified is no objection to Searle's version of the Object-Specific Thesis because these entities are derived social entities and owe their existence to the fundamental social entities, which themselves owe their existence to human beings' collective recognition of their status function.

Searle has in fact articulated a similar view in some of his recent writings on social ontology (Searle 2010, 21–23, 116–117). In particular, this is how he conceives of the mode of existence of economic recession. Conceding (2010, 21) that "such institutional facts as the existence of a recession do not require collective recognition," he adds (2010, 22) that "such facts are facts about systematic fallouts or consequences of ground-floor institutional facts. The ground-facts about the economy are the buying and selling and other economic activities and attitudes of participants."

While not unattractive, this view is problematic in at least three respects. First, to be taken seriously, it needs to be made much more specific. What are these fundamental objects that are the targets of people's (or most people's or some people's) relevant kind of recognition? With respect to this question, it is worth emphasizing that it is not sufficient for these entities to somehow involve mental attitudes and human practices; rather, they must be the targets of the relevant kind of recognition. For instance, for economic activities to play the role hypothesized by Searle, they must not only involve beliefs, desires, and in general attitudes, but they also must be the targets of the proper kind of recognition. In addition, what is the exact nature of the production or dependency relation between fundamental and derived social entities? Is it a causal relation? If not, what kind of relation is it? Searle has little to say in response to these questions.

Second, on this view, fundamental social entities have two properties: Their existence is not produced by any other social entity, and they are the targets of collective recognitions. However, it is dubious that many social entities fulfill both roles. The entities that are plausibly understood by most people to be social do not seem to be fundamental. Red lights, local etiquette norms such as wearing black tie costumes, or patterns of driving (e.g., the Pittsburgh left) are all understood to be social, but they do not seem to be fundamental social entities. In fact, it is plausible that the less fundamental a social entity is, the more likely its mode of existence is to be recognized to be social and that the more fundamental a social entity is, the more likely it is to be reified.

Finally, a single example of a reified social entity that is not plausibly viewed as having been produced by social entities that are themselves the targets of collective recognitions would falsify the amended formulation of Searle's version of the Object-Specific Thesis. Examples of this kind abound. Consider races again or social roles like gender. What social entity that is itself a target of a collective recognition has produced races (whatever production amounts to)?

7.4.4 Restricting the Scope of Searle's Version of the Object-Specific Thesis

As noted above, it is easier to understand the social origins and mode of existence of some social entities than of others. For instance, people know that some local customs are purely conventional. This suggests a fourth way of amending Searle's version of the Object-Specific Thesis: Restrict it to some social entities. This amended version reads as follows:

> *Some* social entities exist if and only if people (or some people) recognize their status function.

This restricted version of Searle's thesis is plausible. It seems true that when partners on a volleyball team design some new hand signals to be used prior to serve (e.g., to indicate what kind of serve will be made or where it will be made), the mode of existence and properties of these signals, qua signals, are wholly determined by the team partners' collective recognition that some hand gestures are to be used to communicate a particular decision. In addition, Searle may be endorsing something like the restricted version of the Object-Specific Thesis discussed here. In Chap. 5 of *Making the Social World*, Searle seems to focus on a particular kind of social entity, which he calls "institutional facts." Furthermore, he seems to acknowledge that his view does not apply to social entities like the calendar, which do not create any "power" (i.e., roughly, norms) (2010, 92).

If by "institutional fact" Searle just means those social facts that satisfy his theory, his theory is obviously true of them. On the other hand, if institutional facts are defined independently from his theory, then it is unclear whether they satisfy it since Searle did not explain what institutional facts are if they are not to be simply identified with social facts.

Furthermore, this restricted formulation says nothing about the reality of many social entities, which limits its interest considerably. It also jeopardizes the unity of the ontology of social entities: If this restricted version is correct, then different social entities exist for different reasons. In light of his claim that human society's "institutional structures are based on exactly one principle" (2010, 6), Searle would not be comfortable with the heterogeneity of social ontology, and, in any case, a unified theory may be preferable on simplicity grounds.

Finally, the restricted version of Searle's Object-Specific Thesis may well be mostly (though perhaps not exclusively) true of (in some sense) superficial social entities, such as red lights and local etiquette traditions. While a good account of the ontology of these social entities would not be nothing, it would cast no light on the mode of existence of the social entities that have the greatest influence on our lives.

7.4.5 No Need to Understand the Social Mode of Existence of the Targets of Collective Recognition

Throughout Chap. 5 of *Making the Social World*, when Searle discusses phenomena related to reification (2010, 107–108, 118–119), he seems to hold that for collective recognition to occur, the entity needs not be viewed as being social; it can be viewed as a purely natural entity or as the product of god's decision. The only thing that is needed is that people agree that the entity has a specific social status that comes with particular normative powers (rights, duties, etc.). For instance, he writes (2010, 119):

> The pope now is believed to have an additional, physical (supernatural) power where the belief goes beyond the fact, and the status function only works as a status function precisely because it is believed not to be a status function but a brute intentionality-independent fact about the universe. The acceptance of an institutional fact, or indeed, of a whole system of status functions, may be based on false beliefs. From the point of institutional analysis, it does not matter whether the beliefs are true or false. It only matters whether the people do in fact collectively recognize or accept the system of status functions. In the extreme case an institutional fact might function only because it is not believed to be an institutional fact.

Searle's response only seems plausible because of an equivocation. If recognizing that some entity *x* has some property P just means judging that *x* has P, then, no doubt, people can recognize that reified social entities have a social status and an attendant function. In that sense, people can recognize, indeed collectively recognize, that water is constituted of H_2O. But, if collective recognition is to be understood on the model of a declaration, then it makes little sense to recognize facts that we believe are natural phenomena. As noted above, we do not recognize, in that sense, that water is H_2O. Because declarations are, for Searle, the basis of the mode of existence of social entities, reification is a genuine problem for his account of social ontology.

7.4.6 *Embracing the Object-General Thesis*

So, perhaps, the response to the objection from reification should be to jettison the Object-Specific Thesis and to embrace the Object-General Thesis. I have no objection to this response since it amounts to abandoning the view criticized in this chapter.

On the other hand, under one reading the Domain-General Thesis seems trivial, while under another reading it is dubious. The Domain-General Thesis is hardly controversial if it asserts that specifically human social entities exist only because human beings have a specific kind of cognition. It is quite dubious if it asserts that the reality of all social entities depends on a particular kind of cognition. Since social entities are found among many species, including insect species with limited cognitive capacities (ants, bees, etc.), the existence of social entities in general cannot require any of the cognitive capacities that distinguish human social cognition (mindreading, etc.). Rather, the existence of social entities in general (though perhaps not of the kind of social entity found in human beings) only requires very simple domain-general forms of cognition, including recognition of conspecifics, the capacity to adapt one's behavior to the behavior of conspecifics (or other animals in the case of mutualism), and very simple forms of learning.

This is not to say that there are no interesting and plausible versions of the Domain-General Thesis. In particular, the claim that specifically human social entities exist only because human beings have a specific kind of cognition stops being trivial as soon as the placeholder "a specific kind of cognition" is replaced with specific hypotheses (mindreading, etc.).

7.5 Conclusion

The social reality of many social entities—from touchdowns, to money, to Pittsburgh left, to marriage, to gender, to races, to etiquette norms—is often hidden in plain sight, and people treat them as if they were natural entities, whose mode of existence and form owe little, and perhaps nothing, to human activity and cognition. Far from being intuitively and spontaneously grasped, the social reality of many social entities is often only revealed after painstaking critical examinations, which often involve the extensive historical investigation of their genealogy and social functions. This phenomenon—the widespread reification of our social world—is incompatible with the view that the mode of existence of many social objects depends on people having particular attitudes toward them; in particular, it is incompatible with the view that their existence depends on people collectively recognizing that these social entities have a particular function, as proposed by Searle. It is thus a serious methodological mistake to take transparently social objects and practices to be paradigmatic social entities and to base a theory of social ontology on the examination of their mode of existence. Rather, the starting point of our theorizing about the social world should be that it often masquerades as natural.

References

Astuti, R., G.E. Solomon, and S. Carey. 2004. Constraints on conceptual development: A case study of the acquisition of folkbiological and folksociological knowledge in Madagascar. *Monographs of the Society for Research in Child Development* 69: vii–135.

Birnbaum, D., I. Deeb, G. Segall, A. Ben-Eliyahu, and G. Diesendruck. 2010. The development of social essentialism: The case of Israeli children's inferences about Jews and Arabs. *Child Development* 81: 757–777.

Gabennesch, H. 1990. The perception of social conventionality by children and adults. *Child Development* 61: 2047–2059.

Gelman, S.A. 2003. *The essential child: Origins of essentialism in everyday thought*. New York: Oxford University Press.

Gil-White, F.J. 2001. Are ethnic groups biological "species" to the human brain? *Current Anthropology* 42: 515–554.

Haidt, J., S. Koller, and M. Dias. 1993. Affect, culture, and morality, or is it wrong to eat your dog? *Journal of Personality and Social Psychology* 65: 613–628.

Haslanger, S. 2000. Gender and race: (What) are they? (What) do we want them to be? *Noûs* 34: 31–55.

Hirschfeld, L.A. 1996. *Race in the making: Cognition, culture, and the child's construction of human kinds*. Cambridge, MA: MIT Press.

Kelly, D., S.P. Stich, K.J. Haley, S.J. Eng, and D.M.T. Fessler. 2007. Harm, affect, and the moral/conventional distinction. *Mind & Language* 22: 117–131.

Lea, S.E., and P. Webley. 2006. Money as tool, money as drug: The biological psychology of a strong incentive. *Behavioral and Brain Sciences* 29: 161–175.
Machery, E. 2012. Delineating the moral domain. *The Baltic International Yearbook of Cognition, Logic and Communication* 7. doi:http://dx.doi.org/10.4148/biyclc.v7i0.1777.
Machery, E., and L. Faucher. 2005a. Why do we think racially? In *Handbook of categorization in cognitive science*, ed. H. Cohen and C. Lefebvre, 1009–1033. Amsterdam: Elsevier.
Machery, E., and L. Faucher. 2005b. Social construction and the concept of race. *Philosophy of Science* 72: 1208–1219.
Medin, D.L., and A. Ortony. 1989. Psychological essentialism. In *Similarity and analogical reasoning*, ed. S. Vosniadou and A. Ortony, 179–185. Cambridge: Cambridge University Press.
Mills, C. 1998. *Blackness visible: Essays on philosophy and race*. Ithaca: Cornell University Press.
Nucci, L., and E. Turiel. 1978. Social interactions and the development of social concepts in preschool children. *Child Development* 49: 400–407.
Omi, M., and H. Winant. 1994. *Racial formation in the United States: From the 1960s to the 1990s*. New York: Routledge.
Prentice, D.A., and D.T. Miller. 2006. Essentializing differences between women and men. *Psychological Science* 17: 129–135.
Rhodes, M., and S.A. Gelman. 2009. A developmental examination of the conceptual structure of animal, artifact, and human social categories across two cultural contexts. *Cognitive Psychology* 59: 244–274.
Sacks, D., Stevenson, B., Wolfers, J. ms. The new stylized facts about income and subjective well-being.
Searle, J.R. 1995. *The construction of social reality*. New York: Free Press.
Searle, J. 2010. *Making the social world: The structure of human civilization*. Oxford: Oxford University Press.
Smetana, J. 1981. Preschool children's conceptions of moral and social rules. *Child Development* 52: 1333–1336.
Taylor, P.C. 2000. Appiah's uncompleted argument: WEB Du Bois and the reality of race. *Social Theory and Practice* 26: 103–128.
Tomasello, M., M. Carpenter, J. Call, T. Behne, and H. Moll. 2005. Understanding and sharing intentions: The origins of cultural cognition. *Behavioral and Brain Sciences* 28: 675–690.
Voltaire. 1756. *Essai sur les mœurs et l'esprit des nations*. Paris: Bordas.

Part II
Perspectives on Social Cognition

Chapter 8
Constraints on Joint Action

Cédric Paternotte

Abstract There exist many competing philosophical definitions of joint action and no clear criteria to decide between them; so far the search for definitions has by and large been a semantical enterprise rather than an empirical one. This chapter describes and assesses several constraints that could help converge towards a set of necessary and sufficient conditions for joint action. The *tightness* constraint favours definitions that fit joint actions in which the links between agents are as relaxed as possible, so as to better pinpoint the conceptual core of jointness. The *developmental* constraint asks for definitions based on realistic psychological states that could be entertained by agents less cognitively developed than ideal human beings. The *motor* constraint holds that definitions should refer to psychological mechanisms involved in actual human coordination. These first three constraints are discussed and dismissed, mainly because they manage to establish vague limits at best (for various reasons). I then introduce a fourth one, the efficiency constraint, based on the fact that most of our joint actions are generally successful, and according to which definitions should involve conditions that help justify this success. Finally, the rational and evolutionary versions of the efficiency constraint are examined and defended against objections.

8.1 The Necessity for Constraints on Joint Action

What relations exist between human individuals who are said to cooperate, to act 'together' or 'jointly'? For the last three decades, philosophers have tried to answer this question by building definitions of joint action. One striking feature of this literature is the multiplicity of available definitions and their apparent irreducibility to

C. Paternotte (✉)
Faculty of Philosophy, Philosophy of Science and Study of Religion,
Ludwig Maximilian University, Munich, Germany
e-mail: cedric.paternotte@lrz.uni-muenchen.de

M. Gallotti and J. Michael (eds.), *Perspectives on Social Ontology and Social Cognition*, Studies in the Philosophy of Sociality 4, DOI 10.1007/978-94-017-9147-2_8,

one another. All agree that some ingredients are essential to joint action while disagreeing on the nature of this conceptual core, which, depending on authors, can be mutually consistent plans of action (Bratman 1992, 1993), normative commitments (Gilbert 1989), collective goals (Miller 2001), irreducible joint intentions (Searle 1990, 1995) or collectively built reasons to act (Tuomela 2007) (the list is not exhaustive).

Most often, such accounts are based on paradigmatic real-life examples involving people walking, painting houses, singing duets, cleaning up backyards or running towards shelters together, to cite only the most famous ones. All are intuitively bona fide cases of joint action and thus equally compelling. As a consequence, they naturally lead theorists to sets of *sufficient* conditions for joint action. Unfortunately, none of them are necessary, let alone necessary and sufficient. Depending on definitions, the core ingredients of joint action can be of normative, teleological or axiological nature; their fundamental relations can be that of mutual consistency or of mutual justification; their properties can be reducible or irreducible to individual ones.[1]

Overall, the apparent incommensurability of competing definitions has caused a somewhat palpable paralysis of the field, currently stuck under the shadow of the 'big four' (Bratman, Gilbert, Searle, Tuomela – the 'classical definitions/accounts'), unable to determine which approach is right or to provide objectively preferable new ones – because no general objective criterion is available.

So far, joint action theory has been a mostly semantic enterprise, striving to identify the reference of the expression 'joint action'. Still, many theorists hold that the problem is not merely to define what we mean when we say that people act together – in which case the reign of intuition would not be problematic. For them, joint action theory crucially impinges on what is called social ontology. The idea is that the more jointly agents act, the more the group they form resembles an individual agent and acts 'as a unit'. Understanding joint action is thus tied to the identification of 'social' entities. This intuitive link between joint action and social ontology provides a starting point for understanding the former. Of course, our daily ascriptions of agency to groups cannot be sufficient for joint actions. We casually talk of groups wanting, believing and doing things or having aims and intentions; and we tend to ascribe agency and intentionality on the basis of purely observational properties, such as apparent coordination of perceivable parts. This strategy – Dennett's (1989) 'intentional stance' – provides some predictive power, but does not guarantee that the entities under consideration are agents. Indeed, following Searle's (1990) famous examples of people running to a shelter together or merely simultaneously, philosophers agree that whatever joint action may be, it is underdetermined by observable behaviour and depends on internal states. Accordingly, a general trend of the literature consists in defining joint intentions, which are supposed to be to joint actions what individual intentions are to individual actions.

[1] I will not survey the existing definitions and their conceptual links, or absence thereof, here. There is already ample literature on this topic, and any such discussion would only be incidental to this paper. For my purpose, acknowledging the absence of a consensus is enough of a starting point.

The irrelevance of observable properties, however, is a matter of degree. The longer an observed action takes, the more subparts of which it is composed, and the more elaborate it is, the more convinced we are that it is intentional rather than a mere superposition of random moves. Similarly, observing groups building houses, football teams striving to win a match, orchestras playing complex symphonies or governments consistently implementing policies leaves us little doubt that we are witnessing joint actions. Such observations buy groups some ontological worth. Indeed, such cases dramatically increase our tendency to see these groups as agents or genuine units. Joint intentions are supposed to be states of things that reliably cause and explain such behaviours. Crucially, a theory interested in identifying actual causes, true explanations and existing entities cannot be only a semantic one and cannot rely chiefly on intuition.[2]

So, how can we prune or at least stake the tree of existing definitions in order to obtain the right one(s)? Ideally, a right definition of joint action should be minimal, that is, it should mark the border between joint and non-joint collective actions. In other words, all of its elements should be individually necessary and jointly sufficient for joint action. Even if this ideal is not reachable, it is at least a useful working hypothesis, as it suggests directions in which current definitions can be improved or replaced. Indeed, the foregoing suggests that the right way to go is to substitute other criteria to intuition, currently the dominant one. How do we find them?

Although the question is rarely explicit, philosophers have strived to come up with minimal definitions, although for different meanings of 'minimal'. Two kinds of approaches are salient. The *top-down* approach starts from existing kinds of joint action, argues that they are too strong and weakens them by eliminating some of their elements or replacing them with more acceptable ones.[3] The *bottom-up* approach builds a definition from scratch, starting from fundamental elements and adding increasingly complex ones until joint action is obtained.[4]

A general worry with such approaches is that their success may only be partial. If pluralism about joint action is right, that is, if there is not one but several kinds of joint actions, then they will only identify one of the correct candidates. There are several starting points and possibly several ways to go down (depending on the order in which elements are suppressed); and there may be several paths up.

This paper adopts an alternative method, which may be called the *adequacy approach*: it aims to identify the type of *constraints* that should bear on definitions of joint action. Rather than building or purifying definitions, it aims to circumscribe the set of possible candidates – and thus is perfectly compatible with pluralism about joint action (an issue on which I do not take a stand here).[5] Even if constraints

[2] Such intuitions will resurface in the later discussion when we examine the justifications for specific constraints on joint action.

[3] See for instance Paternotte (forthcoming).

[4] See Butterfill (submitted), Kutz (2000) and Tollefsen (2005).

[5] Note that a neutralist stance about pluralism is not incompatible with the search for a minimal definition of joint action. Here 'minimal' should be understood in its mathematical sense: a minimal element such that no other element comes 'before' with respect to a given ordering. Just as sets

are rarely explicitly mentioned in the literature,[6] they often lurk in the shadows. For instance, bottom-up or top-down approaches often presuppose the endorsement of such constraints, as there must be a principled way to choose which elements to add to or to delete from a definition.[7]

Does pluralism about joint action not threaten the adequacy approach? Not if various definitions of joint action provide several answers to a unique question. Indeed, a given set of constraints does not have to eliminate all but one candidate. But what if the various accounts of joint action answer different questions and comply with different standards? Each question may necessitate its dedicated set of constraints. However, the fact that the aforementioned theorists have often commented, criticised and compared their respective accounts indicates that they take themselves to be tackling similar issues with competing accounts. Still, these accounts may ultimately be justified and isolated against certain criticisms by emphasising their differences of focus, in which case they may be subject to different constraints. This possibility cannot be dismissed a priori. In any case, it will be apparent that most of the suggested constraints presuppose a focus on particular questions about joint action – so determining which ones apply to which enterprise may be relatively simple.[8]

In the following, three prima facie plausible constraints are successively presented, discussed and rejected: the *tightness constraint* (Sect. 8.2), the *developmental constraint* (Sect. 8.3) and the *motor constraint* (Sect. 8.4). These three constraints reflect often implicit tendencies of the recent literature; there they are discussed and criticised in isolation, as possible guidelines in the search for definition of joint action. I then introduce a fourth one, the *efficiency constraint* (Sect. 8.5), of which two variants – the *rationality constraint* (Sect. 8.6) and the *evolutionary constraint* (Sect. 8.7) – will be examined in turn and defended against several objections. As the efficiency constraint is absent from the literature, these last sections are mostly dedicated to its description, the exploration of its developments and alternative versions, rather than to a detailed conceptual defence. As a consequence they constitute the most speculative part of the paper.

As a preliminary note, it is worth pointing out that whether deemed acceptable or not, all the constraints considered below share a common point: they are to some extent empirically minded. Apart from its already mentioned drawbacks, the semantic nature of joint action theory may be a reason why it has developed as a somehow isolated subfield, cut off from scientific works on cooperation that abound in evolutionary theory, ethology, social psychology, anthropology, biology, game theory, etc. To be relevant to such works, joint action theory needs to go empirical.[9]

---

can have several distinct minimal elements, there could be several minimal definitions of joint action that fit the same general desiderata.

[6] With exceptions to be mentioned below.

[7] In particular, the adequacy approach is not committed to a bottom-up approach. Constraints are not supposed to feature as additional ingredients in definitions but as tools that help assess the adequacy of such ingredients.

[8] For instance, the efficiency constraint presupposes that 'joint action' refers to reliably successful collective action (see Sect. 8.5). I thank an anonymous referee for raising this issue.

[9] This does not mean that other kinds of constraints on joint action are to be excluded. The paper does not aim to provide an exhaustive list of possible constraints, but to discuss those that are at

8.2 The Tightness Constraint

A first dissatisfaction with existing definitions arises from their neglect of intuitively compelling examples of joint action. For instance, some authors have argued that mass actions (such as demonstrations, flash mobs, etc.) or one-shot interactions in which agents are anonymous and cannot communicate can be cases of joint action, although not covered by the classical accounts (Kutz 2000; Paternotte 2014).[10] In such situations, direct knowledge of individual mental states is typically absent, because the set of participating agents is not fixed beforehand; and there is no common knowledge between them.[11] They cannot build collective goals or check that their plans of action are consistent. However, philosophers have traditionally deemed such conditions necessary ingredients of accounts of joint action.[12] In other words, classical definitions only fit cases in which the links between agents are tight enough; when too loosely constituted, groups are typically deemed unable to perform joint actions. Therefore, the reasoning goes, classical accounts need to be amended or replaced.

This approach naturally suggests a general constraint for such definitions:

Tightness constraint: A minimal definition should fit cases of joint action in which the tightness of links between agents is minimal.

Allegedly, the tightness constraint thus formulated is vague, as there is no general characterisation of what 'tightness' is and of what such 'links' are. Still, its principle is clear enough: one should look for situations of interactions in which agents are as 'disjoint' as possible, as their neglect has caused existing definitions to be too strong. This increases the chances of finding necessary conditions. However, the constraint immediately falls prey to three objections.

First, nothing guarantees that the surviving ingredients will collectively constitute a joint action. This is because there may exist several kinds of such minimal situations – several ways to strip a joint action. Maybe a joint action with minimal epistemic conditions can only exist if agents have a collective goal; but weaker collective goals may not be necessary if the epistemic conditions stay strong. In other words, if some links are minimal, joint action may be preserved only by keeping other links tight enough. This can only be determined from the investigation of concrete examples, which goes beyond the limits of this paper. The point is this: there is no reason to assume that one can build a definition of joint action by

least implicitly present in the literature and/or for which empirical data can be relevant (more on this in the concluding section).

[10] Unless stated explicitly, criticisms of the possible constraints on joint action are not criticisms of the works I take to exemplify these constraints, which do not aim to constrain joint action and so should not be assessed with regard to their failure to do so.

[11] There is common knowledge of a fact when it is public or transparent among a group; or, as the traditional description goes, when everyone knows that everyone knows (ad lib.) that everyone knows it.

[12] Bratman, Gilbert, Tuomela and Miller all include common knowledge in most of their definitions.

cherry-picking the ingredients still present in minimal cases of joint action, because such definitions are – unsurprisingly – holistic. The tightness constraint naturally stems from a top-down approach and so naturally inherits its flaws.

Second and relatedly, even if we could cherry-pick ingredients independently, as there exists no exhaustive list of minimal joint actions, we may have failed to consider all possible ingredients. This would lead to a set of necessary but collectively non-sufficient conditions. The tightness constraint does not necessarily provide elements of satisfactory definitions, because there is no certainty that they are not too weak.

Third, although the tightness constraint may seem empirically minded, intuition still is the name of the game. The constraint tells us to look actively for real situations in which human agents manage to act jointly despite the extreme poverty of their knowledge and beliefs about others, plans, means of communication, commitments, etc. This, however, does not make it empirical, as intuition crucially decides whether the impoverished situations are still cases of joint action. The procedure still depends on what we count as minimal joint action: the tightness constraint is semantic after all.[13]

8.3 The Developmental Constraint

Joint action is a kind of *human* collective action. Animals have many ways to cooperate successfully, but our unique cognitive abilities make human cooperation markedly different, if not clearly better or worse. Obviously, definitions of joint action should fit human cognition – one would not accept a definition of joint action of which telepathy, parallel processing or radar sense is the central tenet. As human beings are not cognitively identical, since many cognitive abilities admit of degrees, definitions should fit 'normal' human beings. No problem so far.

Recently, several philosophers have insisted that agents with weaker cognitive abilities than that of human adults can act jointly. In particular, children do manage to coordinate and play together, although they are far less cognitively sophisticated than adults (Tollefsen 2005; Butterfill 2011).[14] In particular, young children do not entertain highly nested mental states, although they do feature in classical definitions of joint action. So the latter should be weakened in order to fit child joint action.

Basically, the general argument can be stated as follows: as (1) human children exhibit a cooperative behaviour that is similar to that of human adults, and (2) because the cognitive abilities of the former are similar to but lesser than that of the latter, then definitions of joint action should fit the set of children's cognitive abilities. This is all the more relevant as some works imply that classical definitions

[13] In effect, the tightness constraint targets minimality by extending the number of admissible cases and thus decreasing their common features. The other constraints are more deserving of their name, as they affect such ingredients directly rather than indirectly.

[14] Such claims typically concern 12–18-month (and possibly older) children, whose ability for joint action is assessed by evidence of coordinated behaviour, as they lack a theory of mind (Tollefsen 2005) or are not able to 'think about minds' (Butterfill 2011) yet.

seem too demanding even for normal human beings, mostly because almost all presuppose common knowledge, often considered to be a psychologically unrealistic concept (Peacocke 2005).

Regardless of the success of such arguments,[15] they do suggest a constraint that may bear on definitions of joint action:

Developmental constraint: A minimal definition of joint action should fit the abilities of the cognitively less developed (or weaker) human-like agents that are capable of acting jointly.

Why 'human-like agents'? If cognitive similarity with human beings was not imposed, then behavioural similarity would be the only condition under which the constraint has to be applied. However, it is difficult to linearly order the cooperative behaviour of human beings and of animals (e.g. primates but also social insects) along one dimension, as they accomplish different outcomes in different ways and with varying degrees of success. Overall, many animal species live in groups and manifest task specialisation and division of labour, all of which are conditions for efficient cooperation. But we do need a principled way to warrant a lower limit to acceptable cognitive abilities. No one would expect the success of ant cooperation to impose constraints on the cognitive abilities that are essential to human cooperation.

More generally, the developmental constraint relies on an intuition of continuity in joint action: as human joint action depends on certain crucial cognitive abilities, cognitive limitations that imply little or no loss of these abilities should still be compatible with joint actions.

The developmental constraint is definitely empirically minded. Where the tightness constraint told us to look at extreme cases of joint action, it focuses on agents that act like normal human adults in certain contexts and are cognitively close to them; and cognitive similarity is not an a priori matter.

Still, the conditions of application of the constraint are vague. Like the tightness constraint, the developmental constraint presupposes that we know and can externally recognise cases of joint action without access to the agents' internal processes. But since Searle's (1990) famous example of individuals running to a shelter, it is well known that the concept of joint action is underdetermined by observable behaviour. So the developmental constraint is partly based on intuition again, as it depends on what cooperative behaviour *in* general counts as joint action, in such a way that renders it circular.

Consider, for instance, cooperating psychopaths. Among other characteristics, psychopaths are supposed to act for purely selfish motives. However, most definitions of joint action imply the collective adoption of common goals. A psychopath could cooperate because she has the goal of joining a group in order to better exploit it later. She would then *behave* exactly as if she was acting jointly; but as she cannot adopt collective goals, the developmental constraint entails that collective goals should not be part of a joint action (as a human psychopath is obviously human-like).

---

[15] I argue in Paternotte (2011) that the accusations of unrealism based on common knowledge are misguided.

Maybe the developmental constraint could escape the objection once conjoined with another constraint that would replace intuition in selecting genuine cases of joint action. This possibility cannot be excluded a priori. However, this section at least shows that the developmental constraint is not the first or main way to go when trying to constrain joint action.[16]

The developmental constraint has one even more important drawback. The behaviour of cognitively weaker agents may seem similar to that of human adults only because such agents interact only between themselves or in specific restrained contexts. Children do cooperate and exhibit many of the adults' cooperative tendencies (Olson and Spelke 2008), but they obviously would not be successful if they had to face adult partners trying to exploit or deceive them – strategies that adults would more easily fend off. Sophisticated exploitation of young children can be easy, as they cannot track others' mental states as closely as human adults ordinarily do (Wimmer and Perner 1983). In other words, even if we do accept that children can act jointly, it may be because some of the ingredients of definitions are realised automatically due to the restricted context in which they operate. In general, the range of situations faced by cognitively weaker agents may be so restricted that the behaviour we observe appears similar to ours even though it results from dispositions to act that considerably differ from ours.

8.4 The Motor Constraint

Social psychologists have recently started investigating the psychological mechanisms at work when human agents coordinate. As such research is still new and has hardly pervaded the joint action literature yet, it deserves a brief description.[17] For instance, Knoblich et al. (2011) have surveyed the 'perceptual, cognitive and motor processes that enable individuals to coordinate their actions with others' (59) and introduced a distinction between emergent and planned coordination. *Emergent* coordination '[involves] multiple individuals acting in similar ways, thanks to common perception-action couplings' (66). More precisely, emergent coordination involves processes such as entrainment (temporal coordination or synchronisation), affordances (objects increasing the likelihood of similar actions), perception-action matching (when the observation of an action elicits a similar action) and action simulation (leading to common expectation of the continuation of an action). All these processes tend to increase the similarity of several individuals' actions and thus facilitate coordination between agents.

[16] Likewise for the sections on the tightness and motor constraint. The paper's conclusion touches upon possible combination of constraints.

[17] Most authors that study the motor mechanisms implied in human cooperative activity does not make strong claims about the consequences for definitions of joint action should be. So here again, the criticisms made against the motor constraint do not jeopardise – or even concern – these often very interesting results.

By contrast, *planned* coordination involves the representation by agents of a joint action goal and is thus closer to joint action, in that it allows groups of agents to manifest behaviours that are more intricate and sustained, which as stated in the introduction typically leads us to more confident ascriptions of intentionality or claims of existence of collective entities. For instance, the representation of others' actions or the adoption of their perspectives both facilitate coordination. One interesting aspect is that even if only planned coordination seems to concern joint action, as it favours coordination when based on plans of action (an ingredient of definitions such as Bratman's), 'emergent coordination and planned coordination each supports joint action [...] Most forms of joint action likely require both emergent and planned coordination because there are complementary limits on what each can achieve' (Knoblich et al. 2011: 91).

In other words, all these processes seem to be implied in most proper joint actions (see also Knoblich and Sebanz 2008); they should therefore be of interest to anyone trying to provide realistic definitions or to identify necessary ingredients for joint action. However, most of these processes – especially those involved in emergent coordination – do not explicitly figure in definitions of joint actions. This suggests another constraint:

Motor constraint (a): A minimal definition of joint action should refer to the mechanisms or processes by which agents actually manage to act jointly.

The motor constraint is more empirical than the previous ones. It tells us to look at the ways in which humans beings cooperate and coordinate, to identify the processes that underpin the realisation of such actions and to import them in definitions. Unlike the tightness and developmental constraints, the motor constraint directly impinges on the *content* of definitions by dictating what some of its elements should be.

The motor constraint has another advantage: it does not rely on intuition and does not presuppose any concept of joint action. This is because the psychological mechanisms or factors discovered in the aforementioned studies are implied in cooperative or coordinated behaviours, which can be defined externally, rather than in joint action. If, as the above quote suggests, joint action involves these processes, then mechanisms present in the latter should be present in the former, and there is no conceptual obstacle to their bearing on the definition of joint action.

Still, is the motor constraint not too severe? Many processes underlie any of our collective actions and even our individual actions (only think of all the neural mechanisms governing perception, attention, etc.), all of which cannot possibly appear in a definition. This suggests an alternative formulation:

Motor constraint (b): A minimal definition of joint action should be compatible with the mechanisms or processes by which agents actually manage to act jointly.

However, the constraint now threatens to become empty. If joint actions are a subset of all instances of cooperation and coordination, then the processes present in the latter will necessarily be present in the former and a fortiori compatible with any definition of joint action that entails the same behaviour. As a consequence, one cannot neither mention nor ignore all the relevant processes. One last variant is:

Motor constraint (c): A minimal definition of joint action should only contain elements that are part of mechanisms or processes by which agents actually manage to act jointly.

Now recall that Knoblich et al. were careful to say that only 'most forms of joint actions' (not all) involve the aforementioned processes. Indeed, we are sometimes inclined to talk of joint action even in the absence of physical coordination – think of tasks of joint action accomplished through computers such as public good games ran in laboratories or mass actions. Sometimes a joint action seems to be nothing more than a superposition of similar individual actions triggered separately. If so, this significantly reduces the generality of the motor constraint. Of course, as we are looking for a definition of joint action, it is impossible to determine a priori whether motor processes are involved in few or many joint actions. Still, recall that our initial intuitions concerning joint action linked it to the ascription of collective agency, which increases with the intricacy of the actions of individuals. Consequently, it seems reasonable to claim that most joint actions do involve motor processes. However, we also tend to ascribe agency when a salient outcome results from the accumulation of many similar individual actions, which prevents us from claiming that motor processes are *necessary* for joint action.

There is a deeper worry with the motor constraint: it appears to mix the definition of joint action with its explanation. All perception-action couplings and processes involved in emergent and planned coordination *facilitate* the production of similar or complementary behaviours and thus the success of coordination and cooperation. At best, they are ways by which some possibly relevant ingredients for joint action – such as mutual plans of action or individual intentions to act – appear. However, joint action should still be characterised by these ingredients rather than by the causal processes from which they result.

One general motivation for defining joint action is to become able to explain it: once we know what constitutes it, we become able to investigate its causes. Most theorists actually try to define not joint action but joint intention, which is supposed to straightforwardly lead to it, so that the two expressions are usually used interchangeably. Intentions are not actions, but they ordinarily suffice to explain them. A more complete explanation should involve a description of the mechanisms through which the intention successfully leads to the appropriate body movements. In the collective case, this is where the perception-action couplings play a role: they facilitate the formation of some ingredients – they smooth up the transition between intertwined mental states and joint action. However, a definition of joint action need not refer to them anymore than a definition of intentional action needs to refer to mechanisms that ensure muscle coordination.

Perception-action couplings belong to the explanatory dimension; at best they can serve as heuristics for finding ingredients that we may not have thought of; but they may not impact definitions directly. Overall, there is no compelling reason to use the motor constraint.

8.5 The Efficiency Constraint

Even if the previous constraints are unsatisfactory, they contain a sliver of truth. Mass actions strike us as cases of joint actions because we frequently observe them. They succeed often enough for us to consider them as genuine cases of joint action, which motivates the tightness constraint. Likewise, the developmental constraint stems from the observation of numerous successful cases of cooperative actions that imply children or cognitively weak agents. The motor constraint focuses on cases of successful coordination between agents and suggests that we pay attention to the mechanisms responsible for such success. In other words, each constraint is motivated by the success of cooperative or coordinated actions of various kinds. Indeed, regular or frequent success in human cooperation or coordination is what usually indicates that a joint action is going on – that people act 'together' is manifested by the likely success of their cooperative endeavour. So we do *recognise* joint actions partly from the success or reliability of cooperative actions.

This makes efficiency an epistemically relevant feature of joint action, but not a constitutive one. However, one distinctive characteristic of joint action – and of cooperation in general – is to lead to outcomes that are unattainable, or less easily attainable, by isolated agents, so that everyone ends up better off than by acting alone.[18] Witnessing an outcome that could not have been accomplished by a classical individual agent (or not in the same way) provides a reason to think that another kind of agent is involved. Joint action differs from happenstance cooperation but is based on the same efficiency basis. Whatever defines human cooperation, it is by and large successful, not by being automatic or wired but by being reliable. We are routinely very good at cooperating, and examples of successful cooperation abound in our daily life; overall, cooperative behaviour benefits us.

Of course, many situations offer considerable incentives for agents not to cooperate, for instance, with opportunities to reap others' benefits without making an effort, as shown by the prisoner's dilemma and public good games (Rapoport and Chammah 1965). By and large, the ingredients of joint action describe cases in which agents have reasons to cooperate, even if the structure of such incentives is often only implicit. For instance, in Bratman's (1993) account of shared intention, agents' intend to do their part 'because' of others' similar intentions and of meshing subplans of action (106). Definitions of joint intention at least specify some causes of the individual intentions to participate. When there is joint action, cooperation is guaranteed because of links between agents that motivate them to do their part. Reliable success of cooperation does constitute joint action.[19]

The role of efficiency is apparent even in some recent efforts to constrain definitions of joint action or build minimal ones. For instance, Butterfill (submitted), probably the best example of a bottom-up approach, does include considerations

[18] Where 'better off' may depend on subjective standards

[19] In what follows, I talk equivalently of regular/frequent/general/reliable success or of reliability *tout court*. Differences between these expressions are irrelevant to the general argument.

of efficiency. He considers that what he calls a collective goal, taken to be necessary to the concept of joint action, is an outcome of actions such that '[these actions are coordinated]' and that 'coordination of this type would normally facilitate occurrences of outcomes of this type' (19). It is revealing that a consideration about efficiency enters even a 'deflationary approach',[20] but hardly surprising after all. Butterfill intends his characterisation to be compatible with various kinds of cooperation and coordination, such as resulting from 'joint intentions', 'team reasoning', 'dynamical properties of the agents' bodies', 'motor systems', 'behavioural patterns' and 'pheromonal signals' (19). This echoes and supports the previous claim that the concept of efficiency lurks behind any attempt to constrain or characterise joint action.

Butterfill actually mentions one constraint for his investigation of the nature of joint action: it 'must be at least potentially relevant to the tangle of scientific and philosophical questions commonly taken to be questions about joint action' (2), namely, questions about its psychological, developmental, conceptual, phenomenological, metaphysical and normative aspects. So a constraint based on efficiency would have unifying virtues, as it is likely to connect the otherwise scattered literature on joint action.

The constraint may be formulated as follows:

Efficiency constraint: A minimal definition of joint action should consist in conditions that explain or justify why it is generally successful or why agents generally benefit from it.

In other words, any account of joint action should include components that help justify this general efficiency. This constraint escapes mere semantics: whether a possible type of joint action leads to success often enough is a matter of fact. Still, it can explain our semantic intuitions, as success is evidence for joint action.

Of course, what counts as efficiency depends on the benefits or payoffs under consideration, of which I will introduce two kinds in the next sections, thus introducing two subspecies of the efficiency constraint. Before that, a preliminary worry must be addressed. As it stands, the efficiency constraint appears to lead to maximal definitions rather than minimal ones. Consider Bratman's (1993) definition of a shared intention, involving individual intentions partly justified by meshing subplans. Suppose we now add to the mix more ingredients, such as agents promising or committing to do their part and enjoying to do things together (for instance). Then the joint action should become even more efficient. In a nutshell: more ingredients make joint actions more likely to be successful (cooperative behaviour more likely to be observed). The more complex, the better! However, we were supposed to aim at minimality.

This objection neglects the fact that increasing the number of requirements for joint action decreases the number of situations that meet them all. This in turn

[20] 'Our deflationary aim is to identify a notion of joint action which can be characterised without appeal to shared intention or any other distinctive ingredient' (Butterfill submitted, 7), where 'a *distinctive ingredient* is one not required for characterizing individual action' (Ibid.).

hinders the explanatory power of a definition of joint action, as it will fit less examples of cooperative or coordinated behaviour. Adding ingredients damages the scope of a definition. In any case, the efficiency constraint does not recommend that we look for the most efficient kinds of joint action. Rather, it tells us to assess any candidate definition of joint action, as impoverished as it may appear, in the light of its efficiency. The previous constraints affected definitions that are too adorned, warning us: don't forget simple situations, cognitive weaknesses, and elementary coordination. This, however, does not reflect how constraints must operate in general; the efficiency constraint is a case in point, as it forbids the choice of definitions that are too bare.

8.6 The Rationality Constraint

Joint actions can be efficient in the sense that agents are provided more often with higher benefits, where these are understood of material payoffs. This leads to a first subspecies of the efficiency constraint, in which 'successful' and 'benefit' refer to such material payoffs. Agents who manage to act jointly will simply be better off that people that do not because they will obtain more resources, more often or more reliably. Of course, such agents are not *unconditional* cooperators, but *conditional* ones (knowing when and in what context to cooperate), so as to avoid exploitation from cheaters trying to reap the result of their efforts. The rationality constraint thus claims that definitions of joint action should contain ingredients that, when realised, make it rational for agents to cooperate.

In a way, insofar as cooperation is partly defined by a mutual benefit, the rationality constraint – that is, the efficiency constraint in which success is based on material payoffs – is almost built-in. Does that not make the constraint tautological and hence vacuous? It does not, because efficiency is not just about the existence of a mutual benefit but about its regular or reliable acquisition.[21]

According to the rationality constraint, a cooperative action can only be a joint action if it is rational to participate in it (although some agents may not realise it). However, rationality has traditionally been kept away from classical definitions. Rational joint action is often considered as a subcategory of joint action, in which some conditions are rationally obtained or justified (Tuomela 2000). That is, rationality is a welcome but non-necessary feature that does not affect the nature of joint action.[22] There are three reasons for the reluctance to bring rationality within joint action theory, all of which are unconvincing.

First, the rationality constraint may seem unduly restrictive, as only rational agents may act jointly. But most agents are only boundedly rational and certainly not up to the standards set by classical rational choice theory (which is well known

[21] Also note that a mutual benefit is not a shared or common goal; rather, it provides an opportunity for a common goal to arise.

[22] There are at least two exceptions to this trend, to be discussed below.

since the pioneering work of Kahneman and Tversky (1979)).[23] However, as seen above, the rationality constraint is normative – it tells us that participation should be the right choice for rational agents, whether they exist or not. Moreover, rational components can be included in a definition without being completely explicated as parts of a detailed reasoning mechanism; this allows for occasional departures from rationality. Reliability is not constant success and admits of degrees.

Second, many cases of joint action involve no clear material payoff (think of Gilbert's (1989) paradigmatic example of people walking together). In such cases, the mutual benefit can only be defined in terms of agents' subjective preferences (or utilities). Again, this confuses the rationality constraint with a constraint on actually observed cases. Joint action is such that it would lead to reliable or efficient acquisition of benefits in situations in which consequences of actions are defined by material payoffs. Efficiency with regard to material payoffs indicates a joint action, but does not define it.[24]

Third and more importantly, does the rationality constraint not operate an illegitimate mix of explanatory and defining features, which was deemed a sound objection against the motor constraint? To recall, the motor constraint imposed the reference to many causally relevant processes in a definition. The rationality constraint escapes this worry, as it only pleads for the inclusion of ingredients that participate in the explanation of the efficiency of a joint action. Complete causal explanations are possibly infinite; partial rational explanations are not. Moreover, as seen previously, the inclusion of explanatory features into definitions is not illegitimate, as even classical definitions share this characteristic. Reasons to form intentions and beliefs are constitutive of joint actions; the rationality constraint only imposes that some of these reasons appear in rational explanations.

Still, rationality may not be reducible to mere efficiency. According to game theory, which aims to elucidate the nature of rational strategies in situations of interaction, rational solutions are always *equilibria*: sets of strategies such that no agent has any incentive to deviate if all others play according to the equilibrium. In other words, sets of rational strategies are stable. So far we have considered efficiency understood as optimality; what about stability? Chant and Ernst (2007) have argued that joint intentions are indeed equilibria, more precisely epistemic ones: agents only act jointly when they have acquired enough (costly) knowledge about one another to offset the risks of failure. However, this is less about defining joint action than about claiming that cost-related considerations matter to the realisation of collective action and should be part of its (context-dependent) explanation. By contrast, my claim is that a rationality constraint bears on the definition of joint action because efficiency is one of its intrinsic properties.

---

[23] Recalling the discussion on developmental constraint, it may seem that the objection vanishes as agents with weak cognitive abilities may not be able to act jointly. However, this only concerned agents such that their abilities create doubts as to whether they can act jointly. We have no such doubt for normal human adults, as their very behaviour is what motivates the concept of joint action.

[24] In Sect. 8.5, the discussion of efficiency makes clear that benefits can be defined subjectively.

How should the rationality constraint be used? So far, only a few theorists have tried to put rationality back into definitions of joint action. A recent example is provided by Hakli et al. (2010), according to which there are structural similarities between Tuomela's (2007) we-mode characterisation of joint action and Bacharach's (1999, 2006) team reasoning. While Bacharach's work belongs to game theory, Hakli et al. integrate it by showing how agents involved in joint actions à la Tuomela do engage in team reasoning. Although they do not mention general constraints, this exemplifies the tacit use of the rationality constraint to select acceptable definitions. Recognition of this constraint should lead to more work along these lines.

8.7 The Evolutionary Constraint

I now come to the last and, I think, most interesting constraint on definitions of joint action, although to my knowledge an utterly ignored one so far. In the efficiency constraint, the terms 'successful' and 'benefit' do not have to be understood as material payoffs that agents obtain immediately, but can also be cashed out in terms of *biological fitness* – that is, of survival and reproductive success. This interpretation leads to a second subspecies of the efficiency constraint, namely, the evolutionary constraint.

In evolutionary theory, there is no doubt that the appearance and further evolution of the ability to cooperate have been important (if not the most important) steps in the history of the human species. Humans have started to live in groups and cooperate regularly tenths of thousands of years ago, and this ability has not been selected out since; far from it, it has led to increasingly impressive accomplishments. Efficiency is even more obviously a characteristic of cooperation – and hence of joint action – from the evolutionary point of view.

Evolutionary studies of cooperation abound, for it is even harder to justify cooperation in an evolutionary setting as it is in a rational one (Gintis 2009). Each classical social dilemma can receive an evolutionary interpretation and be used to model the evolution of cooperation.[25] However, they have always – understandably – ignored the literature on joint action. The reciprocal neglect is more surprising: evolutionary considerations have almost never entered definitions of joint actions.[26]

The proposal here is not that conditions for joint action should mention biological fitness and natural selection, but that they should refer to abilities and mechanisms for which we can display evolutionary explanations as to the biological or cultural selective benefits they provide. In other words, the conditions for joint action should be part of an explanation that shows how and why such conditions have been beneficial in the evolutionary history of the human species – in evolutionary terms, that shows that these abilities and mechanisms are adaptations. By definition, adaptations must have been efficient in bringing the effect (here, joint action) they were selected for.

[25] See for instance Skyrms 2003 for an evolutionary analysis of Stag Hunt situations.

[26] Tuomela (2007) is a notable exception.

Why bring evolutionary considerations in? After all, it seems enough to have a definition of joint action based on efficient ingredients or mechanisms, where efficiency is understood in terms of material payoffs. This, however, is not sufficient, for the following reasons. First, the reliability of a kind of joint action may not be measurable in terms of material payoffs, as it requires repeated observations of success in a range of situations which may be difficult to define precisely. An evolutionary story as to the past adaptiveness of certain elements would add weight to claims regarding their efficiency. Second, that a cognitive mechanism has been selected because of its past reliability does not mean that it ensures reliable success in current environments.[27] By focusing on current reliability, we risk to eliminate crucial elements (which we should not as long as they do not drag the reliability of current joint actions too far down).

The evolutionary constraint can be explored, or made explicit, in at least two ways. One can look for mechanisms or abilities that are *compatible with* or *result from* evolutionary processes. One can also look at mechanisms that generate biological cooperation and unity (organismality) and select those that are *analogous to* them at the human intentional level. Let us describe these two strategies, which I deem possible, compatible and necessary. As they are new, the following describes existing options and avenues.

8.7.1 The Evolution of Abilities for Joint Action

Following the first strategy, we can look for the cognitive abilities that are likely to have evolved through natural and cultural selection, that is, that are adaptations dedicated to joint action. Three major current trends deserve to be mentioned here. First, defenders of the Machiavellian intelligence hypothesis hold that life in groups has favoured the emergence of strategic faculties, such as deception, lie detection, coalition formation, etc. (Byrne and Whiten 1988; Whiten and Byrne 1997). This approach entails the necessity of nested mental states (e.g. beliefs about beliefs) or, more generally, of metarepresentations (Sperber 2000). Second, developmental theorists and ethologists have focused on the ability to share emotions, goals and joint attention, which are taken to characterise human cooperation as opposed to other kinds of animal cooperation (Tomasello et al. 2005). Third, philosophers such as Sterelny (2012) have emphasised the role of assisted learning: humans learn to cooperate from repeatedly facing cooperative challenges in controlled environments.

Of course, the choice of the right theory(ies) concerns evolutionary psychologists and not joint action theorists. But in principle, each ingredient featuring in a definition should be backed up by an evolutionary explanation, and the explanations of all ingredients within one definition should be compatible. Then, in order to choose between rival definitions, one should investigate whether what precise evolutionary advantages and vulnerabilities follow from an increased ability to, say, form nested beliefs about others' mental states or to become able to make promises.[28]

[27] This is the familiar point that *adapted* traits are not necessarily still *adaptive*.

[28] Skyrms (2010) is a good example in the case of communication.

One method may consist in checking which possibly relevant ingredients can be explained by group selection – the principles of natural selection applied to groups rather than individuals (Okasha 2006). Group selection, which had been considered as refuted after Williams' (1966) famous attack, has been enjoying a renewed interest and is now considered by many as a major selective force in the history of life and in the evolution of social behaviours (Sober and Wilson 1998). However, there are still heated discussions as to whether it has played a significant role in the evolution of human social abilities.[29]

A first objection against this strategy is that it rules out the possibility of joint action among living forms that have not evolved, say, of Martian joint action.[30] However, we are discussing definitions for human joint action, which would not fit cases of cooperation among most terrestrial animals, let alone among possible extraterrestrial ones. Human beings have evolved and have been subject to some amount of natural selection, hence the evolutionary constraint. Other kinds of population would require different constraints based on whatever processes led to their appearance.

A second objection is that the evolutionary constraint is not much of a constraint. Most of the cognitive abilities we currently possess have evolved; many are arguably the result of natural or cultural selection; at least they have not been selected out. So they are bound to be evolutionary efficient at best, not inefficient at worst. Moreover, selective pressures may be compatible with any proximate mechanism(s) leading to a reliable cooperative behaviour; ultimate explanations usually allow for multiple proximate ones. However, the fact that theorists struggle to come up with evolutionary theories such as the previously mentioned ones and do not agree on the nature of the selective forces that most influenced our evolution shows that building explanations is not that straightforward. The challenge is not only to show that a given mechanism has been efficient, but that it has stayed so for thousands of years in a changing environment.

8.7.2 Social Ontology and Biological Organisms

The second strategy is markedly different: it consists in seeking systematic analogies between joint action and biological individuality. Joint actions make groups appear like individuals – hence the social ontology tag. Similarly, for decades the biological literature has been ripe with analyses and definitions of organismality or biological individuality, the relevant components of which have been listed with far more precision than in the joint action case (Buss 1987; Godfrey-Smith 2009). The evolutionary episodes of emergence of higher-level organisms – the so-called major transitions (Maynard and Szathmáry 1995) – are now a widely explored topic in philosophy of biology. Interestingly, these are seen as cases in which cooperation between individuals evolves and tightens to such a degree that groups become new individuals; in this case the link between individuality and cooperation is immediate. The idea here is thus not to look for adaptations for joint action anymore, but for mechanisms that have led to higher levels of organismality and for this reason are

[29] Pinker (2012) and the following replies provide a nice overview of the current state of the debate.

[30] Here I am indebted to an anonymous referee.

highly efficient with regard to cooperative behaviour. When do biological entities form an organism – a higher-level individual? Intuitively, an organism should possess the properties of spatial contiguity and of genetic unity. There are, however, a considerable number of counterexamples to this, for instance, among plants (Clarke 2011).

As a result, theorists have been led to consider more elaborate criteria, such as division of reproductive labour (Michod 1999), bottlenecks (Dawkins 1982), degrees of cooperation and conflict between subunits (Queller and Strassmann 2009), immune systems (Pradeu 2010) or repression of competition (Gardner and Grafen 2009). There is no consensus on any set of criteria, and the answer may be a pluralist one (Godfrey-Smith 2009; Clarke 2013). Still, theorists are increasingly focusing on the search for common mechanisms underlying organismality; this is motivated by the recent view that almost all living beings have appeared from the aggregation of lower-level units. The history of life is now seen as a sequence of *evolutionary transitions* (Maynard and Szathmáry 1995; Calcott and Sterelny 2011) from lower to higher levels of organismality (bluntly put, molecules, cells, multicellular organisms, societies), all resulting from similar processes (Bourke 2011).

As a result, we have at our disposal a list of mechanisms, for the efficiency of which there is ample evidence. The interesting point is that most of these evolutionary ingredients have close counterparts in the joint action literature. For instance, there are respective conceptual similarities between Bratman's meshing subplans and division of labour, collective goals and clonality or repression of competition, Gilbert's normative aspects and policing and Tuomela's we-mode and group selection.

The proposal is thus as follows. If the evolutionary constraint is to bear on definitions of joint action, such fruitful parallels have to be explored systematically, because they allow us to identify mechanisms that are or have been efficient for cooperation, as they participate in the formation and stabilisation of new units. The aim is not to be content with mere analogies, but to use them as evidence that there are only so many ways to make cooperation between agents efficient and reliable. This should limit the kinds of ingredients used in definitions of joint action, insofar as they are submitted to the efficiency constraint.

There is one last objection to the use of the evolutionary constraint, under both its guises: nothing proves that evolutionary mechanisms and cognitive processes that have allowed cooperation and organismality to evolve in the past are still relevant to our current cooperative behaviour. Maybe it depends so much on new technologies and new cognitive mechanisms – the evolutionary efficiency of which we cannot assess yet – that the old ones have been replaced and their effects swamped. However, nothing supports this hypothesis. The cognitive abilities previously discussed (lie detection, communication, learning, joint attention) and the mechanisms underlying organismality are so fundamental that they are still present in most, if not all, cases of cooperation and joint action. New technologies may modify the way in which we gather information but not that in which we process it. Anyway, ultimately the proof will be in the pudding; if the efficiency of new ingredients can be determined, there would be no reason not to consider them as well. The rationality and evolutionary constraints are not mutually exclusive but compatible and should be applied simultaneously.

8.8 Concluding Remarks

Definitions of joint action are too semantic and not susceptible enough to objective comparison and assessment. The paper has studied several possible constraints for them, such as the tightness, motor and developmental constraints, finding them all unsatisfactory. The most compelling constraint is the efficiency one, which tells us to select ingredients only if they can help explain why joint action is generally successful or reliable. Such success can be cashed out in terms of immediate material payoffs or of biological fitness; in both cases, I have described several ways in which the constraints could be applied concretely.

Regardless of my own preference, I want to emphasise the need for constraints in general. To my knowledge, this approach to definitions of joint action has never been explicitly undertaken, although the above reasons strongly suggest it should.

Note that the paper does not exhaust the list of possible constraints. As said in the outset, I have focused on empirically minded constraints that are discernible in the existing literature. Still, other candidates could be considered in principle, and some have been implicit in the foregoing. For instance, the discussion of the links between joint action and social ontology can be seen as promoting the constraint that definitions of joint action should conform to some extent with our intuitions about ascriptions of collective agency. Moreover, the motor and developmental constraints could be discussed once gathered under the mantle of a constraint of compatibility with mechanisms by which cooperative and coordinated behaviours are implemented. It is also possible that several defects of the tightness, developmental and motor constraints would disappear once conjoined with the efficiency constraint. Ultimately, all plausible constraints are not supposed to be exclusive but complementary and should ideally be combined.

Moreover, I cannot think of any principled way to determine what qualifies as an acceptable constraint. It seems obvious that a constraint such as 'a joint action should refer to a joint goal' would be question begging. Surely, direct mention to the explicit content of definitions should be avoided; but we cannot know a priori what future definitions may refer to. In short, at this stage I do not see how to find meta-constraints for joint action.[31]

These issues, however, are for another time. It will be enough that this paper succeed in its primary tasks, that is, to establish the search for joint action constraints as a promising research programme and to show the importance of the efficiency constraint. A natural next step would consist in building an exhaustive list of compatible constraints.

Acknowledgments This work was supported by the Alexander von Humboldt Foundation. I thank the audience of the Fifth Joint Action Meeting (Berlin, 2013).

[31] I am grateful to an anonymous referee for bringing up these points.

References

Bacharach, M. 1999. Interactive team reasoning: A contribution to the theory of co-operation. *Research in Economics* 53: 117–147.

Bacharach, M. 2006. In *Beyond individual choice: Teams and frames in game theory*, ed. N. Gold and R. Sugden. Princeton: Princeton University Press.

Bourke, A. 2011. *Principles of social evolution*. Oxford: Oxford University Press.

Bratman, M. 1992. Shared cooperate activity. *The Philosophical Review* 101(2): 327–341.

Bratman, M. 1993. Shared intention. *Ethics* 104: 97–113.

Buss, L. 1987. *The evolution of individuality*. Princeton: Princeton University Press.

Butterfill, S.A. 2011. Joint action and development. *Philosophical Quarterly* 62(246): 23–47.

Butterfill, S.A. submitted. What is joint action? A modestly deflationary approach.

Byrne, R.V., and A. Whiten (eds.). 1988. *Machiavellian intelligence – Social expertise and the evolution of intellect in monkeys, apes and humans*. Oxford: Oxford University Press.

Calcott, B., and K. Sterelny (eds.). 2011. *Major transitions in evolution revisited*. Cambridge, MA: MIT Press.

Chant, S., and Z. Ernst. 2007. Group intentions as equilibria. *Philosophical Studies* 133(1): 95–109.

Clarke, E. 2011. Plant individuality and multilevel selection theory. In *The major transitions revisited*, ed. K. Sterelny and B. Calcott. Cambridge, MA: MIT Press.

Clarke, E. 2013. The multiple realizability of biological individuals. *The Journal of Philosophy* CX(8): 413–435.

Dawkins, R. 1982. *The extended phenotype*. Oxford: W. H. Freeman.

Dennett, D. 1989. *The intentional stance*. Cambridge, MA: MIT Press.

Gardner, A., and A. Grafen. 2009. Capturing the superorganism: A formal theory of group adaptation. *Journal of Evolutionary Biology* 22: 659–671.

Gilbert, M. 1989. *On social facts*. Princeton: Princeton University Press.

Gintis, H. 2009. *Game theory evolving: A problem centered introduction to modeling strategic interaction*. Princeton: Princeton University Press.

Godfrey-Smith, P. 2009. *Darwinian populations and natural selection*. Oxford: Oxford University Press.

Hakli, R., K. Miller, and R. Tuomela. 2010. Two kinds of we-reasoning. *Economics and Philosophy* 26(3): 291–320.

Kahneman, D., and A. Tversky. 1979. Prospect theory: An analysis of decisions under risk. *Econometrica* 47: 313–327.

Knoblich, G., and N. Sebanz. 2008. Evolving intentions for social interaction: From entrainment to joint action. *Philosophical Transactions of the Royal Society B* 363: 2021–2031.

Knoblich, G., S.A. Butterfill, and N. Sebanz. 2011. Psychological research on joint action: Theory and data. In *The psychology of learning and motivation*, vol. 54, ed. B. Ross, 59–101. Burlington: Academic.

Kutz, C. 2000. Acting together. *Philosophy and Phenomenological Research* 61(1): 1–31.

Maynard, Smith J., and E. Szathmáry. 1995. *The major transitions in evolution*. Oxford: W. H. Freeman (now Oxford University Press).

Michod, R.E. 1999. *Darwinian dynamics: Evolutionary transitions in fitness and individuality*. Princeton: Princeton University Press.

Miller, S. 2001. *Social action – A teleological account*. Cambridge, MA: Cambridge University Press.

Okasha, S. 2006. *Evolution and the levels of selection*. New York: Oxford University Press.

Olson, K.R., and E. Spelke. 2008. Foundations of cooperation in young children. *Cognition* 108: 222–231.

Paternotte, C. 2011. Being realistic about common knowledge: A Lewisian approach. *Synthese* 183(2): 249–276.

Paternotte, C. 2014. Minimal cooperation. *Philosophy of the Social Sciences* 44(1):45–73.

Peacocke, C. 2005. Joint attention: Its nature, reflexivity and relation to common knowledge. In *Joint attention: Communication and other minds*, ed. N.M. Eilan, C. Hoerl, T. McCormack, and J. Roessler. Oxford: Oxford University Press.
Pinker, S. 2012. The false allure of group selection. *Edge*. http://edge.org/conversation/the-false-allure-of-group-selection.
Pradeu, T. 2010. What is an organism? An immunological answer. *History and Philosophy of the Life Sciences* 32: 247–268.
Queller, D.C., and J.E. Strassmann. 2009. Beyond society: The evolution of organismality. *Philosophical Transactions of the Royal Society of London B* 364: 3143–3155.
Rapoport, A., and A.M. Chammah. 1965. *Prisoner's dilemma*. Ann Arbor: University of Michigan Press.
Searle, J. 1990. Collective intentions and actions. In *Intentions in communication*, ed. P. Cohen, J. Morgan, and M.E. Pollack. Cambridge, MA: MIT Press.
Searle, J. 1995. *The construction of social reality*. New York: The Free Press.
Skyrms, B. 2003. *The stag hunt and the evolution of social structure*. Cambridge, MA: Cambridge University Press.
Skyrms, B. 2010. *Signals: Evolution, learning, and information*. Oxford: Oxford University Press.
Sober, E., and D.S. Wilson. 1998. *Unto others: The evolution and psychology of unselfish behaviour*. Cambridge, MA: Harvard University Press.
Sperber, D. 2000. Metarepresentations in an evolutionary perspective. In *Metarepresentations: A multidisciplinary perspective*, ed. D. Sperber, 117–137. Oxford: Oxford University Press.
Sterelny, K. 2012. *The evolved apprentice: How evolution made humans unique*. Cambridge, MA: MIT Press.
Tollefsen, D. 2005. Let's Pretend! Children and joint action. *Philosophy of the Social Sciences* 35(1): 75–97.
Tomasello, M., M. Carpenter, J. Call, T. Behne, and H. Moll. 2005. Understanding and sharing intentions: The origins of cultural cognition. *Behavioral and Brain Sciences* 28: 675–691.
Tuomela, R. 2000. *Cooperation – A philosophical study*. Dordrecht: Kluwer.
Tuomela, R. 2007. *The philosophy of sociality – The shared point of view*. Oxford: Oxford University Press.
Whiten, A., and R.V. Byrne (eds.). 1997. *Machiavellian intelligence II: Extensions and evaluations*. Cambridge: Cambridge University Press.
Williams, G.C. 1966. *Adaptation and natural selection: A critique of some current evolutionary thought*. Princeton: Princeton University Press.
Wimmer, H., and J. Perner. 1983. Beliefs about beliefs: Representation and constraining function of wrong beliefs in young children's understanding of deception. *Cognition* 13(1): 103–128.

Chapter 9
How Objects Become Social in the Brain: Five Questions for a Neuroscience of Social Reality

Cristina Becchio and Cesare Bertone

Abstract Social objects have been at the centre of philosophical discussion and debate over the last decade. So far, however, little empirical work has been conducted on social objects and we are still at the very early stages of understanding how the brain permits us to represent, recognize, and constitute a social reality. In this chapter, we consider five core questions for a neuroscience of social objects: Are social objects a category of objects in the brain? When we use money or see it being used, do we employ similar representations as those of concrete tools such as screwdrivers? How do status functions emerge? Do social objects depend on a uniquely human ability to share goals and intentions? Do social objects influence the sensory-motor system? We speculate on ways in which these questions might be addressed combining behavioural, developmental, neuropsychological, and neuroimaging approaches.

9.1 Social Objects and the Brain

Social objects include money, property, universities, driving licences, chess games, and elections. As highlighted by John Searle (1995), a peculiarly puzzling feature of these objects is that they exist because *we think* they exist. Consider a ten dollar bill. It is an objective fact that the piece of paper in my hand is a ten dollar bill. But the objective fact only exists in virtue of collective acceptance. What makes the piece of

C. Becchio (✉)
Center for Cognitive Science, Department of Psychology, University of Turin, Turin, Italy

Robotics, Brain and Cognitive Sciences, Istituto Italiano di Tecnologia, Genova, Italy
e-mail: cristina.becchio@unito.it

C. Bertone
Center for Cognitive Science, Department of Psychology, University of Turin, Turin, Italy

Centre for Theoretical and Applied Ontology (CTAO), University of Turin, Turin, Italy

M. Gallotti and J. Michael (eds.), *Perspectives on Social Ontology and Social Cognition*, Studies in the Philosophy of Sociality 4, DOI 10.1007/978-94-017-9147-2_9,

paper count as money is the fact that we, collectively, accept and recognize that the piece of paper has the status of money (Searle 1995, 1998; Smith and Searle 2003). But how can 'collective acceptance or recognition' create a social reality? What is the nature of this creation? Are social objects part of physical reality? What is the ontology, the mode of existence, of social institutional reality?

Social objects have been at the centre of philosophical discussion and debate over the last decade. So far, however, little empirical work has been conducted and we are still at the very early stages of understanding how the brain permits us to represent, recognize, and constitute social objects. In this chapter we consider five core questions for a neuroscience of social objects and speculate on ways these questions might be addressed combining data from a variety of different approaches, including behavioural, developmental, neuropsychological, and neuroimaging studies.

9.1.1 Are Social Objects a Category of Objects in the Brain?

Questions about the organization of conceptual knowledge in the human brain can be addressed by studying category-specific semantic deficits, in which the ability to identify specific categories of objects can be selectively impaired, while performance with other categories remains relatively intact (Caramazza and Mahon 2003; Mahon and Caramazza 2011). Category-specific semantic deficits have been demonstrated for animals, fruits and vegetables, and artefacts (Capitani et al. 2003). An open question is whether category-specific semantic deficits for nonliving things fractionate into more fine-grained deficits. The domain-specific hypothesis assumes that conceptual domains in the brain are restricted to those domains for which rapid and efficient identification could have had survival and reproductive advantages (Caramazza and Shelton 1998). Plausible candidate categories in this view are thus 'animals', 'fruit/vegetables', 'conspecifics', and possibly 'tools'. The existence of subcategory of artefacts, including 'social objects', is however implausible. In contrast to this viewpoint, the sensory-functional models assume that object concepts are not explicitly represented, but rather emerge from weighted activity within property-based brain regions (Warrington and McCarthy 1987; Martin 2007). Category-specific knowledge disorders occur when a lesion disrupts information about a particular property or set of properties critical for defining that object category and for distinguishing among its members. For example, damage to regions that store information about object form will produce a disorder for musical instruments, but not for tools, because visual appearance is a critical property for defining musical instruments, but not tools (Masullo et al. 2012; see also Siri et al. 2003). In this view, the question is not whether social objects form an object category in the brain, but whether there is a critical property or set of properties defining social objects in the brain.

Finkelnburg (1870) described the inability to recognize the values of coins and military marks observed in aphasic as a form of asymbolia, implying that the ability to symbolize, i.e. imbue object configurations with an arbitrary meaning, is crucial not only to recognize words but, more generally, symbolic objects. In this interpretation, social objects should be associated with words because, as for words, the source of knowledge that critically contributes to their construction is symbolic. An alternative possibility (see below) is that social objects are recognized by their function and are thus more similar, in terms of properties, to tools than words.

9.2 Tool Theory of Social Objects: Is a Ten Dollar Bill a Tool?

Although many animals use simple tools to extend their physical capabilities (e.g. sticks for reaching), only humans seem to posses the ability to manufacture and use complex artefacts to perform specific *functions*. Neuropsychological evidence and contemporary findings in functional neuroimaging indicate that this ability arises from a temporo-parietal network encoding critical knowledge of the functional use of tools (Johnson-Frey 2004). Activation within this network has been demonstrated for familiar tools such as screwdrivers, knifes, fountain pens, and nutcrackers (Vingerhoets 2008). Is this network also associated with knowledge of the *function* of social objects? Consider the case of money. As a screwdriver is *for* screwing, money is *for* representing the value of goods and services. In contrast to a screwdriver, a ten dollar bill, however, does not perform its function on the basis of its physical characteristics, but in virtue of the fact that we have a certain set of attitudes towards it. Only our social practices tie the function to that physical substrate. We acknowledge the piece of paper the *status* of money, and we count it as money and, in virtue of this, impose on it a function which could not be performed without the collective acceptance of that status (Searle 1995, 1998; Smith and Searle 2003). The fact that social objects are special in this way raises the question of whether brain regions associated with complex tool use also subtend functional knowledge associated with social objects. When we use money or see it being used, do we employ similar representations as those of concrete tools such as screwdrivers? Despite the material substrate is clearly of far less importance for money than for concrete tools, does the brain treat money as a tool? Using functional MRI, Becchio et al. (2011) demonstrated that observing banknotes being cut up or torn, a critical violation of their function, elicits activation within the left temporo-parietal tool network. This activation was the greater the higher the value of the banknote manipulated, suggesting value modulated activations within functional use areas. These findings lend plausibility to tool theories of money, interpreting money as a tool for parametrically symbolizing exchange (Lea and Webley 2006). However, studies with more sophisticated experimental designs are needed before any strong conclusions can be advanced regarding the representation of functional knowledge associated with social objects. Are activations within the tool network reflecting properties specific to money or to all social objects? What specifically differs in the attribution of physical functions and collectively assigned status functions? A crucial next step will involve comparing, within the same design, neural activation on the presentation of tools, money, and social objects other than money (e.g. chess pieces, passes). Complementary to this, future research should examine whether and how the perception of affordances offered by social objects differs from the perception of affordances offered by tools (see Fiebich in Chap. 11 of this volume).

9.3 How Do Status Functions Emerge?

Another approach to studying the possible mechanisms of status function assignment is to examine how children develop this ability (see also Paternotte, Chap. 8). Children's use of language—a system of status functions—has been proposed to involve some appreciation of status and normativity (Kalish 2005). For example, the fact that children by 18 months of age will correct a speaker who mislabels an object (Pea 1982) seems to suggest that they appreciate the normative structure of language. As noted by Rakoczy and Tomasello (2007), however, the case of language is difficult to interpret because children may use language even without appreciating the logical structure of status function assignment. Clearer cases are games of pretence involving objects which children know and which get additional status in the context of the game, for example, a banana used as a telephone receiver. In contrast to the case of language, in games of pretence involving familiar objects, children have to be aware that of the dual structure of status function assignment: 'X count as Y in C'. This banana counts as a telephone receiver in the context of this pretence (Rakoczy et al. 2005; Rakoczy and Tomasello 2007; Rakoczy 2008).

Children begin to engage in pretend play from 18 months. From 24 months they understand that one or even several different fictive identities can be assigned to an object in pretence; they can follow simple pretence scenarios, join in with appropriate own pretence actions, and produce normatively appropriate inference acts (Rakoczy and Tomasello 2006; Rakoczy et al. 2004). For example, they pretend to drink from a cup into which the experimenter had pretended to pour into (Harris and Kavanaugh 1993). When a third joins the game, but does not respect the pretence status of the object, they protest and criticize him/her, displaying a clear understanding of the normative status of the practice (Rakoczy 2008). In embryonic and isolated form, games of pretending of 2-year-olds seem thus to have the basic structure of institutional reality. However, it remains an open question as to how the awareness of status and normativity in pretend games relates to children's developing an understanding of "serious" status in areas of institutional reality such as money and private property. Children think and talk about money, norms, roles, and ownership. But how do they understand about such things?

Research using a verbal interview methodology has usually not revealed much competence until age 7 (e.g. Kalish et al. 2000). For example, while 7-year-old children understand that statements about pretences ("This bear is now called George") and conventions about property ("This horse in now yours") have different truth values, 3- and 5-year-old children fail to evaluate that conventions, but not pretences, change reality. This might indicate that in young children normative awareness of status only reaches as far as the very limited pretence game context.

However, it is also possible that young children understand *in action* more about conventionality and normativity than what they are able to distinguish *in words* (Rakoczy et al. 2006). Rossano et al. (2011) addressed this possibility by using a novel interactive measure of normative awareness based on spontaneous protest against property right violations. Children watched as an actor took possession and attempted to dispose of an object. What varied was who owned the object: the actor himself, the child subject, or a third party. While both 2- and 3-year-old children protested when their own object was involved, 3-year-old children also stood up when a third party's object was involved. This suggests that by 3 years of age, children have some implicit understanding of the basic normative structure of property and property rights violations. Whether these results generalize to other social objects and which factors are important in the development from early implicit to later explicit understanding of normativity are questions for future research.

9.4 Do Social Objects Depend on a Uniquely Human Ability to Share Goals and Intentions?

Approaches from a developmental and comparative viewpoint have gone some way towards addressing this issue, suggesting that creation and maintenance of social objects may critically depend on 'shared intentionality' (Tomasello et al. 2005) or 'we intentionality' (Becchio and Bertone 2004). Already at 14 months of age, human infants show some rudimentary skills for engaging in cooperative activities (Warneken and Tomasello 2007). During the second year of life, they become progressively more adept and active as social partners, and by their second birthday, they engage various kinds of collaborative activities in which they flexibly adapt their individual intentions and actions towards their partner's intentions and actions based upon an intention to act jointly (Warneken et al. 2012). This—as it has been proposed—creates the possibility of culturally constituted entities that exist because *we* believe and act as if they do (Tomasello and Herrmann 2010).

Nonhuman primates show some understanding of the goals and the perception of social partners, but they seem to lack the social skills and motivations for shared intentionality (Tomasello et al. 2005). For example, they do not try to direct the attention of conspecifics by pointing, showing, or offering (Call and Tomasello 2008). Moreover, although they can learn to use human artefacts, they do not engage in pretend play or in any other behaviour suggesting that they understand the normativity in those artefacts. One hypothesis is therefore that nonhuman primates lack the type of collective intentionality needed to create the structure of institutional reality (Tomasello and Herrmann 2010).

An alternative view, inspired by field studies of primates in their natural environments, suggests that nonhuman primates may share a symbolic culture. In chimpanzees, for example, some communicative traits have been shown to follow group-specific norms (Boesch 2008, 2011). The most complex example is the leaf-clipping behaviour: In Taï chimpanzees, leaf clip is used by adult males just before a display to signal their intention; in Bossou chimpanzees, it is used by youngsters to get others' attention and invite others to play; and in Mahale chimpanzees, it is used by sexually active males to attract estrus female to mate with them (Nishida 1987; Sugiyama and Koman 1979; Boesch 1995). The actions themselves are arbitrary; the significance of the behaviour is defined by the individuals within the group to create a convention. Using a diffusion approach, Bonnie et al. (2007) demonstrated that arbitrary conventions can spread among chimpanzees as a result of social learning. Different conventions concerning a sequence of arbitrary actions were seeded in two chimpanzee groups. Each sequence spread in the group in which it was seeded, with many individuals adopting the sequence demonstrated by a group member. Although one individual in one group consistently performed an alternative action sequence and was rewarded for doing so, no other member of the group adopted the alternative sequence, showing an unprecedented fidelity to the experimentally seeded convention. These and other observations (Boesch 2011) support the idea that object-directed behaviours in nonhuman primates may follow specific social norms. In this view, the human uniqueness would not reside so much on shared social practices and conventions, as on cultural transmission modes not available to other species (e.g. speech, writing, radio, Internet).

9.5 Do Social Objects Influence the Sensorimotor System?

An increasingly important theoretical notion in cognitive psychology and neuroscience is the idea that high-level cognitions rely in part on embodied conceptualizations and can therefore be reflected in and influence bodily states (e.g. Barsalou 2008; Niedenthal 2007). In the social domain, 'embodiment' has been demonstrated for affective judgements (Beilock and Holt 2007; van den Bergh et al. 1990), stereotypes (Mussweiler 2006), persuasion (Sherman et al. 2010), and helping behaviour (Liljenquist et al. 2010). Moreover, there is evidence that moral cleanness may be metaphorically linked to physical cleanness. For example, it has been demonstrated that cleaning one's hands with soap or an antiseptic wipe can alleviate the guilt of moral transgressions (Zhong and Liljenquist 2006) and influence one's moral judgement (Schnall et al. 2008a, b). Other work has highlighted the impact of metaphorical links between verticality and power (e.g. 'high in the hierarchy'; Schubert 2005) and spatial concepts, such as left and right, and political attitudes (Oppenheimer and Trail 2010). For instance, it has been demonstrated that participants who are oriented to their right report more conservative political attitudes, while those who are oriented towards their left report more liberal attitudes (Oppenheimer and Trail 2010), suggesting that, to the extent that strong association exists between spatial concepts and political ideology, bodily orientation can influence political attitudes. Taken together, these studies indicate that common metaphors in which abstract target concepts are described may use concrete concepts derived from sensorimotor experience. However, as recently noted by Meier et al. (2012), it remains controversial whether such metaphors are a manifestation, a reinforcement, or the cause of embodiment effects in social judgement and behaviour.

Adopting a somewhat different approach, Constable et al. (2011) asked whether the concept of ownership may exert an influence on the action system. In a first experiment, participants performed natural lifting actions with mugs that differed in terms of ownership. Analysis of trajectory and acceleration as the mugs moved through space revealed that participants lifted the mug owned by the experimenter with greater care and moved it slightly more towards the experimenter, while they lifted their own mug more forcefully and drew it closer to their own body. In a second experiment, the same participants responded to stimuli presented on mug handles in a computer-based stimulus–response compatibility task. Overall, they were faster to respond in trials in which the handles were facing in the same direction as the response location. However, this compatibility effect was abolished when stimuli were presented on the experimenter's mug—as if the action system were blind to the potential for action towards objects owned by others (Constable et al. 2011). A similar approach could be used to investigate the sensorimotor grounding of money, passports, signs, and flags, i.e. social objects that have some physical realization. According to Searle (1995), however, all social objects are ultimately 'place holders for patterns of activities': they are associated with deontic powers (right, duty, obligation, and requirement) and deontic powers create reasons for action. This holds both for social objects that have a physical realization and for objects that have no physical realization or whose physical realization is partial, scattered, or intermittent, such as marriage, government, and universities (Smith 2003). If this is correct, then also social objects that have no physical realization—free-standing social objects, as Smith (2003) calls them—might be expected to influence the action system.

9.6 Concluding Remarks

So far social cognitive neuroscience has been mainly, if not exclusively, focused on interaction between minds and brains. The above questions force us to think about the complex interactions that tie minds and brains to material objects. Brains—as it has been proposed—help make new objects, which in turn help create new brains (Gosden 2008). This proves especially true for social objects. Being material and social at once, social objects may serve as a platform to understand how interacting minds/brains can establish new ontologies, which in turn may expand and create new possibilities for thinking.

References

Barsalou, L.W. 2008. Grounded cognition. *Annual Review of Psychology* 59: 617–645.

Becchio, C., and C. Bertone. 2004. Wittgenstein running: Neural mechanisms of collective intentionality and we-mode. *Consciousness and Cognition* 13(1): 123–133.

Becchio, C., J. Skewes, T.E. Lund, U. Frith, C.D. Frith, and A. Roepstorff. 2011. How the brain responds to the destruction of money. *Journal of Neuroscience, Psychology and Economics* 4(1): 1–10.

Beilock, S.L., and L.E. Holt. 2007. Embodied preference judgments: Can likeability be driven by the motor system? *Psychological Science* 18(1): 51–57.
Boesch, C. 1995. Innovation in wild chimpanzees. *International Journal of Primatology* 16(1): 1–16.
Boesch, C. 2008. Taking ecology and development seriously. *Journal of Comparative Psychology* 122(4): 453–455.
Boesch, C. 2011. From material to symbolic cultures: Culture in primates. In *The Oxford handbook of culture and psychology*, ed. J. Valsiner, 677–694. Oxford: Oxford University Press.
Bonnie, K.E., V. Horner, A. Whiten, and F.B. de Waal. 2007. Spread of arbitrary conventions among chimpanzees: A controlled experiment. *Proceedings of the Royal Society of London. Series B* 274(1608): 367–372.
Call, J., and M. Tomasello. 2008. Does the chimpanzee have a theory of mind? 30 years later. *Trends in Cognitive Science* 12(5): 187–192.
Capitani, E., M. Laiacona, B. Mahon, and A. Caramazza. 2003. What are the facts of semantic category-specific deficits? A critical review of the clinical evidence. *Cognitive Neuropsychology* 20(3): 213–261.
Caramazza, A., and B.Z. Mahon. 2003. The organization of conceptual knowledge: The evidence from category-specific semantic deficits. *Trends in Cognitive Sciences* 7(8): 325–374.
Caramazza, A., and J.R. Shelton. 1998. Domain-specific knowledge systems in the brain the animate-inanimate distinction. *Journal of Cognitive Neuroscience* 10(1): 1–34.
Constable, M.D., A. Kritikos, and A.P. Bayliss. 2011. Grasping the concept of personal property. *Cognition* 119(3): 430–437.
Finkelnburg, F.C. 1870. Sitzung der Niederrheinischen Gesellschaft in Bonn. *Medizinische Section. Berliner Klinische Wochenschrift* 7: 450–462, 460–462.
Gosden, C. 2008. Social ontologies. *Philosophical Transactions of the Royal Society of London. Series B, Biological Sciences* 363(1499): 2003–2010.
Harris, P.L., and Kavanaugh, R.D. 1993. *Young children's understanding of pretense*, Monographs of the Society for Research in Child Development, 58(1, Serial No. 231).
Johnson-Frey, S.H. 2004. The neural bases of complex tool use in humans. *Trends in Cognitive Sciences* 8(2): 71–78.
Kalish, C.W. 2005. Becoming status conscious: Children's appreciation of social reality. *Philosophical Explorations* 8: 245–263.
Kalish, C.W., M.D. Weissman, and D. Bernstein. 2000. Taking decisions seriously: Young children's understanding of conventional truth. *Child Development* 71(5): 1289–1308.
Lea, S.E.G., and P. Webley. 2006. Money as tool, money as drug: The biological psychology of a strong incentive. *The Behavioral and Brain Sciences* 29(2): 161–209.
Liljenquist, K., C. Zhong, and A.D. Galinsky. 2010. The smell of virtue: Clean scents promote reciprocity and charity. *Psychological Science* 21(3): 381–383.
Mahon, B.Z., and A. Caramazza. 2011. What drives the organization of object knowledge in the brain? *Trends in Cognitive Sciences* 15(3): 97–103.
Martin, A. 2007. The representation of object concepts in the brain. *Annual Review of Psychology* 58: 25–45.
Masullo, C., C. Piccininni, D. Quaranta, M.G. Vita, S. Gaudino, and G. Gainotti. 2012. Selective impairment of living things and musical instruments on a verbal 'Semantic Knowledge Questionnaire' in a case of apperceptive visual agnosia. *Brain and Cognition* 80(1): 155–159.
Meier, B.P., S. Schnall, N. Schwarz, and J.A. Bargh. 2012. Embodiment in social psychology. *Topics in Cognitive Science* 4(4): 705–716.
Mussweiler, T. 2006. Doing is for thinking! Stereotype activation by stereotypic movements. *Psychological Science* 17(1): 17–21.
Niedenthal, P.M. 2007. Embodying emotion. *Science* 316(5827): 1002–1005.
Nishida, T. 1987. Local traditions and cultural transmission. In *Primate societies*, ed. S.S. Smuts, D.L. Cheney, R.M. Seyfarth, R.W. Wrangham, and T.T. Strusaker, 462–474. Chicago: University of Chicago Press.

Oppenheimer, D.M., and T.E. Trail. 2010. Why leaning to the left makes you lean to the left: Effect of spatial orientation on political attitudes. *Social Cognition* 28(5): 651–661.

Pea, R.D. 1982. Origins of verbal logic: Spontaneous denials by two- and three-year olds. *Journal of Child Language* 9(3): 597–626.

Rakoczy, H. 2008. Taking fiction seriously: Young children understand the normative structure of joint pretend games. *Developmental Psychology* 44(4): 1195–1201.

Rakoczy, H., and M. Tomasello. 2006. Two-year-olds' grasp the intentional structure of pretense acts. *Developmental Science* 9(6): 558–565.

Rakoczy, H., and M. Tomasello. 2007. The ontogeny of social ontology: Steps to shared intentionality and status functions. In *Intentional acts and institutional facts: Essays on John Searle's social ontology*, ed. S.L. Tsohatzidis, 113–137. Berlin: Springer.

Rakoczy, H., M. Tomasello, and T. Striano. 2004. Young children know that trying is not pretending – a test of the "behaving-as-if" construal of children's early concept of "pretense". *Developmental Psychology* 40(3): 388–399.

Rakoczy, H., M. Tomasello, and T. Striano. 2005. On tools and toys: How children learn to act on and pretend with 'virgin' objects. *Developmental Science* 8(1): 57–73.

Rakoczy, H., M. Tomasello, and T. Striano. 2006. The role of experience and discourse in children's developing understanding of pretend play actions. *British Journal of Developmental Psychology* 24(2): 305–335.

Rossano, F., H. Rakoczy, and M. Tomasello. 2011. Young children understanding of violations of property rights. *Cognition* 121(2): 219–227.

Searle, J.R. 1995. *The construction of social reality*. New York: Free Press.

Searle, J.R. 1998. *Mind, language and society: Philosophy in the real world*. New York: Basic books.

Siri, S., E.A. Kensinger, S.F. Cappa, K.L. Hood, and S. Corkin. 2003. Questioning the Living/Nonliving Dichotomy: Evidence from a patient with an unusual semantic dissociation. *Neuropsychology* 17(4): 630–645.

Smith, B. 2003. John Searle: From speech acts to social reality. In *John Searle*, ed. B. Smith, 1–33. Cambridge: Cambridge University Press.

Smith, B., and J.R. Searle. 2003. The construction of social reality: An exchange. *The American Journal of Economics and Sociology* 62(1): 285–309.

Schnall, S., J. Benton, and S. Harvey. 2008a. With a clean conscience: Cleanliness reduces the severity of moral judgments. *Psychological Science* 19(12): 1219–1222.

Schnall, S., K. Harber, J. Stefanucci, and D.R. Proffitt. 2008b. Social support and the perception of geographical slant. *Journal of Experimental Social Psychology* 44(5): 1246–1255.

Schubert, T.W. 2005. Your highness: Vertical positions as perceptual symbols of power. *Journal of Personality and Social Psychology* 89(1): 1–21.

Sherman, D.K., C. Gangi, and M.L. White. 2010. Embodied cognition and health persuasion: Facilitating intention–behavior consistency via motor manipulations. *Journal of Experimental Social Psychology* 46(2): 461–464.

Sugiyama, Y., and J. Koman. 1979. Tool-using and -making behavior in wild chimpanzees at Bossou, Guinea. *Primates* 20: 513–524.

Tomasello, M., and E. Herrmann. 2010. Ape and human cognition: What's the difference? *Current Directions in Psychological Science* 19(1): 3–8.

Tomasello, M., M. Carpenter, J. Call, T. Behne, and H. Moll. 2005. Understanding and sharing intentions: The origins of cultural cognition. *The Behavioral and Brain Sciences* 28(5): 675–691.

van den Bergh, O., S. Vrana, and P. Eelen. 1990. Letters from the heart: Affective categorization of letter combinations in typists and nontypists. *Journal of Experimental Psychology: Learning, Memory, and Cognition* 16(6): 1153–1161.

Vingerhoets, G. 2008. Knowing about tools: Neural correlates of tool familiarity and experience. *NeuroImage* 40(3): 1380–1391.

Warneken, F., and M. Tomasello. 2007. Helping and cooperation at 14 months of age. *Infancy* 11(3): 271–294.

Warneken, F., M. Gräfenhain, and M. Tomasello. 2012. Collaborative partner or social tool? New evidence for young children's understanding of joint intentions in collaborative activities. *Developmental Science* 15(1): 54–61.
Warrington, E.K., and R.A. McCarthy. 1987. Categories of knowledge. Further fractionations and an attempted integration. *Brain* 110(Pt 5): 1273–1296.
Zhong, C.B., and K. Liljenquist. 2006. Washing away your sins: Threatened morality and physical cleansing. *Science* 313(5792): 1451–1452.

Chapter 10
Materializing Mind: The Role of Objects in Cognition and Culture

Kristian Tylén and John J. McGraw

Abstract If mind is investigated as the set of interactions that accomplish a cognitive task, that is, *if mind is more than that which occurs inside the head*, then how does the interplay of biological and environmental resources produce human cognition? Informed by active externalism, joint action, and distributed cognition, we review and classify a set of cognitive processes mediated by material representations. Specifically, we ask how—in a range of everyday cognitive and cultural practices—we employ objects (1) to scaffold memory, (2) to alter cognitive complexity, (3) to facilitate epistemic experimentation, (4) to enable the division of cognitive labor, (5) to promote confidence and trust, (6) to consolidate social structure, and (7) to support dialogical coupling. We conclude that through cultural practices the stable, "manipulable", and public properties of objects have come to afford unprecedented modes of extended and distributed cognition.

10.1 Introduction

What is the relation between cognition and the material world? Traditional approaches in psychology and the philosophy of mind treat the material world as "context" or "input," essentially separating human cognition from its environment. Others have challenged these assumptions, claiming that the environment plays a *constitutive* role in cognition (Clark and Chalmers 1998; Mesquita et al. 2010).

It has been famously observed how the ontology of some objects derives from their assigned status functions: money, marriage, and law do their work not by virtue of the material properties of currency, wedding rings, or documents, but by anchored and reified social practices (Searle 1995). Perhaps more radically, though, it has been

K. Tylén (✉) • J.J. McGraw
Interacting Minds Centre, Aarhus, Denmark
e-mail: kristian@cfin.dk

M. Gallotti and J. Michael (eds.), *Perspectives on Social Ontology and Social Cognition*, Studies in the Philosophy of Sociality 4, DOI 10.1007/978-94-017-9147-2_10,

suggested that certain engagements of objects and properties of the environment are basic and essential for cognition (Latour 1996). This idea builds on the observation that many everyday cognitive processes unfold in close interaction with the social and material environment (including objects, artifacts, and other people) where these make irreducible, continuous contributions. It is this idea we will explore in our chapter. In particular we ask: *What is the role of the material environment in human cognitive processing? What do objects and artifacts contribute? And what kinds of processes do they engage?*

10.2 Extending and Distributing Cognition

The idea that human thinking may rely on material structure beyond skin and skull is not new, but has found expression in Peirce, Dewey, Heidegger, Vygotsky, and Bateson, among others. More recently, philosophical discussions about *externalism* have been challenging prevalent assumptions regarding bounded, individual minds (see Menary 2010). Most of these debates can be traced to Clark and Chalmers's (1998) provocative article, "The Extended Mind." Their argument regarding an "active externalism" hinges on what later became known as "the parity principle," derived from this statement:

> If, as we confront some task, a part of the world functions as a process which, *were it done in the head*, we would have no hesitation in recognizing as part of the cognitive process, then that part of the world *is* (so we claim) part of the cognitive process.

According to the parity principle, when you consult a dictionary, it becomes as constitutive a part of your current cognitive processing as, say, your cerebral cortex. There is nothing *more cognitive* about your cerebral cortex's role in reading the dictionary—just because it is inside your head—than the actual text itself. If a mad scientist could somehow disable your cerebral cortex, and thus prevent your capacity to read the book, it would, in principle, be no different, in terms of the overall cognitive process, than had a bully taken your dictionary from you.

Given the implications of "the extended mind hypothesis" (as it is sometimes called), even the phrase "individual mind" appears to be a contradiction in terms since everything that is *in the head* was once outside of it (Vygotsky 1978), be that the language a person speaks, the belief system she holds dear, or the image she may conjure up, in her mind's eye, of the Mona Lisa. According to active externalism, then, cognition is neither bound to the circuits of the brain nor isolated in individual minds.

Through the enaction of a cognitive task, resources both internal and external to the person are coordinated in a way that diminishes inside/outside and individual/group distinctions (Varela et al. 1992). Following this line of thought, the brain *participates* in cognitive processes as part of the assemblage of biological and environmental components. The brain is *necessary* for the person to accomplish cognition, but it is not *sufficient*. A brain must develop in a body which must develop in a culture in order to enact thought, use language, make decisions, and participate in society.

Real-world cognition does not derive from a Cartesian mind receiving input from the world, cognitively processing that input, and then transmitting an output to the world in the form of behavior or language. The "input-output" model of human cognition needs to be replaced by a more naturalistic approach that perceives cognition to be an emergent property of a system composed of people, knowledge, and objects engaged in a "traffic of representations" (see Peirce 1982). Cognition needs to be studied *in context* to fully understand a particular function, such as decision making (McGraw 2011). Cognition is not Cartesian meditation (at least most of the time), but practical "thinking–doing" in complex environments.

Such an approach is exemplified in Hutchins's, *Cognition in the Wild*. Based on a series of investigations far from the domesticating lab, Hutchins describes the numerous people, tools, and practices that went into the navigation of a large Navy ship before the days of GPS. This study of "distributed cognition" offers a rich account of the way that people, artifacts, and cultural practices interact in, and indeed emerge from, systems.

In the book, Hutchins makes a useful distinction between "mediating artifacts" and "mediating structures," but only for the purpose of subsuming the former into the latter. Mediating artifacts are conveyances of thought external to the body. These include such things as charts, calendars, calculators, and keyboards. Mediating structures relate to a larger class: all the components brought into coordination for the accomplishment of the task. This includes not only the mediating artifacts but resources inside the body, like the thalamus and the hippocampus. A complete description of a cognitive task would detail the sequence of processes as they are accomplished by various media, be they biological or environmental. This is an especially important point since the mediating structures coordinated for the accomplishment of a task, particularly if it is a repetitive, highly functional task, tend to "educate" one another, improving the speed and efficiency of their coordination through practice (De Jaegher and Di Paolo 2007: 487). The capacity of the biological and environmental to educate one another—for the maker to mark his tools and vice versa—confirms that a softening of the internal/external boundary is required when studying human cognition.

10.3 Tools for Thought

The role of objects in cognitive processes is commonly discussed using the analogy to manual tool use. Just as a well-crafted tool engages and enhances our bodily capacities, so can objects and artifacts substitute and augment our cognitive powers (Clark 2003). A person can learn how to do complicated math in his head, but the use of a calculator for the same purpose radically improves mathematical performance. And though people can rely on robust systems of biological memory to store information, it takes an institutionalized writing system to organize the countless details and events that make up a narrative like *Anna Karenina*.

Crucially, the tool metaphor can take us a step further. Just as a carpenter requires different tools for different tasks, people use objects and artifacts in distinctive "functional assemblies" to enact cognitive processes. This focus on function needs to be emphasized since it is the functional relationships among different components, rather than the elemental make up of the components themselves, that accomplish cognition. To the extent that componentry matters qua componentry in a system, it matters because of relationally determined properties or "affordances" (Gibson 1977; Zhang and Patel 2006).

For example, people have used clay, bark, papyrus, wax tablets, stone, vellum, napkins, hands, and bleached wood pulp as writing surfaces. All of these quite varied media possess qualities that permit the recording of script (some better than others). However, to analyze molecules of sandstone or cellulose in search of a particular *writing essence* is the wrong scale of analysis, if not a "category mistake" (Ryle 1949). Rather, it is a set of *functional properties*—durability, transportability, or other such practical aspects—that favor a particular medium for conveying a particular message.

Similarly, understanding how tools for thought work requires attending to the material affordances of things without falling into the trap of reifying those affordances into fixed *types*: a hammer is a hammer not by virtue of some metallurgical ratio nor precise form nor trademark. Many objects can become hammers and do so whenever they function well for that purpose. Along similar lines, in the following we identify different kinds of *functional roles* that material representations play in cognitive processes.

10.3.1 Material Representations Store Information

Structuring the environment can serve to scaffold memory, radically expanding the capabilities of our brains. This works in different fashions. Vygotsky (1978) discussed how simple mnemonic techniques like tying a knot in one's handkerchief can be used for self-cue, thus enhancing recall. And Beach (1993) pointed out how the deliberate arrangement of glassware on a counter helps bartenders keep track of their drink orders. However, beyond mere cuing of biological memory, notations—in particular, writing and numeral systems—serve as valuable information stores. By engaging these kinds of mediating structures, people develop cognitive capacities that far exceed the abilities of their brains alone and, indeed, change how their brains work. A culture of libraries, recordkeeping, and monuments enables people to access and harness information in a qualitatively new way (Donald 1991). And once a set of practices for information processing and storage becomes institutionalized, the *accumulation* of information rapidly accelerates and increases. The ability to coordinate with this kind of information is an *essential* aspect of our species, part of the process of "niche construction" that changed human evolution (Sterelny 2003).

Clark and Chalmers (1998) used a vivid example in "The External Mind" related to this point. They imagined a memory-impaired person by the name of Otto who organized basic aspects of his daily life using an ever-present notebook filled with schedules, names, telephone numbers, and addresses. By efficient use of his notebook, Otto was able to perform key cognitive tasks nearly as quickly as, and perhaps more reliably than, people who had full use of their "onboard" biological memory. In the foreword to Clark's (2008: ix–xvi) more recent book, *Supersizing the Mind*, Chalmers discussed his own use of the iPhone as an example of how perfectly healthy, unimpaired people can transform into "Otto-like" beings who quickly lose many basic abilities when deprived of their "smart" devices. The example of Otto's notebook and Chalmers's iPhone underscores the more obvious, but perhaps less intuitive, point that all of us make use of environmental resources to accomplish cognitive processes on a daily basis.

10.3.2 Material Representations Alter Cognitive Complexity

A classic in cognitive psychology, Miller's (1956) "The Magical Number Seven, Plus or Minus Two" was among the first publications to challenge the notion that humans were the "paragon of animals…noble in reason…infinite in faculty" (Shakespeare 1992: 103) since the bottleneck of working memory seemed to be capped at seven plus or minus two "chunks" of information. As Miller's paper made clear, limits on human cognition only permit people to exercise what some scholars have called "bounded rationality" (Gigerenzer and Selten 2001). This approach, related to the work on "heuristics and biases" by Tversky and Kahneman (1974), believes cognition to be composed of various shortcuts that lead to "quick and dirty" solutions. Luckily, people had recognized the limits of "bare naked" cognition long before psychologists had worked out the details; numerous techniques and technologies for surpassing those limits were bequeathed by each generation to the next (Barnier et al. 2008; Roberts 1964; Rubin 1995).

Among the most commonly used, checklists, instructions, and schedules reduce "cognitive load" by setting up complex tasks as sequences of more manageable units (Paas et al. 2003; Simon 1996). This has typically been discussed as the *reduction* of cognitive complexity (e.g., Histon and Hansman 2008) since it makes tasks less demanding on limited biological resources. However, it might be better conceived as *altering* cognitive complexity since it involves shifting processes and attention to different mediating structures within the system. Additionally, there is merit to the idea that such steps ultimately *increase* cognitive complexity overall as progressively more complex forms of cognition are enabled through the orchestration of biological and environmental resources (see Kirsh 2009).

Even tasks which seem to rely on purely *mental* operations are often solved more effectively when transformed to an external, *manipulable* representation. In their seminal study, Kirsh and Maglio (1994) showed that expert players of Tetris tended to use manual rotation of Tetris tiles significantly more than mental rotation, while the opposite was true for less skilled players. The novice strategy involved more simulation, mentally rotating and placing the tiles in various ways in search of the optimal move. In contrast, the expert strategy utilized a series of manual rotations and thus relied on the actual visual matching rather than the imagined one. This coordination of biological and environmental resources in a cognitively demanding task demonstrates how expertise may be better identified as more efficient *coupling* rather than mightier brain power (see also Haier et al. 1992).

In addition to his cognitive ethnographic studies of ship navigation, Hutchins (1995b, 2000) has pursued aeronautics as a site of inquiry. As in the navigation of a ship, piloting a plane requires the extensive coordination—through expert knowledge—of a variety of mediating structures both internal and external to the pilot's body. The coordination ultimately produces a system in which the properly adjusted cockpit possesses such redundancy of processing and memory that the pilot's cognitive load is greatly reduced. This reduction allows the pilot's cognitive resources to be better employed in supervisory review and correction. For instance, pilot review and correction is especially important in safety procedures. Since flying has such an unforgiving tolerance of error, the fastidious adherence to preflight checklists greatly increases overall safety. And for certain classes of aircraft, the division of cognitive labor and the redundancy of procedures among multiple pilots ensure levels of confidence that surpass most other forms of travel, in spite of the tremendous risk of racing a behemoth heavier-than-air machine, laden with combustible fuel, through the skies.

10.3.3 Material Representations Permit Exploratory Manipulation

Brooks (1991: 15) famously insisted that "the world is its own best model." This maxim indicated that one of the central assumptions of representationalism (or "indirect realism") might be errant; instead of the human mind building up complex mental representations about the world and acting upon those representations, a great deal of cognition may be accomplished without such extensive computation—the world itself providing more information than could ever be reproduced by the nervous system's limited capacities. Once again, the idea emerges that cognition might be best understood by emphasizing the importance of coordinating biological and environmental resources toward realizing cognitive goals rather than expending limited mental resources to reproduce what is immediately accessible in the environment (see also Gibson 1979).

Mediating artifacts function by seamlessly coupling with biological processes in situated cognitive tasks. In many cases, performance depends on the degree to which tools become fully integrated, "transparent" parts of the system. When coupling works smoothly, little attention is devoted to the tool; instead, efficient coupling (as exhibited in expert tool usage, for instance) permits attention to be more lavishly spent on the performance of the task rather than on the instruments necessary for the performance. This notion of the tool's transparency is derived from Heidegger's (1962) work on "readiness to hand" versus "unreadiness to hand" (see also Harman 2002). Recently, Dotov and colleagues (2010) experimentally tested Heidegger's notions and demonstrated that the perturbation of coupling processes severely disrupted task performance. By manipulating a tool's reliability, experimenters drew attention to the instrument and, as a consequence, intermittently decoupled tool from tool user. In sum, they empirically validated Heidegger's conception of the readiness to hand of objects in use by skilled practitioners.

Nevertheless, there are also situations where this principle is reversed and *decoupling* is preferred, where an object's cognitive benefit is achieved precisely by attending to the tool. These are cases where the benefits of material representations emerge from their physical affordances, such as the manipulability they provide. Material representations can quite literally be poked, prodded, pulled apart, and reassembled. Such epistemic experimentation often leads to unforeseen insights. The properties of material objects enable a different set of organism–environment affordances than do mental operations on their own. Additionally, manual experimentation introduces an element of unpredictability that potentially disrupts functional fixedness and other constraining biases (Duncker 1945).

In a study of Scrabble players, Maglio and colleagues (1999) demonstrated better performance when people used their hands to shuffle Scrabble tiles for purposes of word search than when they were prevented from using their hands. Similar findings by Valée-Tourangeau and Krüsi Penney (2005) showed that performance in a classical problem-solving paradigm was significantly improved if participants were allowed to manipulate material representations. The widespread use of physical models in a variety of industries and disciplines also suggests an intuitive appreciation of the cognitive possibilities that only artifacts can provide by virtue of their manipulability. The shuffling and juxtaposition of numerous components in a model may be challenging, if not impossible, to reproduce without access to these mediating structures.

10.4 Thinking Together

While the previous examples generally capitalize on manipulability, another salient property of material representations is their *public* nature. While mental imagery is necessarily bound to individuals, material representations are potentially accessible by several people, thus affording unprecedented modes of collective thinking. When put out in the public, thoughts can be negotiated, elaborated, and tested. Shared calendars, whiteboards, and diagrams enable people to stimulate each other's minds in ways that can make a group perform better—*as a whole*—than the mere sum of its members' contributions. In these cases, mediating structures permit the formation of socially distributed cognitive systems.

Moreover, the instantiation of cognitive processes in material representations forms "trails" that come to guide, constrain, and reify particular practices for thinking and acting. This is—in essence—*material culture*. Take Hutchins's (1995a) aforementioned study of ship navigation: a lot of demanding math is required in order to compute logarithmic relationships between time, speed, and distance. However, the development of a simple mediating artifact—the Three-Scale Nomogram—transforms the complex computational task into a simple perceptual one. Knowing any two of the three values allows one to determine the third by simply placing a straight edge across the three scales; lining up the two known values intersects the correct third value. This materially mediated shortcut to identify the third value requires essentially no computational effort. Such practices allow novices to reap the benefits of their ancestors' labor by simply learning how to follow "the material trail" rather than discovering a new path each and every time. This immersion in distributed cognitive practices facilitates cognition by relying on the accumulated store of hard-won routines (Hutchins 2008; Sterelny 2005). In the following, we enumerate different aspects of socially distributed cognition, from the way objects and artifacts distribute cognitive labor to the role of language in coupling cognitive systems.

10.4.1 Material Representations Enable the Division of Cognitive Labor

Hutchins (1995a) asserts "division of labor" to be among the most important ideas in the social sciences (Durkheim 1984; Smith 1776). He expresses surprise that this same insight has not been more rigorously applied in the study of cognition. Just as society orchestrates labor to create institutional action, so must cognition be socially distributed to enact complex cognition at the institutional level (Douglas 1986).

The division of cognitive labor requires a variety of mediating structures and can take two forms: (1) the coordination of multiple people for *collective* cognitive goals and (2) the coordination of multiple people for *individual* cognitive goals. That is, some goals cannot be achieved without the combined cognitive resources of many people, while other goals can easily be achieved by an individual, yet the individual may benefit by distributing cognitive tasks among many people in order to improve performance or free up time and effort for other purposes.

The use of a conventionalized set of practices and tools allows multiple people to coordinate their cognition so that a single person's limitations (e.g., time, skills, productivity) need not constrain the overall system; this is the beginning of the institution as a meaningful unit of analysis. With the proper organization, not only can labor be coordinated toward a never-ending 24 h, 7 days a week cycle, but additionally, the labor can be multiplied by as many participants as are available. Through such actions, productivity toward a collective goal can reach *millions* of labor hours, equivalent to countless *lifetimes* of cognitive effort.

For example, the production of scientific knowledge is conceived of as a collective endeavor in which the observations of many people are recorded and shared so that a much larger set of observations—the accumulated efforts of numerous people over time—can be assembled for the benefit of the community (Fleck 1979:42). The importance of publications in science is derived from the essential interdependence of this enterprise, and, even more specifically, the careful exposition of methodology in such publications improves reliability across the set of practitioners by ensuring the use of similar tools and practices when performing related experiments.

In addition to the roles that material representations play in coordinating people toward collective goals, they also permit people to distribute labor for accomplishing individual goals. Examples of "offloading" memory to free up one's biological resources for other processes are intuitive and mundane, though they may require coordinating people and objects in complex ways. Consider the practice of telling a friend to remember a phone number before reciting it out loud, so that one can perform an additional set of cognitively demanding tasks. Peoples' daily routines are punctuated by innumerable such practices, clever techniques which are so commonplace that their significance for understanding the way minds work is often overlooked. Similarly, a partner of any variety—whether for business, travel, or romance—functions well by complementing the other's cognitive labor in order to reduce the demands on each and to foster more robust cognition than either could accomplish alone.

Though this discussion has focused on interpersonal coordination, since division of labor is typically conceived of this way, these ideas are hinged on the coordination of people and technologies since the human niche, including the ways that people coordinate interpersonally, is *essentially* technological. The natural habitat for human beings involves a variety of "cognitive ecosystems" in which each component of cognition depends on and creates the environment for the others (Hutchins 2010).

10.4.2 Material Representations Promote Confidence and Trust

Material representations, and operations upon those representations, possess the virtue of being public. For instance, when a calculation is done in the head during a financial exchange, it may be looked upon with suspicion, particularly if the person doing the calculation has something to gain by erring in his own favor. The trader may be capable of performing complex calculations in his head, but his customer will be more trusting if he can see the calculations performed with pencil and paper right in front of him. Similarly, the possibility for exchange-related disputes is greatly minimized if records that include acknowledgment by each party are kept on file. Such practices, if not based on distrust, certainly prevent the frailty of self-interested memory processes from creating "bad blood" between people. Trust, confidence, and faith in the cognitive labor are enhanced as more and more of the processes are rendered public.

A similar phenomenon has emerged in the present economic climate in regard to money. Though money has long since been detached from material commodities (such as gold) and even material forms (such as cash), trust in the binary codes that represent our financial holdings waxes and wanes with confidence in the economy as a whole. Over the last few years, the price of gold shot upward serving as an index of pessimism regarding the world's financial systems. Such movements into gold exhibit the kind of uncertainty people experience when they consider how much of their wealth resides in nonmaterial form. The conversion of the essentially private representations within financial institutions into more public representations, like gold, demonstrates peoples' greater confidence in material forms of money. A similar "gold standard" occurs as people transform private cognition into public cognition through the use of material representations such as ledgers, logs, and bills of lading.

10.4.3 Material Representations Consolidate Social Structure

In the contemporary social sciences, the reintroduction of such seemingly basic topics as "embodiment" and "materiality" bears witness to a marginalization of the nonsocial during the recent past (see Appadurai 1986; Csordas 1990; Ingold 2000; Miller 1998). In other words, sociality had become the sole means of relationality—or *mediation*—in cultural settings (Strathern 1995). Nevertheless, every ethnography before and after documents the importance of "things" (e.g., objects, places, and texts) as mediators of relations as well. Is there a Greek culture without sheep or olives? Is there a Bedouin culture without deserts? And what is Judaism without Torah? Nevertheless, all these other mediators became subservient to "the social," the true engine of human action. This hegemony of the social implies a nonmaterial ontology. Latour (2005: 70) challenges the sensibility of this model:

> As soon as you believe social aggregates can hold their own being propped up by 'social forces', then objects vanish from view and the magical and tautological force of society is enough to hold *every thing* with, literally, *no thing*.

Given the marginalization of material representations described above, it may come as a surprise that Durkheim (1965), a foundational figure in the study of society, considered objects to be one of the constituent elements of culture:

> Moreover, without symbols, social sentiments could have only a precarious existence. Though very strong as long as men are together and influence each other reciprocally, they exist only in the form of recollections after the assembly has ended, and when left to themselves, these become feebler and feebler... But if the movements by which these sentiments are expressed are connected with something that endures, the sentiments themselves become more durable. These other things are constantly bringing them to mind and arousing them; it is as though the cause which excited them in the first place continued to act. Thus these systems of emblems, which are necessary if society is to become conscious of itself, are no less indispensable for assuring the continuation of this consciousness.

In this excerpt, Durkheim describes the materialization of social life in emblems. The affordances of their materiality, their service as physical cues of experience and their enduring nature, *reify* concepts into percepts. A god becomes an idol and vice versa. A flag becomes a nation and excites collective identity. The land itself becomes a country "from sea to shining sea." In short, conceiving social life without material culture is no different than conceiving mind without body.

10.4.4 Material Representations Support Dialogical Coupling

So far, one of the most important mediating structures—*language*—has not received appropriate attention in this chapter. Clark (1997) has suggested language to be the "ultimate artifact," emphasizing its centrality as a tool for thought. Like the other tools discussed here, language seems to mediate cognitive processes in a variety of ways. One influential position holds that language—drawing upon its phonetic or orthographic instantiations—is another material resource that individuals can engage for individual thought (Clark 2006; Roepstorff 2008). However, a complementary perspective holds that language should be conceived of as the "coupling link" that enables socially distributed cognition. Or, to say it another way, language enables a person to become someone else's "cognitive extension" (Fusaroli et al. 2012, 2014a; Tylén et al. 2010). By engaging in dialogical interactions, individuals coordinate joint apprehension and manipulation of representations, thus creating *interpersonal synergies* which potentially exceed the sum of individual contributions (Fusaroli et al. 2014b). A number of recent studies support such claims.

In a simple psychophysical task, Bahrami and colleagues (2010) showed that when pairs of participants were allowed to discuss freely among themselves, they performed significantly better than the best member of the pair alone. However, not all pairs performed equally well and a follow-up study (Fusaroli et al. 2012) revealed that more linguistically coordinated pairs (i.e., those who developed a shared vocabulary attuned to the task demands) reached higher levels of performance.

Similar observations were made by Dale and colleagues (2011) who had dyads of participants solve a joint task matching ambiguous tangram figures while recording their eye and computer mouse movements. As they evolved a shared vocabulary for referring to the figures, not only did participants' eye movements and mouse movements become increasingly coordinated, but cross-modal coordination between the eye movements of the "director" and mouse movements of the "matcher" significantly increased. In sum, the dyad became a coupled, tangram recognition system.

10.5 Conclusion

Numerous researchers have pursued investigations of cognition informed by the same sensibilities we share, but there has been little synthesis of the findings in terms of clarifying the role of objects in cognition and culture. We have identified two central properties of material representations that have enabled unprecedented modes of cultural cognition: their manipulable and public characteristics. Due to their manipulability, objects can store information, alter cognitive complexity, and offer novel opportunities for search and experimentation. Because of their public nature, objects facilitate the division of cognitive labor, promote trust, consolidate social structure, and through language—the "ultimate artifact"—provide the coupling link for socially distributed cognition.

Though it has not always been foregrounded, properties of the material environment are as essential to human cognition as they are to our other abilities. As a distinctive trait, humans have come to rely on inherited environments constituted by material representations and cultural practices that kindle their usage. Archaeologists have marked entire eras of human history using labels derived from the novel lithic and metallurgical technologies of the time in recognition of the critical importance these materials held in shaping the course of events. Though mediating structures like language, writing, and numerals are more difficult to identify in the archaeological record than are the first appearances of ceramics, bronze, or iron artifacts, our tools and technologies punctuate cultural evolution and remain the most powerful agents of change right up to the present. Just looking around our contemporary world, it is easy to see that smartphones, computers, and the Internet are more than "tools at our disposal"; they are, in fact, basic technologies for our involvement with each other and our shared world. Our tools constantly shape and define us, permitting us to exercise a plasticity that, more than anything, expresses our human natures.

References

Appadurai, Arjun (ed.). 1986. *The social life of things: Commodities in cultural perspective*. Cambridge: Cambridge University Press.

Bahrami, Bahador, et al. 2010. Optimally interacting minds. *Science* 329(5995): 1081–1085.

Barnier, Amanda J., et al. 2008. A conceptual and empirical framework for the social distribution of cognition: The case of memory. *Cognitive Systems Research* 9(1–2): 33–51.

Beach, King. 1993. Becoming a bartender: The role of external memory cues in a work-directed educational activity. *Applied Cognitive Psychology* 7(3): 191–204.

Brooks, Rodney A. 1991. Intelligence without reason. *Artificial Intelligence* 47(1–3): 139–159.

Clark, Andy. 1997. *Being there: Putting brain, body, and world together again*. Cambridge, MA: MIT Press.

Clark, Andy. 2003. *Natural-born Cyborgs: Minds, technologies, and the future of human intelligence*. Oxford: Oxford University Press.

Clark, Andy. 2006. Material symbols. *Philosophical Psychology* 19(3): 291–307.

Clark, Andy. 2008. *Supersizing the mind: Embodiment, action, and cognitive extension*. Oxford: Oxford University Press.

Clark, Andy, and David Chalmers. 1998. The extended mind. *Analysis* 58(1): 7–19.

Csordas, Thomas J. 1990. Embodiment as a paradigm for anthropology. *Ethos* 18(1): 5–47.

Dale, Rick, Daniel C. Richardson, and N.K. Kirkham. 2011. In *Proceedings of DUET (Dual Eye-Tracking Workshop): How two people become a tangram recognition system*. European Conference on Computer-Supported Cooperative Work, 2011. Aarhus University, Aarhus, Denmark.

De Jaegher, H., and E. Di Paolo. 2007. Participatory sense-making. *Phenomenology and the Cognitive Sciences* 6(4): 485–507.

Donald, Merlin. 1991. *Origins of the modern mind: Three stages in the evolution of culture and cognition*. Cambridge, MA: Harvard University Press.

Dotov, Dobromir G., Lin Nie, and Anthony Chemero. 2010. A demonstration of the transition from ready-to-hand to unready-to-hand. *PLoS ONE* 5(3): e9433.

Douglas, Mary. 1986. *How institutions think*. Syracuse: Syracuse University Press.

Duncker, Karl. 1945. *On problem-solving*. Washington, DC: American Psychological Association.

Durkheim, Emile. 1965. *The Elementary Forms of Religious Life*. Trans. J.W. Swain. New York: The Free Press.

Durkheim, Emile. 1984. *The Division of Labor in Society*. Trans. W.D. Halls. New York: Free Press.

Fleck, Ludwik. 1979. *Genesis and Development of a Scientific Fact*. Trans. F. Bradley and T. Trenn. Chicago: University of Chicago Press.

Fusaroli, Riccardo, et al. 2012. Coming to terms: Quantifying the benefits of linguistic coordination. *Psychological Science* 23(8): 931–939.

Fusaroli, Riccardo, Joanna Rączaszek-Leonardi, and Kristian Tylén. 2014a. Dialog as interpersonal synergy. *New Ideas in Psychology* 32: 147–157.

Fusaroli, Riccardo, Nivedita Gangopadhyay, and Kristian Tylén. 2014b. The dialogically extended mind: Language as skillful intersubjective engagement. *Cognitive Systems Research* 29–30: 31–39.

Gibson, J.J. 1977. The theory of affordances. In *Perceiving, acting, and knowing: Toward an ecological psychology*, ed. R.E. Shaw and J. Bransford. Hillsdale: Lawrence Erlbaum Associates.

Gibson, J.J. 1979. *The ecological approach to visual perception*. Boston: Houghton Mifflin.

Gigerenzer, Gerd, and Reinhard Selten. 2001. *Bounded rationality: The adaptive toolbox*. Cambridge, MA: MIT Press.

Haier, Richard J., et al. 1992. Intelligence and changes in regional cerebral glucose metabolic rate following learning. *Intelligence* 16(3–4): 415–426.

Harman, Graham. 2002. *Tool-being: Heidegger and the metaphysics of objects*. Chicago: Open Court.

Heidegger, Martin. 1962. *Being and time*. New York: Harper.

Histon, Jonathan M., and R. John Hansman. 2008. *Mitigating complexity in air traffic control: The role of structure-based abstractions*. Cambridge, MA: Aeronautics and Astronautics/ Massachusetts Institute of Technology.

Hutchins, Edwin. 1995a. *Cognition in the wild*. Cambridge, MA: MIT Press.

Hutchins, Edwin. 1995b. How a cockpit remembers its speeds. *Cognitive Science* 19(3): 265–288.

Hutchins, Edwin. 2000. The cognitive consequences of patterns of information flow. *Intellectica* 1(30): 53–74.

Hutchins, Edwin. 2008. The role of cultural practices in the emergence of modern human intelligence. *Philosophical Transactions of the Royal Society of London. Series B, Biological Sciences* 363(1499): 2011–2019.

Hutchins, Edwin. 2010. Cognitive ecology. *Topics in Cognitive Science* 2(4): 705–715.

Ingold, Tim. 2000. *The perception of the environment: Essays on livelihood, dwelling & skill*. London: Routledge.

Kirsh, David. 2009. Interaction, external representations and sense making. In *Proceedings of the 31st annual conference of the Cognitive Science Society*, ed. N.A. Taatgen and H. van Rijn, 1103–1108. Austin: Cognitive Science Society.

Kirsh, David, and Paul Maglio. 1994. On distinguishing epistemic from pragmatic action. *Cognitive Science* 18(4): 513–549.

Latour, Bruno. 1996. On interobjectivity. *Mind, Culture, and Activity* 3(4): 228–245.

Latour, Bruno. 2005. *Reassembling the social: An introduction to actor-network-theory*. Oxford: Oxford University Press.

Maglio, Paul, et al. 1999. Interactive skill in scrabble. In *Proceedings of the twenty-first annual conference of the cognitive science society*, 326–330. Mahwah: Lawrence Erlbaum Associates.
McGraw, John J. 2011. *Divination & decision-making: Ritual techniques of distributed cognition in the Guatemalan Highlands*. Ph.D. dissertation, Anthropology, University of California San Diego.
Menary, Richard (ed.). 2010. *The extended mind*. Cambridge, MA: MIT Press.
Mesquita, Batja, Lisa Feldman Barrett, and Eliot R. Smith. 2010. *The mind in context*. New York: Guilford Press.
Miller, George A. 1956. The magical number seven, plus or minus two: Some limits on our capacity for processing information. *Psychological Review* 63(2): 81–97.
Miller, Daniel (ed.). 1998. *Material cultures: Why some things matter*. Chicago: University of Chicago Press.
Paas, Fred, et al. 2003. Cognitive load measurement as a means to advance cognitive load theory. *Educational Psychologist* 38(1): 63–71.
Peirce, Charles S. 1982. *Writings of Charles S. Peirce: A chronological edition*. Bloomington: Indiana University Press.
Roberts, John M. 1964. The self-management of cultures. In *Explorations in cultural anthropology: Essays in honor of George Peter Murdock*, ed. W. Goodenough, 433–454. New York: McGraw-Hill.
Roepstorff, Andreas. 2008. Things to think with: Words and objects as material symbols. *Philosophical Transactions of the Royal Society, B: Biological Sciences* 363(1499): 2049–2054.
Rubin, David C. 1995. *Memory in oral traditions: The cognitive psychology of epic, ballads, and counting-out rhymes*. New York: Oxford University Press.
Ryle, Gilbert. 1949. *The concept of mind*. London/New York: Hutchinson's University Library.
Searle, John R. 1995. *The construction of social reality*. New York: Free Press.
Shakespeare, William. 1992. *Hamlet*. New York: Washington Square Press.
Simon, Herbert A. 1996. *The sciences of the artificial*. Cambridge, MA: MIT Press.
Smith, Adam. 1776. *An inquiry into the nature and causes of the wealth of nations*, 2 vols. London: W. Strahan and T. Cadell.
Sterelny, Kim. 2003. *Thought in a hostile world: The evolution of human cognition*. Malden: Blackwell.
Sterelny, Kim. 2005. Cognitive load and human decision, or, three ways of rolling the rock uphill. In *The innate mind*, Evolution and cognition, ed. P. Carruthers, S. Laurence, and S. Stich, 218–233. Oxford: Oxford University Press.
Strathern, Marilyn. 1995. *The relation: Issues in complexity and scale*. Cambridge: Prickly Pear Press.
Tversky, Amos, and Daniel Kahneman. 1974. Judgment under uncertainty: Heuristics and biases. *Science* 185(4157): 1124–1131.
Tylén, Kristian, et al. 2010. Language as a tool for interacting minds. *Mind & Language* 25(1): 3–29.
Vallée-Tourangeau, Frédéric, and Andrea Krüsi Penney. 2005. The impact of external representation in a rule discovery task. *European Journal of Cognitive Psychology* 17(6): 820–834.
Varela, Francisco J., Evan Thompson, and Eleanor Rosch. 1992. *The embodied mind: Cognitive science and human experience*. Cambridge, MA: The MIT Press.
Vygotsky, Lev. 1978. *Mind in society: The development of higher psychological processes*. Cambridge, MA: Harvard University Press.
Zhang, Jiajie, and Vimla L. Patel. 2006. Distributed cognition, representation, and affordance. *Pragmatics and Cognition* 14(2): 333–341.

Chapter 11
Perceiving Affordances and Social Cognition

Anika Fiebich

Abstract Navigating successfully through the environment requires perceiving what action possibilities the ecological environment affords to us. Though ecological affordances have been discussed intensively in the Gibsonian tradition, little attention has been paid to the role that social cognition plays for our perception of ecological affordances. The present chapter aims to fill this gap in the debate. In a first step, I will provide a relational account of affordances according to which perceiving affordances are perceiving one's own action possibilities (i.e. the 'animal relatum') in relation to particular aspects of the environment (i.e. the 'environment relatum'), including physical, intentional, and institutional aspects. In a second step, I discuss the role of social cognition for the perception of ecological affordances in social and institutional contexts. Here, I distinguish between 'social cognition in a narrow sense' that is required to understand the attitudes and intentions of a particular person in a social context and 'social cognition in a broad sense' that is required to understand the shared intention of a social group in an institutional context.

Navigating successfully through the environment requires perceiving what action possibilities the environment affords to us. Basically, we can distinguish between ecological affordances and interpersonal affordances. 'Ecological affordances' are action possibilities we perceive whilst navigating through the ecological environment. 'Interpersonal affordances', in contrast, are action possibilities we perceive whilst navigating through the interpersonal environment, for example, what interactive responses another person affords to us. As a bodily being, another person also provides us ecological affordances. When you are standing as stiff as a statue in front of a cupboard, I may perceive the ecological affordance to climb onto your shoulder in order to get the pan from the top shelf. In this sense, interpersonal affordances might be regarded as a subcategory of ecological affordances. That is, the

A. Fiebich (✉)
Ruhr-University Bochum, Bochum, Germany
e-mail: anifiebich@gmail.com

M. Gallotti and J. Michael (eds.), *Perspectives on Social Ontology and Social Cognition*, 149
Studies in the Philosophy of Sociality 4, DOI 10.1007/978-94-017-9147-2_11,

interpersonal environment is a part of the ecological environment. However, the distinctive feature of persons who offer not only ecological but also interpersonal affordances to other people is that the other person's body is typically not static but animate and in motion. I perceive your physical aspects, such as your body scale, in relation to mine when interacting with you and I coordinate my bodily movements accordingly. For example, kissing you, I bend down slightly, because you are smaller than me. Interpersonal affordances are, in contrast to ecological affordances, perceived within the interactive *reciprocal* processes; the behaviour of the other person affords behavioural responses to me. Furthermore, social-cognitive skills come into play in order to grasp the meaning of the other person's bodily expressions.

But also the perception of ecological affordances might require social-cognitive skills. Although ecological affordances have been discussed intensively in the Gibsonian tradition, little attention has been paid to the role that social cognition plays for the perception of ecological affordances. The present chapter aims to fill this gap in the debate. I provide a relational approach to affordances and analyse the role of social cognition for the perception of ecological affordances in social and institutional contexts.

11.1 Towards a Relational Account of Affordances

The term 'affordance' goes back to James Gibson ([1979] 1986, p. 127) who defines it as follows:

> The affordances of the environment are what it offers the animal, what it provides or furnishes, either for good or ill. The verb is found in the dictionary, but the noun affordance is not. I have made it up. I mean by it something that refers to both the environment and the animal in a way that no existing term does. It implies the complementarity of the animal and the environment.

Gibson describes affordances as animal-related properties of the ecological environment. He considers the body scale of the animal as the essential aspect of the animal and affordances are relative to the body scale; for example, a surface that is horizontal, flat, extended, rigid, and knee-high relative to the perceiver affords the possibility to sit upon it. Notably, 'knee-high' for a child is not the same as 'knee-high' for an adult; that is, perceived affordances are relative to the body scale of the individual perceiver. Gibson distinguishes between different kinds of affordances of the terrestrial environment (such as medium, substance, surface, person, and place) and highlights that some affordances are positive and beneficial whereas others are negative and injurious. For example, some substances that afford ingestion afford also nutrition for the animal, others in turn afford poisoning, and some are neutral. Of course, the benefits and injuries an object affords to an animal may be misperceived by the animal; for example, poison ivy may be mistaken for ivy that affords nutrition. According to Gibson, affordances exist prior to and independently of the perception of single individuals.

Reed (1996) and Heft (1989, 2001) follow Gibson's approach to conceive affordances as properties of the environment, which are relative to the animal's body scale. Warren's (1984) classical study of stair-climbing affordances has shown that although the ruler measured riser of a stairway as climbable differs across participants, the ratio of riser height to leg length remains common to all observers. Thus, people observe affordances (such as climbable stairs) in their own spatial dimensions.

A recent study of Cesari et al. (2003) has shown, however, that it is not just their own body scale upon which participants base their perception of stairs as climbable but also their own climbing competencies in terms of energy and motor flexibility; thus, older adults who have different stair-climbing abilities than young adults used the ratio differently and perceive climbing affordances in terms of ability. The evidence indicates that there are affordances as Chemero (2003) defines them. Chemero's (2003) definition of affordances takes not just the environment's properties but also the animal's ability into account. More precisely, Chemero argues for affordances as relations between the abilities of an animal and some feature of the situation (see also Stoffregen 2003 for a similar approach to affordances).

Following Chemero, I defend a relational approach to ecological affordances. To perceive affordances is to perceive one's own action possibilities that depend on one's own action capabilities (the 'animal relatum') in relation to particular aspects of the ecological environment (the 'environment relatum'), including physical, intentional, and institutional aspects. This account also includes the perception of negative affordances in the sense that I may perceive my inability to meet particular challenges.[1] Notably, I remain neutral to the question of whether perception should be regarded as being enactive or representational and do not defend any specific approach to perception in this chapter.

In the following, I will outline the peculiarities of these relata as well as their interrelations (see Sects. 11.2 and 11.3). Furthermore, I discuss the role of social cognition for perceiving affordances. On my account, social cognition plays two roles for the perception of ecological affordances. First, social cognition plays a role in social learning which is often required for understanding what action possibilities particular aspects of the ecological environment afford (see Sect. 11.2.1). Second, social cognition may shape an individual's perception of ecological affordances in a way that it determines whether or not an individual perceives himself or herself as being capable of making use of the affordances that he or she perceives. Here, we can distinguish between 'social cognition in a narrow sense' that is required to understand the attitudes and intentions of a particular person in a given situation (see Sect. 11.4.1) and 'social cognition in a broad sense' that is required to understand the shared intention of social group members who constitute a particular institution (see Sect. 11.4.2).

[1] Other approaches to affordances deny the notion of negative affordances. Michaels (2003, p. 137), for example, defends the view that affordances need to be action related. Basically, Michaels distinguishes between two categories of 'affordances'; (1) action-related affordances such as stairs that afford climbing and (2) affordances in which actions are conspicuously absent such as a cliff or a snake that might afford danger or particular substances that afford nutrition. Since danger and nutrition are not actions in the sense of movements that are coordinated in order to achieve some goal, Michaels does not rank them among affordances.

11.2 The Environment Relatum: Physical, Intentional, and Institutional Aspects

I distinguish between three aspects that an individual may perceive in an ecological object: ‘physical aspects’, ‘intentional aspects’, and ‘institutional aspects’. The ‘physical aspects’ of an object include its physical features such as size, weight, shape, etc. Sensorimotor knowledge is acquired by sensorimotor exploration of the physical aspects of an object. Perceiving the physical aspects of an object involves so-called sensorimotor knowledge for which purpose[2] these aspects can (reasonably) serve. For example, when aiming to destroy a window to break into your house, I may make use of the heavy secateurs I found in your garden by throwing it at the window considering the weight and size of the secateurs as being suited for that purpose. Considering the leaves on the earth for this purpose, in contrast, would not be sensible.

Obviously, the secateurs have not been designed to serve the purpose of breaking windows. They have been designed to cut the plants. When you are gardening, you typically focus on those physical aspects that can serve the purpose for which the secateurs have been designed (i.e. the scissor blades that are suitable to cut the plants when pressing the handle); call those aspects ‘intentional aspects’ (Tomasello 1999a). To perceive the purpose for which an object has been designed is to perceive the purpose for which an object has been designed *for us*, that is, the *conventional* use of the object; call this *conventional knowledge*. Furthermore, the knowledge of this conventionality may be implicit in the sense of being nonconscious but accessible. For example, you may not be consciously aware of the conventionality of a fork when you perceive its intentional affordance to use it as a tool for eating your dish. But when you are asked about it, you are well capable of indicating that using a fork for eating is a conventional use, and you may also be capable of indicating the society in which this use is conventional (e.g. Western but not Eastern cultures).

Finally, you may focus on the ‘institutional aspects’ of an ecological object. Imagine, for example, that the secateurs (being a special kind of scissors) are part of a modified version of the game *Paper, Scissors, Stone* in which gamblers choose among these three options not by making manual gestures. Instead, each gambler has one box containing a paper, a scissor, and a stone and has to choose one item. Within this game, the secateurs have what Searle (2011) calls a ‘status function’ (i.e. the scissors win over the paper but lose against the stone), and to perceive this function is to perceive the ‘institutional aspects’ that this object affords within an institutional context, that is, the game.

[2] Of course, the perceived ‘flexibility’ of the use of an object’s physical aspects ‘for whatever purpose’ is relative to the perceiving system. That is, although the secateurs may, in general, be perceived as being heavy and big enough to be a tool for breaking the window, I may not perceive this sensorimotor affordance because I do not think I am strong enough to pick up and throw the secateurs.

The crucial difference between perceiving what the 'intentional aspects' of an object afford in a conventional context and perceiving what the 'institutional aspects' of an object afford in an institutional context is that the latter, though not the former, presupposes the existence of an institution involving other agents. Following Kono (2009, p. 357), I propose that social institutions produce and maintain the institutional aspects of the ecological environment and construct the 'niche' for human beings. Without explicit reference, Kono seems to adopt Gibson's ([1979] 1986, p. 128) conception of 'niche', according to which 'a niche refers more to *how* an animal lives than to *where* it lives. I suggest that a niche is a set of affordances'. Gibson provides the example of a postbox that affords letter-mailing to a person living in a community with a postal system. Thus, by the postal system the letter-mailing affordance of the postbox is produced and maintained.

I perceive the intentional aspect of an object, that is, the purpose for which it has been designed, without taking into account the institutional context (in which it may have been designed). When perceiving institutional affordances, in contrast, I perceive the institutional aspect of an object always by taking the institutional system into account. An institutional system typically involves a set of social rules and roles which I need to know (call this *institutional knowledge*) and to follow in order to actualize the perceived affordance; I need to affix the appropriate postage stamp on the letter to perceive that the postbox in which I throw the letter affords transferring my letter. Furthermore, the postal system involves a number of agents who contribute to actualizing my perceived affordance whereas I do not need any other agent within an institutional system to actualize the intentional aspects I perceive of an object; for example, I may use an alarm clock to wake up even if I am on a desert island, far away from any institutional systems whereas I don't perceive the postbox I brought with me on my stranded ship as affording letter-mailing anymore. That is, perceiving institutional affordances presupposes the *belief* in the existence of a particular institution such as the post (which is not given on a desert island).

One and the same object can have (in principle) a variety of affordances for the perceiver. Depending on which perceived aspect is of significance to the animal in a given situation, the animal perceives what I call 'sensorimotor affordances' (when the physical aspects are significant), 'intentional affordances' (when the intentional aspects are significant), or 'institutional affordances' (when the institutional aspects are significant) of the ecological environment. Following Fröse and Di Paolo (2011), I propose that 'significance [...] constitutes a concern which is relative to the current situation of the system and its needs' (p. 7). For example, the physical aspects of an object (say, a postbox) may be of significance to me in a given situation (e.g. when I aim to pick an apple from a tree by climbing on the postbox) whereas in other situations, different aspects of that very object may be significant (such as the institutional aspect of the postbox that affords mail-lettering).

11.2.1 The Role of Social Learning

An individual's understanding of what the various aspects of the ecological environment may afford develops throughout ontogeny via individual exploration or social learning.

Infants acquire sensorimotor knowledge of the physical aspects of objects by individual exploration at the very beginning of ontogeny. From birth onwards infants are engaged in touching and sucking at objects. Within the first weeks of life, they are able to modify their sucking behaviour in a fitting manner to the object they are sucking at (Piaget [1970] 2003). Three-month-olds reach for objects not just on the basis of visual stimuli but also auditory ones (Clifton et al. 1993). From the fifth month onwards, infants are even capable of accounting for the object's distance in their grasping behaviour (Field 1976) indicating a first implicit awareness of their own body scale and grasping abilities in relation to another physical object or person.

At about age 1, infants acquire social-cognitive competencies that enable them to learn about the physical aspects of the environment in situations of so-called social referencing. In social referencing, infants refer to an adult in ambiguous situations and adopt the emotional attitude of the adult towards a particular situation or an (inanimate or animate) object in order to determine whether the situation or object in question is 'safe' or 'unsafe' to approach, or (more basically) 'good' or 'bad' (Striano and Rochat 2000; Moses et al. 2001). Via social referencing, infants may get a grasp, for example, of whether surfaces are 'crawable'. In the so-called visual cliff paradigm, 1-year-old infants were put on the covered part of a glass table and they saw their mothers at the far end of the table. The mother either smiled at the infant or showed him or her fearful facial expressions. Infants, unsure whether or not it is safe to crawl over the glass table to get to their mothers, mostly crossed the 'visual cliff' when their mothers smiled at them whereas none of the infants ventured over the visual cliff when they saw their mothers' fearful expressions (Gibson and Walk 1960).

To be engaged in social referencing, infants need to have a grasp of another person's emotional attitudes and attention to entities in the ecological environment, and they need to be capable of joint attention. Joint attention can be defined as the awareness that oneself and another agent are attentive towards the same ecological entity and that this awareness is mutually shared or is mutual common knowledge among the agents (see Triesch et al. 2006 for a discussion). Joint attention has been found to be developed at the same age in infants from different cultures (Tomasello 1999b), suggesting that it relies on a cognitive module that is innate but emerges in the course of development which is determined by its own developmental timetable rather than interaction with the culture-specific social environment (Baron-Cohen 1995). Furthermore, infants need to account for another person's emotional attitude towards objects or other people in situations of social referencing.

By social referencing infants enter the conventional world in which they grow up. Though an infant might not fully understand the complex set of conventional beliefs that underlie the adult's emotional attitude towards particular entities (e.g. an infant growing up in a Muslim family may not understand initially that his or her mother shows a facial expression of disgust towards pork due to religious reasons), she simply adopts that negative attitude and integrates it into his or her behavioural repertoire by avoiding eating pork henceforward.[3] Infants adopt the emotional attitudes of close adults, mostly their parents, independently of whether that attitude is shaped by the conventional or personal beliefs of the adults; in either way, the infants become a social being and part of the social group they live in (the family in a narrow and the society in a broader sense). By the adoption of emotional attitudes towards situations and objects, the perception of these entities gains a normative connotation and in this way modulates what we perceive as affordances. As recent studies have shown, a communicative setting is required to yield this effect (see Csibra 2010 for a review). Communicative settings are established by ostensive cues such as waving to the observer, calling him or her by name, or simply looking at him or her.

An understanding of the 'intentional aspects' or 'institutional aspects' of objects is typically acquired via different forms of social learning. Many objects infants deal with are artificial and designed for specific purposes. I agree with Tomasello (1999a, p. 154) that 'in many instances, the purpose of an artifact can only be discerned through adult demonstration or instruction that establishes what 'we' do with it, after which the artifact possesses intentional affordances – that is, in addition to the natural affordances for sensory-motor action that have so occupied Gibsonians'. One glance is sufficient to find Tomasello's claim supported that most (or at least many) of the ecological objects we are surrounded by are artificial. Tomasello makes a distinction between natural objects such as rocks and material artefacts such as tools that are designed for a specific purpose. Although I follow Tomasello in calling those affordances that a material artefact affords to fulfil the purpose for which it has been designed 'intentional affordances', I do not only use the term 'sensorimotor affordances' for the affordances of natural objects. On my account, perceiving different affordances is dependent on perceiving different *aspects* of an ecological object, independent of whether this object is artificial or not.

Infants may, for example, discover that drapes afford help in pulling themselves up in their first attempts to standing upright ('sensorimotor affordances') without knowing about the intentional affordances of drapes to darken the room. Likewise an infant may explore that a chair is sitable without understanding that it has been designed for precisely this purpose. Of course, infants may explore accidently that drapes can be used to darken the room, but as long as they are not aware of this as an intentional rather than a physical aspect, they do not perceive the intentional affordances of drapes. Perceiving the 'intentional affordances' of an object requires one to perceive the purpose an object has been designed for *as* the purpose an object has been designed *for us*; perceiving the intentional aspects of an object is to perceive aspects that are designed for a conventional use. That is, it involves conventional knowledge.

[3] This does not necessarily presuppose the possession of a linguistic concept of pork, but only the capability to categorize pork according to specific physical aspects (colour, consistency etc.). Already 11-month-olds have been found to be able to categorize ecological objects (Pauen 2002).

Following Tomasello (1999a), I distinguish between two kinds of social learning: emulation learning and imitative learning. In emulation learning, we learn something about the intrinsic physical features of an object by observing another conspecific dealing with that object. This kind of learning is also observable in non-human primates; for example, observing a conspecific's cracking open a nut might lead the observer to use this information to crack open the nut. The observer solves the problem not by using the own strategy but rather by emulating the other's problem-solving strategy (p. 156). In emulation learning, we learn about the *physical aspects* of an object, that is, what the object affords to us sensorimotorically. In imitative learning, in contrast, we learn about the *intentional aspects* of an object, that is, the conventional use for which a particular object has been designed, or the *institutional aspects* of an object, that is, the use of a particular object in an institutional context. We imitate actual behavioural strategies of another person due to our attribution of normativity to the other's action, which is human-specific and needs to be distinguished from a blind mimicry of the other's sensorimotor actions such as when a parrot mimics human speech or a human or non-human primate newborn mimics the adult poking out his tongue.

In general, imitating how another person deals with an object to achieve a specific goal presupposes an understanding of another person as an intentional agent who represents a particular means-end relation in order to achieve that goal. Of course, another person's action plan might not always be the best to achieve a particular goal. As a result of understanding this, 18-month-olds imitate not the specific movements they observe an actor performing who is unsuccessfully attaining a specific goal but rather novel actions that lead to the actor's desired result (Meltzoff 1995). Carpenter et al. (1998) have found that 14- to 18-month-old infants imitate twice as many purposeful rather than accidental actions they observe. In line with this research, 15-month-olds have been found to choose that out of two artefacts that they have observed to be more efficient for a specific purpose than the other one (Elsner and Pauen 2007). Whereas children acquire an understanding of how to make use of tools via imitation early in ontogeny, children's tool innovation is developed much later. For example, Beck et al. (2011) have found that children do not choose a hook tool to retrieve a bucket from a tube until age 7.

Two-year-olds exhibit an understanding of the intentional aspects of ecological objects also by being engaged in so-called pretend plays in which they make use of the physical and intentional aspects of objects playfully (Rakoczy 2008). According to Tomasello (1999a), infants being engaged in pretend play must be able to (1) understand and adopt the adult's conventional use of objects and artefacts and (2) 'decouple' the intentional affordances from the objects playfully; for example, the infant might use a banana as a telephone.

The ability to make use of the various aspects of an object playfully may be required for perceiving the institutional aspects of an object. In the institutional context of playing games, for example, gamblers may 'decouple' the intentional affordances of an object playfully and assign a particular 'status function' to it. On my account, the status function of an object is determined by its relation to other objects within the institutional system, and the relations among these objects are typically specified by a set of rules. In chess, for example, the rook has a status function which is determined by the rules of chess that assign different status functions to the different pawns in the game. Perceiving the institutional aspects of a rook in the context of playing chess is to perceive the institutional affordances of the rook as a particular pawn in the game. Children may acquire (institutional) knowledge of a set of (institutional) rules by imitating another person's demonstration (Rakoczy et al. 2009; Williamson et al. 2010). As pointed out by Rakoczy et al. (2009), when children learn rules in an institutional context such as a game, they preferentially imitate the demonstrations of particular rules of familiar persons who have previously appeared to the children as being reliable.

In general, perceiving institutional affordances involves perceiving an institutional context. Perceiving an institutional context, in turn, involves being aware not just of oneself but also of other (may be currently non-present) agents as part of that institution. As I will argue later, this awareness involves what I call 'broad social cognition' (see Sect. 11.4.2).

If agents are engaged in an institutional context that involves social rules and norms, commitments to obey these rules come into play. When playing chess, for example, you would protest if I used the tower like the queen. Developmental studies have shown that 2-year-old children can learn about the institutional affordances of the pawns in a particular game and the conventional rules of that game via demonstration and explanation of their interaction partner. At this age, children are well aware of the joint commitments that exist in institutional contexts. When playing a particular game entailing a specific set of rules, they protest if their interaction partner breaks the joint commitment to obey these rules (Rakoczy et al. 2008).

11.3 The Animal Relatum: Body Default and Deviant Body Percept

When perceiving different kinds of ecological affordances, we do not only focus on particular aspects of the ecological environment (environment relatum) but also take into account our ability to make use of the action possibilities those aspects afford to us (animal relatum).

On my account, what I call a 'body default' and a 'body percept' may play a role in the perception of any kind of affordances insofar as sensorimotoric actions are required to use them. In perceiving our own action abilities in terms of what the environment affords us, one needs to take into account one's own body scale, as it has been demonstrated, for example, nicely by Warren's (1984) stair-climbing experiment. Furthermore, our general physical capability (in terms of energy and motor flexibility) and skills to perform a particular action need to be taken into account. When individuals perceive affordances, they do so by taking into account their 'body default' that is uninfluenced by their deviant body percept and the given social context in which they perceive the affordances.

The individual's 'body default' involves the unity of (i) body features of his or her body scale (properties such as body height, weight, shape, etc.), (ii) general physical action capabilities in terms of energy and motor flexibility, and (iii) general action skills (i.e. simple skills such as walking as well as sophisticated skills such as playing the piano).

Moreover, the body scale does not just involve the body height of a given individual but also other bodily properties such as weight or muscularity. Even pieces of clothing that I wear regularly such as my watch may be part of my body scale. My default body scale (which is part of my body default) might be shaped by the clothes I wear in a particular situation and that influence my perception of affordances in a crucial way; how deep I feel capable of diving into a 15 m deep lagoon may depend on whether I wear a snorkel or a diving bell. It may also depend on my general diving skills. Our more or less general skills to perform particular actions may impact our (unconscious as well as conscious) perception of ecological affordances. As a professional swimmer, diving as deep as 15 m is no problem at all for me, and I perceive the lagoon affording me diving to the bottom with ease. As a non-swimmer, in contrast, I perceive the lagoon affording the possibility of rather drowning than swimming in it and even less of diving in it.

As pointed out by Cesari et al.'s (2003) follow-up study of Warren's (1984) experiment, our general physical action capabilities might change with age in terms of motor flexibility and/or energy; the latter involves a perceptual aspect, that is, how I perceive my body perceptually. Let's call this, following Gallagher (2005), 'body percept'. This is part of what Gallagher calls 'body image' that involves attitudes and beliefs about our body. According to Gallagher (2005, p. 25), the body image entails three different sorts of intentional contents: (1) a 'body percept' that involves our perceptual experience of our own body, (2) a 'body concept' that involves a conceptual folk and/or scientific knowledge about our body in general, and (3) a 'body affect' that involves our subjective emotional attitude towards our own body.

In the present investigation, I focus on the body percept (even though the body concept and body affect may also play a role in the perception of affordances). In general, the body percept is crucial in order to judge whether we are in a good physical condition to perform a certain action such as climbing a hill. The body percept is always experienced in the present. I distinguish between a 'deviant body percept' and a 'general body percept'. The general body percept is characterized by how we *typically* experience our body. For example, it is defined by a specific level of energy/tiredness that we typically experience in everyday life. On my account, the general body percept is part of the body default. The deviant body percept, in contrast, is characterized by a phenomenal bodily experience that deviates from the default, for example, when a person feels tired or excited.

Crucially, if you experience your body consistently over time in a particular way, it may become part of your body default, for example, if you have recurring back pain. That is, I account for the general body percept as being part of the body default that we typically take into account when we perceive our action abilities in relation to aspects of the environment. Growing older, I may perceive my body's physical fitness as restricted consistently over time so that this constraint becomes part of my general body percept and my sense of my body default which influences my perception of affordances. As pointed out by Bhalla and Profitt (1999), judging hill slants and walking distances is indeed influenced by the perceiver's age and physical condition.

The deviant body percept deviates *by definition* from the general body percept. Judging hill slants and walking distances may be influenced by our deviant body percept when we are fatigued (Proffitt et al. 1995) or wearing a heavy backpack (Proffitt et al. 2003). Furthermore, we are able to manipulate our deviant body percept and thereby the perception of affordances; Schnall et al. (2010) have shown that those participants who had consumed a glucose drink perceived the slant of a hill to be less steep than participants who had consumed a drink containing noncaloric sweetener. In general, these studies indicate that the deviant body percept only comes into play if we are more fatigued or excited than usual or if we feel bodily impaired in terms of energy and motor flexibility because of wearing a heavy backpack. If our bodily experiences do not deviate from the standard, the body default is taken into account whilst navigating through the environment.

11.4 The Role of Social and Institutional Contexts

Living in a society, we often perceive ecological affordances in a socio-situational context. Broadly, I distinguish perceiving between affordances in a *social context*, that is, in the (imagined or actual) presence of other people, and in an *institutional context*, that is, in the presence of an institution in which other people are involved. Social cognition may shape the perceived action abilities in both contexts; whereas what I call 'social cognition in narrow sense' may come into play in social contexts, 'social cognition in a broad sense' plays a central role in the perception of affordances in institutional contexts.

11.4.1 Social Contexts and Social Cognition in a Narrow Sense

Our perception of affordances may be modulated by the social context in which we perceive the affordances in a given situation. Karmack et al. (1990) have shown that cardiac stress reactions are reduced in task situations if the participant is accompanied by a supportive other person rather than alone. Similarly, Schnall et al. (2008) pointed out that participants accompanied by a friend perceived a hill as less steep compared to perceiving the hill alone. Furthermore, the quality of the social relationship to the person who accompanies us in perceiving affordances plays a crucial role, even if this person accompanies us just in imagination: participants who thought of a supportive friend whilst perceiving a hill perceived it as less steep than those participants who thought of a neutral or disliked person.

On my account, 'social cognition in a narrow sense' is required to understand the attitudes and intentions of a particular person in a given situation. 'Social cognition in a broad sense', in contrast, is tied not to understanding the individual attitudes and intentions of particular persons in a specific context but to the shared attitude and intention of social group members who constitute a particular institution (see Sect. 11.4.2).

Which cognitive procedure people use when attributing mental states to other people has been discussed in the so-called theory of mind debate. There are two main schools in this debate: (i) Theory Theory (TT) and (ii) Simulation Theory (ST). According to theory theorists (Perner 1999; Gopnik 2003), we understand other minds by means of folk psychological rules such as 'if A wants p and believes that doing q will bring about p, then ceteris paribus, A will do q' (Borg 2007, p. 6). Proponents of so-called Simulation Theory, in contrast, claim that we put ourselves imaginatively 'into the shoes' of another person and simulate the thoughts and feelings we would experience in his or her situation (Goldman 2006).

Rather than there being a single default procedure that people use whenever attempts are being made to explain an agent's behaviour, I defend a pluralistic approach to social understanding and propose that it is more likely that individuals use different procedures to achieve such understanding dependent on the particular situation of social understanding and cognitive effort. There are some indicators that might help to determine which procedure has been used in predicting or explaining another person's behaviour. Individuals make use of a folk psychological theory, for example, in situations that allow for psychological generalizations. Theory theorists propose that a folk psychological theory involves a conceptual understanding of mental states such as beliefs and desires and how they interrelate and motivate agents to act. In line with what Saxe (2005) has called 'the argument from error', I propose that in tasks that presuppose a conceptual understanding of mental states, errors that hinge on a congruency between the observer's failure or success in behaviour prediction and his or her theory about how minds work may serve as an indicator of theory use. Simulation processes, in contrast, are not proposed to rely on psychological generalizations. Rather, simulation theorists argue that individuals are engaged in running simulation routines each time anew when it comes to understanding other minds in a given situation. As pointed out by Goldman (2006), egocentric biases in the domains of knowledge, evaluation, and feeling may serve as an indicator of simulation.

However, I propose that social understanding cannot only be achieved by theory or simulation. Studies on so-called stereotype activation have shown that people automatically associate particular attitudes and character traits with members of social groups that are categorized along, for example, gender or race (Eagly and Steffen 1984; Lin et al. 2005). Notably, the stereotyping process often occurs automatically without the perceiver's intention or awareness (Macrae and Bodenhausen 2000) and may even diverge from the perceiver's intention. Empirical studies suggest that associations only become integrated in mental state or character trait attribution when they do not diverge from the perceiver's intention. If the perceiver becomes aware of that divergence, he or she may be able to override undesirable implicit processes (Cunningham et al. 2004).

Analogous to associations that become automatically activated when people face members of social groups, I propose that people associate also specific peculiarities (attitudes, character traits, habits, etc.) with a familiar person on the basis of their interactive or observational experiences with the person in the past or due to what a third party has told them about this person (call this 'associations with person identity'). I propose that an individual associates a friend typically with a positive attitude towards himself or herself and that it is precisely this association that comes into play when an individual's perception of ecological affordances (e.g. the climbability of hills) is supported by the presence of a friend (see above). Even though this has not been tested empirically yet, I assume that also the presence of a foreign person may yield a supportive or inhibitive effect on the perceived action possibilities by impacting the body percept in situations in which the attitude of this person is derivable by either theory or simulation or experientially accessible by means of lower-cognitive empathetic processes.

11.4.2 Institutional Contexts and Social Cognition in a Broad Sense

Following Searle (2011), I propose that the *creation* of the institutional aspects of an object presupposes an awareness of the object being part of an institutional context in which other people are involved and agree upon and recognize the status function of the object in question (call this 'constitutive condition'). For example, the existence and validity of a social fact such as money is created by a group of agents who collectively recognize a wad of notes *as* money. Notably, once a social fact is in place, the agents may forget about its social origin and treat it as a natural fact. Searle (2011, p. 58) writes:

> Cooperation requires the collective intention to cooperate. But collective recognition need not be a form of cooperation and thus does not require a collective intention to cooperate. [...] Rather, what it requires is that each participant accepts the existence and validity of money in the belief that there is mutual acceptance on the part of the others. So we have an interesting result; namely, that the existence of an institution does not require cooperation but simply collective acceptance or recognition. Particular acts within the institution such as buying or selling or getting married or participating in an election require cooperation.

Thus, collective recognition but not collective intentionality is required for the *creation* of the institutional aspects of an object (constitutive condition). The status function Y of an object X in an institutional context C is defined by what Searle (2011) calls the constitutive rule 'X counts as Y in C'. Insofar as X *represents* Y in C, I agree with Searle that for perceiving institutional facts as such, linguistic skills 'or at least some form of symbolism' (p. 95) are required.

Institutional aspects of ecological objects are status functions that are created only in virtue of the collective acceptance and recognition of that very status by a group of people who constitute the institution. Tuomela (2010, p. 202 ff.) provides the medieval case of squirrel pelts taken as money and introduces a useful distinction between what he calls the 'generic institution' of money that refers to the institutional predicate of 'money' generally understood (such as that money involves exchanging activities) and 'tokens' of money such as squirrel pelts. For a squirrel pelt to have the institutional aspect or status function of money, a social group (e.g. a particular society who lived in the Middle Ages) needs to accept this status function under conditions of mutual common knowledge and needs to collectively recognize that status function in a context in which this institutional aspect becomes relevant (e.g. on a market where exchanging activities come into play). Insofar as these requirements presuppose an understanding of the psychological states of the other group members, what I call 'social cognition in the broad sense' is involved. I call it social cognition in the *broad sense*, because the social-cognitive processes being involved are devoted not to a particular person in a specific context (as it is the case in social cognition in the narrow sense; see previous section) but to any member of the group in a stereotypical institutional context.

Social cognition in a broad sense is involved not only in the collective recognition of a status function but also in the collective intention to cooperate. To perceive which actions the institutional aspects of an object afford within an institutional context requires the collective intention to cooperate insofar as *making use* of these aspects is part of a cooperative action among a number of agents (call this 'executive condition'). A particular act within an institution such as the post requires the collective intention to cooperate which might be structured by a set of rules and roles. For example, when I make use of the institutional aspect of a postbox, namely mail-lettering, I need to affix the appropriate postage stamp on the letter. In addition, I need to believe in the existence of the postal system that involves a number of agents who contribute to actualizing my perceived affordance which is not given on a desert island (see Sect. 11.2 for a discussion).

The psychological states of the members of an institution like the post have been discussed in the framework of so-called shared or collective intentionality (Searle 1990; Bratman 1993; Tuomela 2010). Bratman (1993), for example, defines a 'shared intention' as 'a state of affairs consisting primarily of appropriate attitudes of each individual participant and their interrelation' (p. 99) in which each participant represents his or her contribution (*as* contribution) to the group activity being performed. Perceiving institutional affordances requires an awareness of the shared intention the cooperating agents of the institution have even if these agents are not present in a given context of perceiving the institutional affordances; such awareness also amounts to 'social cognition in a broad sense'. Notably, shared intention and cooperation are involved not only in institutional frameworks but also in basic joint actions such as intentional joint attention (Fiebich and Gallagher 2012).[4]

Finally, an awareness of being a member of a social group ('social identity') who is engaged in an institutional context is required to perceive one's own socio-normative ability to make use of institutional affordances. For example, I may

[4] That is, social cognition in a broad sense also comes into play when the interacting agents form a shared intention outside of an institutional setting. This, however, is not the focus of the present investigation.

perceive a particular stone as a boundary and negative affordance to cross the landscapes when I perceive myself as a member of a particular tribe. Perceived social identity may also involve perceiving one's status or role within the group. Imagine, for example, that only the two chiefs of the tribes are allowed to cross the stone that functions as a border for the other tribe members. Being a chief, the stone might then afford crossing the boundary of the landscapes whereas it does not so for the other members of the tribe.

11.5 Summary

To sum up, in the perception of ecological affordances, we perceive the environment in terms of the relation between, on the one hand, our own abilities (the animal relatum) based upon our body default which might be shaped by our deviant body percept (perceived bodily abilities) and based upon our social identity (socio-normative abilities) and, on the other hand, the physical, intentional, and institutional aspects of the ecological environment (the ecological environment relatum) (Fig. 11.1).

Furthermore, perceiving ecological affordances may take place in social contexts, that is, in the (imagined or actual) presence of other people, or institutional contexts, that is, in the presence of an institution in which other people are involved. If so, social cognition may shape the perceived action abilities. 'Social cognition in a narrow sense' is understanding the intentions, feelings, and attitudes of a particular person that may support the perceived bodily abilities in a given social context. 'Social cognition in a broad sense', in contrast, is tied not to understanding the individual attitudes and intentions of particular persons in a specific context but to the shared intention of social group members who constitute a particular institution. It is a presupposition for the perception of socio-normative abilities in institutional contexts.

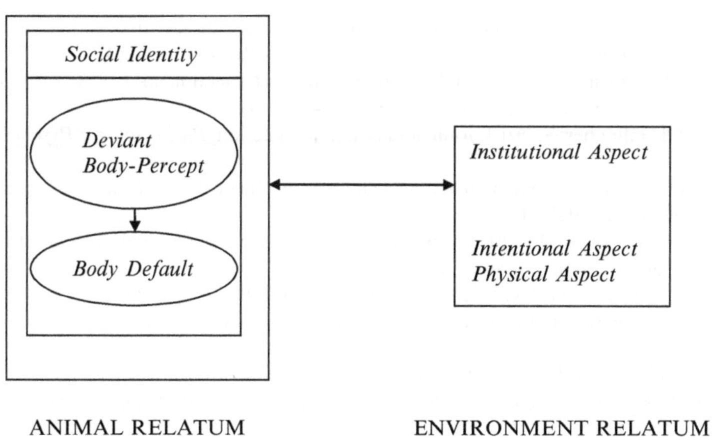

Fig. 11.1 Perceiving ecological affordances

Acknowledgements I acknowledge the support provided by the Humboldt Foundation and Albert Newen for a research stay in Memphis, USA, where I finished this chapter. I would like to thank Shaun Gallagher, Steve Butterfill, Nivedita Gangopadhyay, John Michael, and one anonymous reviewer for helpful comments on an earlier draft of this chapter as well as Deborah Tollefsen and the auditory of the colloquium of the Philosophy Department of the University of Memphis for fruitful discussions. Finally, I would like to thank Adrian Smith and Joel Krueger for organizing a conference on affordances at the Center for Subjectivity Research in Copenhagen, 2010, which inspired me to dip deeper into that debate.

References

Bhalla, M., and D.R. Profitt. 1999. Visual-motor recalibration in geographical slant perception. *Journal of Experimental Psychology. Human Perception and Performance* 25: 1076–1096.

Baron-Cohen, S. 1995. *Mindblindness: An essay on autism and theory of mind.* Cambridge: MIT Press.

Beck, S.R., I.A. Apperly, J. Chappell, C. Guthrie, and N. Cutting. 2011. Making tools isn't child's play. *Cognition* 119: 301–306.

Borg, E. 2007. If mirror neurons are the answer, what was the question? *Journal of Consciousness Studies* 14: 5–19.

Bratman, M.E. 1993. Shared intention. *Ethics* 104(1): 97–113.

Carpenter, M., N. Akhtar, and M. Tomasello. 1998. Fourteen-through 18 month-old infants differentially imitate intentional and accidental actions. *Infant Behavior and Development* 21(2): 315–330.

Cesari, P., F. Formenti, and P. Olivato. 2003. A common perceptual parameter for stair climbing for children, young and old adults. *Human Movement Science* 22: 111–124.

Chemero, A. 2003. An outline of a theory of affordances. *Ecological Psychology* 15(2): 181–195.

Clifton, R.K., D.W. Muir, D.H. Ashmead, and M.G. Clarkson. 1993. Is visually guided reaching in early infancy a myth? *Child Development* 64: 1099–1110.

Csibra, G. 2010. Recognizing communicative intentions in infancy. *Mind & Language* 25: 141–168.

Cunningham, W.A., M.K. Johnson, C.L. Raye, J.C. Gatenby, J.C. Gore, and M.R. Banaji. 2004. Separable neural components in the processing of black and white faces. *Psychological Science* 15: 806–813.

Eagly, A.H., and V.J. Steffen. 1984. Gender stereotypes stem from the distribution of women and men into social roles. *Journal of Personality and Social Psychology* 46(4): 735–754.

Elsner, B., and S. Pauen. 2007. Social learning of artifact function in 12- and 15-month-olds. *European Journal of Developmental Psychology* 4(1): 80–99.

Fiebich, A., and Gallagher, S. 2012. Joint attention in joint action. *Philosophical Psychology*, ifirst, 1–17.

Field, J. 1976. The adjustment of reaching behavior to object distance in early infancy. *Child Development* 47(1): 304–308.

Fröse, T., and E.A. Di Paolo. 2011. The enactive approach. Theoretical sketches from cell to society. *Pragmatics and Cognition* 19(1): 1–36.

Gallagher, S. 2005. *How the body shapes the mind.* Oxford: University Press.

Gibson, J. [1979] 1986. The theory of affordances. In *Ecological approach to visual perception*, pp. 127–143. Hillsdale: Lawrence Erlbaum Associates.

Gibson, E.J., and R.D. Walk. 1960. The "visual cliff". *Scientific American* 202: 67–71.

Goldman, A. 2006. *Simulating minds: The philosophy, psychology, and neuroscience of mindreading*. Oxford: Oxford University Press.

Gopnik, A. 2003. The theory theory as an alternative to the innateness hypothesis. In *Chomsky and his critics*, ed. L. Antony and N. Hornstein, 238–254. Oxford: Blackwell.
Heft, H. 1989. Affordances and the body: An intentional analysis of Gibson's ecological approach to visual perception. *Journal for the Theory of Social Behavior* 19: 1–30.
Heft, H. 2001. *Ecological psychology in context: James Gibson, Roger Barker, and the legacy of William James' radical empiricism*. Mahwah: Lawrence Erlbaum Associates.
Karmarck, T.W., S.B. Manuck, and J.R. Jennings. 1990. Social support reduces cardiovascular reactivity to psychological challenge: A laboratory model. *Psychosomatic Medicine* 52: 42–58.
Kono, T. 2009. Social affordances and the possibility of ecological linguistics. *Integrative Psychological and Behavioral Science* 43: 356–373.
Lin, M.H., V.S.Y. Kwan, A. Cheung, and S.T. Fiske. 2005. Stereotype content model explains prejudice for an envied outgroup: Scale of anti-Asian American stereotypes. *Personality and Social Bulletin* 31: 34–47.
Macrae, C.N., and G.V. Bodenhausen. 2000. Social cognition: Thinking categorically about others. *Annual Review of Psychology* 51: 93–120.
Meltzoff, A.N. 1995. Understanding the intentions of others: Re-enactment of intended acts by 18-month-old children. *Developmental Psychology* 31: 838–850.
Michaels, C.F. 2003. Affordances: Four points of debate. *Ecological Psychology* 15(2): 135–148.
Moses, L.J., D.A. Baldwin, J.G. Rosicky, and G. Tidball. 2001. Evidence for referential understanding in the emotions domain at twelve and eighteen months. *Child Development* 72: 718–735.
Pauen, S. 2002. Evidence for knowledge-based categorization in infancy. *Child Development* 73: 116–133.
Perner, J. 1999. Metakognition und Introspektion in entwicklungspsychologischer Sicht: Studien zur "Theory of Mind" und "Simulation". In *Hundert Jahre Institut für Psychologie und Würzburger Schule der Denkpsychologie*, ed. W. Janke and W. Schneider, 411–431. Göttingen: Hofgrede.
Piaget, J. [1970] 2003. *Meine Theorie der geistigen Entwicklung*. Weinheim: Beltz.
Proffitt, D.R., M. Bhalla, R. Gossweiler, and J. Midgett. 1995. Perceiving geographical slant. *Psychonomic Bulletin and Review* 2: 409–428.
Proffitt, D.R., J. Stefanucci, T. Banton, and W. Epstein. 2003. The role of effort in perceived distance. *Psychological Science* 1: 110–122.
Rakoczy, H. 2008. Pretence as individual and collective intentionality. *Mind & Language* 23(5): 499–517.
Rakoczy, H., F. Warneken, and M. Tomasello. 2008. The sources of normativity: Young children's awareness of the normative structure of games. *Developmental Psychology* 44(3): 875–881.
Rakoczy, H., F. Warneken, and M. Tomasello. 2009. Young children's selective learning of rule games from reliable and unreliable models. *Cognitive Development* 24(1): 61–69.
Reed, E.S. 1996. *Encountering the world*. New York: Oxford University Press.
Saxe, R. 2005. Against simulation: The argument from error. *Trends in Cognitive Sciences* 9(4): 174–179.
Schnall, S., K.D. Harber, J.K. Stefanucci, and D.R. Proffitt. 2008. Social support and the perception of geographical slant. *Journal of Experimental Social Psychology* 44: 1246–1255.
Schnall, S., J.R. Zadra, and D.R. Proffitt. 2010. Direct evidence for the economy of action: Glucose and the perception of geographical slant. *Perception* 39: 464–482.
Searle, J. 1990. Collective intentions and actions. In *Intentions in communication*, ed. P. Cohen, J. Morgan, and M. Pollack, 401–415. Cambridge, MA: MIT Press.
Searle, J. 2011. *Making the social world. The structure of human civilization*. Oxford: University Press.
Stoffregen, T.A. 2003. Affordances as properties of the animal-environment system. *Ecological Psychology* 15(2): 115–134.
Striano, T., and P. Rochat. 2000. Emergence of selective social referencing in infancy. *Infancy* 1(2): 253–264.

Tomasello, M. 1999a. The cultural ecology of young children's interactions with objects and artifacts. In *Ecological approaches to cognition. Essays in honor of Ulric Neisser*. London: Lawrence Erlbaum Associates.

Tomasello, M. 1999b. *The cultural origins of human cognition*. Cambridge: Harvard University Press.

Triesch, J., C. Teuscher, G. Deák, and E. Carlson. 2006. Gaze following: Why (not) learn it? *Developmental Science* 9(2): 125–147.

Tuomela, R. 2010. *The philosophy of sociality*. Oxford: University Press.

Warren, W.H. 1984. Perceiving affordances: Visual guidance of stair climbing. *Journal of Experimental Psychology. Human Perception and Performance* 10: 683–703.

Williamson, R.A., V.K. Jaswal, and A.N. Meltzoff. 2010. Learning the rules: Observation and imitation of a sorting strategy by 36-month-old children. *Developmental Psychology* 46(1): 57–65.

Chapter 12
Social Cognition as Causal Inference: Implications for Common Knowledge and Autism

Jakob Hohwy and Colin Palmer

Abstract This chapter explores the idea that the need to establish *common knowledge* is one feature that makes social cognition stand apart in important ways from cognition in general. We develop this idea on the background of the claim that social cognition is nothing but a type of causal inference. We focus on autism spectrum disorder (ASD) as our test case and propose that a specific type of problem with common knowledge processing is implicated in challenges to social cognition in this condition. This problem has to do with the individual's assessment of the reliability of messages that are passed between people as common knowledge emerges. The proposal is developed on the background of our own empirical studies and outlines different ways common knowledge might be comprised. We discuss what these issues may tell us about ASD, about the relation between social and nonsocial cognition, about social objects, and about the dynamics of social networks.

12.1 Introduction

Social cognition concerns the representation of states of affairs in the world that, in a wide variety of ways, involve other people's mental states and agency. It is tempting to try to understand the nature of social cognition by assuming that it is essentially different from nonsocial cognition and, consequently, exploring and interpreting behavioural and neurological differences in the light of this assumption. One reason why this assumption is appealing is that creatures with social cognition, like us, seem so different from creatures without much recognisable social cognition. Another reason is that the perception of things like the intentions and beliefs of other people feels more intangible than, for instance, the perception of visual objects. A further reason is that some disorders, in

J. Hohwy (✉) • C. Palmer
Philosophy & Cognition Lab, Monash University, Melbourne, Australia
e-mail: Jakob.Hohwy@monash.edu

M. Gallotti and J. Michael (eds.), *Perspectives on Social Ontology and Social Cognition*, Studies in the Philosophy of Sociality 4, DOI 10.1007/978-94-017-9147-2_12,

particular ASD, seem to have specific differences in certain aspects of social cognition, suggesting that specialised, dissociable circuits in the brain take care of these functions.

Here, we begin with a different assumption, namely that though social cognition is no doubt in part processed in domain-specific areas of the brain, it is *not* essentially different from nonsocial cognition. To substantiate this approach, we will examine how both social and nonsocial cognition are instances of causal, perceptual inference. We then propose that what makes some cognition recognisable as social is related to the emergence of *common knowledge* and explain ways in which underlying problems with cognition in general could lead to profound problems in common knowledge in particular. We explore the consequences of this approach for both our understanding of ASD and social cognition in general.

ASD is an important testing ground for approaches to social cognition because this set of developmental disorders is first and foremost characterised by deficits and differences in social cognition. Individuals with ASD can be deeply socially disabled, with very severe language and communication deficits. Even when language is present, there can be profound challenges in the ability to infer other people's mental states. ASD is also characterised, however, by more subtle and difficult to describe sensory and perceptual differences. In fact, it is an astounding characteristic of ASD that seemingly disparate social and nonsocial symptoms are found together. At times, these sensory differences present as islands of enhanced or superior performance, at other times, performance is diminished relative to the wider population. For example, on one hand individuals with ASD have been found to be less susceptible to some visual illusions than control groups, and on the other hand, they have been found to be less proficient in visual tasks involving the discrimination of coherence between perceptual elements (e.g. motion coherence; reviewed in Happé and Frith 2006). A key question is then whether and how these perceptual differences relate to the social deficits. One possibility is that these features of ASD are independent, another possibility is that the perceptual differences cause the social deficits, a third is that the social deficits cause the perceptual deficits (e.g. through problems with learning). A fourth possibility, which we pursue here, is that the perceptual differences and the social deficits in ASD are different effects of a common cause. We shall understand this common cause to be something afflicting causal inference, which is a process that manifests differently in the perceptual and social domains. The hope is, of course, that this approach will allow for a better understanding of this debilitating and heart-breaking disorder.

The plan of this chapter is to first, in Sect. 12.2, describe why social cognition is nothing but causal inference and then, on the background of this commonality with the nonsocial perceptual domain, identify some notable characteristics of causal inference that occur when applied to the social domain. In Sect. 12.3, we then make the connection between social cognition, understood in this causal way, and common knowledge. Section 12.4 describes ways in which common knowledge can be challenged and compromised and how this would impact on social cognition. In Sect. 12.5, we explore how specific sensory differences hypothesised to occur in ASD could be continuous with compromised common knowledge and how this may account for profound social deficits in this disorder. We exemplify this point with research performed in our own lab. The overall consequences for our conception of social cognition are then discussed in Sect. 12.6.

12.2 Social Cognition as Causal Inference

The paradigm of social cognition that we consider here is *mentalising*, the act of representing other people's mental states. This faculty is invaluable for both predicting and understanding the behaviour of others. For example, if someone says, 'the train leaves at three o'clock', we represent them as having the *belief* that the train leaves at three o'clock. Similarly, if someone says, 'It is very hot today, isn't it? Do you know when the ice cream shop opens', we represent them as having the *desire* for an ice cream.

The representation that occurs in mentalising is entirely analogous to the representation that occurs in nonsocial contexts. For example, if you hear a particular rapid 'tock-tock-tock' noise, then you may well represent the world as having a woodpecker nearby. Similarly, if you see smoke and hear a fire engine, then you represent the world as having a fire nearby. In both mentalising and nonsocial representation of the world, the process begins with some sensory input, which triggers an inference about what the causal origin of the input might be.

Mostly, this inference is unconscious, namely when it concerns perceptual states – this is the unconscious perceptual inference made famous by Ibn al-Haytham and Helmholtz and defended by Neisser, Gregory, and more recently in machine learning and computational neuroscience by Mumford, Dayan, Hinton, Friston, and others (Helmholtz 1867; Neisser 1967; Gregory 1980; Mumford 1992; Dayan et al. 1995; Friston and Stephan 2007, al-Haytham ca. 1030; 1989). On occasion, such inference can of course also be conscious; for example, you could go through in your mind the various hypotheses about what may cause an individual's statement about the hot weather and the ice cream shop or try to imagine different common causes for both the visual input of the smoke and the auditory input from the fire engine. It isn't necessarily the case that the process of inference leading to mentalising is conscious, of course: a mental state attribution may pop into mind as automatically as a visual object does when we shift our gaze. In each case, the ease at which a new perception enters consciousness belies the non-trivial computational demand that an accurate causal inference from the sensory data requires.

If words, gestures, and additional behaviours that we pick up from other people are treated as just being characteristics of sensory input, and if the mental states of other people are treated as the causes of this input, then mentalising can be characterised as causal inference from sensory effects to worldly causes (Wolpert et al. 2003; Kilner et al. 2007). Mentalising is then nothing but the kind of causal inference that the brain is in any case consigned to engage in to make sense of the world. Of course, there are differences between social and nonsocial cognition, but viewed from the perspective of causal inference, we should not expect these differences to be more dramatic than the differences that exist between other kinds of cognition (e.g. the difference between the processing of moving and stationary objects or between 2D and 3D perception). In other words, the dissimilarities between these processes will only pertain to the kind of challenges in performing causal inference specific to a given class of worldly causes of sensory input.

If there are specific difficulties in the application of causal inference to social phenomena, then we are likely to find that they stem from uncertainty in the sensory input. This is because what makes causal inference difficult is the lack of unequivocal one-one relations between cause and effect. Evidence for one-one relations is made uncertain by the presence of noise, ambiguity, and non-linear interactions in general. For example, when we see smoke and hear fire engines, there is ambiguity regarding whether the cause of this sensory input could be a real fire, a pretend-fire in a movie set, or harmless smoke from a chimney co-occurring with a fire engine out on a false alarm.

In order to engage in causal inference in spite of uncertainty, the brain can appeal to both the fit between the sensory input and the different hypotheses about its causes and to prior beliefs about the probability of each hypothesis. For example, I might disregard the 'movie set' hypothesis because it is very unlikely that a movie would be set in my neighbourhood, and I might disregard the hypothesis that the smoke and the fire engine are independent causes of my input because the smoke disappeared very soon after the fire engine sound ceased.

All this is to say that we engage in *Bayesian* reasoning in order to infer the causes of our sensory input (Kersten et al. 2004). Such probabilistic inference is necessary precisely because the sensory input is riddled with ambiguity and uncertainty. The specific manner in which our brains engage in inference in a given context depends heavily on the place of the relevant worldly causes in the overall causal structure of the world. Some causes give rise to their effects in more highly non-linear, context-dependent ways than others, and some causes are hidden deeper in the causal hierarchy than others (e.g. the subprime mortgages that caused the global financial crisis are deeply hidden, and there are numerous non-linearly working factors in the way they cause parts of our sensory input; in contrast, the redness of the apple in front of you is less deeply hidden, though it also depends on contextual factors such as lighting conditions).

It is crucial to add an active element to our understanding of Bayesian perceptual inference, namely in the way we actively test our hypotheses about the causes in the world. For instance, we may engage in more vigorous visual and auditory *search* in order to figure out whether the smoke and the fire engine sound is correlated, or we may check the emergency services on the net to see if a fire is mentioned. Similarly, in the ice cream case, we may *ask* the person whether they feel like an ice cream. This active element is clearly recognised in key treatments of causal inference, where causation is conceptualised in terms of invariant relations under (active) intervention (Pearl 2000; Woodward 2003).

Social cognition, we therefore propose, is nothing but causal, Bayesian inference from sensory input to mental states. To understand social cognition and how it may differ from other areas of cognition, the task is then to specify how uncertainty may arise in the inference from sensory input to mental causes.

Some sources of uncertainty in social causal inference spring quickly to mind. The mental states of other people are quintessentially hidden causes, so hidden in fact that their existence can be doubted on epistemological grounds, leading to scepticism about other minds. This is known as the *other minds problem*. John Stuart Mill famously proposed an inferential solution to this problem, via an argument from analogy with our own, known mental states (Mill 1865). Modern Bayesian accounts of social causal inference merely update Mill's idea. The key observation is that mental causes are deeply hidden, that is, they must be inferred on the basis of various causal links, including observed behaviour. One problem here is that observed behaviour has a rather volatile relation to mental states. Different contexts will make it considerably more or less likely that a particular piece of behaviour is caused by a particular mental state. Famously, this occurs in deception, pretending, and stage-acting, but the point generalises such that a context can be found which makes any kind of mental state a cause of a certain behaviour (e.g. we could assume you have rather bizarre beliefs about what aggressive ice cream shop owners do to force their products on consumers on hot days and assume you fear such aggression and therefore infer that your question about opening hours was motivated by a desire to be far away from ice cream shops on hot days).

It is thus tempting to say that social cognition is special in the sense of being dependent on the context of our existing knowledge regarding the other person's more or less idiosyncratic sets of beliefs and desires. However, this does not seem to set social cognition especially apart from other types of cognition. Context dependence is everywhere and can entail many different degrees of difficulty. Already we have mentioned the example of subprime mortgages and the highly context-dependent ways they cause other phenomena such as low interest rates and high unemployment. But everyday examples of perception are also highly context-dependent. For example, in the visual occlusion of a cat behind a fence, there is a very intricate non-linear interaction between the context of the fence and the observer's movements relative to the fence and the cat, which makes the unconscious perceptual inference of the presence of a cat non-trivial in this specific context. In inference under context dependence, it is crucial to rely on prior statistical expectations about what the cause and the context might be, as well as on an ability to predict how the flow of sensory input will change under various interventions. For example, we expect the world to be populated by many more whole cats than by curiously aligned, detached cat slices, and we expect things like fences to be stationary in the world as we walk past, seeing the whole cat behind it. Similarly, we rely on statistical regularities about the likely beliefs and desires of people around us as we try to infer their mental states. For example, I rarely consider the possibility that you may have somewhat paranoid beliefs about ice cream shop owners.

Hence, even though mentalising is riddled with context dependence, we should not expect this to be what sets it apart from nonsocial cognition.

Another contributor to uncertainty in social causal inference that we will consider is, in fact, specific to the social domain. In general, this factor has to do with the kind of uncertainty that stems from non-linear interactions between causes and as such is of a piece with all other kinds of causal inference (e.g. inferring the whole cat behind the fence). But in the social domain, there is an intricate, special level of non-linear interaction: when we interpret other people, we are often aware that they are also interpreting us and that their behaviour depends in a non-linear way on which mental states they interpret us as harbouring. For example, when, on a hot day, the kids ask for the opening hours of the ice cream shop, you are interpreting their verbal behaviour under a model of the world that includes their model of your mental states; it is crucial for the further negotiations to understand that they ask this question under the hypothesis that you might allow them to get an ice cream – you could therefore lie and say the ice cream shop is closed all day. This aspect of mentalising we might call *meta-mentalising*. It is a fascinating concept because the interaction of mental causes is so pervasive: it can even be necessary to model how other people model you modelling them, and so on. This comes about because other people are agents: that is, their intervention in the causal chain is contingent upon their model of the world, and how they intervene impacts both on what you experience and how you model them.

It is important to recognise that the need for meta-mentalising arises because causal inference in general is challenged by non-linearly interacting causes. It is just that we happen to find ourselves in an environment with sensory input from worldly causes (i.e. other people) who can act, conditional on what our and their own mental states are. This does not mean mentalising is different from causal inference, but there does not seem to be any other area of causal inference where such meta-modelling is required to overcome non-linearity.

In this section, we have argued that social cognition, in particular in the shape of mentalising, is nothing but causal inference on hidden causes of sensory input. We pointed out that, as such, social cognition can only be set apart from other areas of cognition by the way causal inference is challenged by sources of uncertainty and ambiguity. This leads to the suggestion of one factor in particular, which contributes to uncertainty and ambiguity in social cognition: the need to engage in meta-mentalising.

This proposal goes somewhat against an assumption that lies behind much research on social cognition: namely that there are domain-specific elements in social cognition. The benefit of taking our approach is that the nature of social cognition, and the important challenges to social cognition in mental and developmental disorder, can be understood exclusively in terms of how causal inference occurs under uncertainty, which is a well-studied, standard problem set in science. Because this approach makes social cognition continuous with all other areas of causal inference, it holds potential for understanding how, for example, the social deficits in ASD are connected to the more poorly understood perceptual differences in this condition. In other words, social and nonsocial deficits may be different manifestations of an underlying issue with causal inference under uncertainty, where the apparent differences in these symptoms are driven by domain-specific factors creating different constellations of uncertainty. To forestall objections, note that this is not to claim that there are no areas of the brain that are specifically engaged in mentalising, neuroscience evidence certainly suggests that there are such areas or modules; the claim is merely that such areas are engaged in causal inference too, just like areas engaged in other domains of perception; what makes it special are the constraints under which such inference proceeds, as we suggested above and continue to develop below.

More generally, some may object that the reduction of social cognition to causal inference is rather radical and flies in the face of decades of theorising about social cognition. In particular, it sets aside theory-theory, simulation theory, and direct perception theories of social cognition (Heal 1986; Gopnik 1993; Gopnik and Meltzoff 1997; Gallese and Goldman 1998; Meltzoff and Decety 2003; Gallagher 2007; Call and Tomasello 2008; Hutto 2008) and claims that causal inference is explanatorily prior. Further, some may object that this bald reduction fails to explain in what sense social cognition concerns the representation or perception of minds, rather than mere inert environmental causes. We believe these objections can be met efficiently. First, our proposal claim may seem radical, but others have also been critical of the idea that mentalising is domain-specific (Apperly et al. 2005) or have offered domain-general accounts of mentalising (Perner et al. 2011); most relevantly, Bayesian (predictive coding) accounts have been suggested before (Wolpert et al. 2003; Kilner et al. 2007; Kilner and Frith 2008). Second, though occasionally these influential, prior theories of social cognition are presented as being deeply opposed to reductionist views, they are all essentially consistent with the causal inference view, even though they offer only impoverished explanatory resources compared to a full Bayesian account. The theory-theory's appeal to folk psychology is a crude inferential tool for building up models of other's minds, which is something a causal inference account also must do, since building generative models is what inference requires; however, it is done with much more fine-grained, statistical tools than mostly envisaged by theory-theory. Simulation theory can be reduced to theory-theory (as argued by Jackson (1999)) under the assumption that one's own mental state is a probabilistic cue for disambiguating social signals; the key concept of mirror neurons has been explained as a natural outcome of probabilistic notions of causal inference (namely the free energy principle; see Friston 2011). The direct perception view is accommodated easily once we observe that causal inference can be unconscious, in just the way proposed by Helmholtz (1867): thus it can appear phenomenologically as direct but is in fact inferential. So rather than subordinating our account to any of these theories, we like (somewhat provocatively) to view it as a challenge: explain how these prior theories are not mere poor precursors to the fully inferential view. The causal inference view of social cognition is, we believe, also better placed than these earlier views to explain why social cognition is about *minds* specifically. This is because, as we demonstrate throughout this chapter, we can say something about the ways in which causal inference about minds differs from causal inference about other things in the sensorium: mental states are causes that are hidden in a special way in other people's heads, and they causally interact in a special way with our own and other's mental states. These aspects of mental causal inference place special demands on our inference about them – and these demands reflect what *makes* them mental. We don't see similar resources for explaining the nature of mentality in the older theories.

12.3 Common Knowledge in Social Cognition

Having argued that social cognition can be reduced to causal inference, we now proceed to characterise an important purpose of mentalising. Specifically, we focus on what people get out of representing mental states not just as simple causes in the world but as causes that themselves represent and meta-represent other people's mental states including our own. This is an important concept to consider in identifying what people may get out of engaging in causal inference about other people's mental states. With this focus on meta-representation we are able to speak specifically to a factor that we argue makes social cognition a particular kind of causal inference.

The idea we wish to pursue is that the main purpose of representing, and re-representing, other people's mental states, including their representation of our own mental states, is to enable common knowledge. Common knowledge is a technical notion, deriving from economics, semantics, and epistemology. We can introduce the idea with a famous example from one of the first treatments of this concept.

> When a man loses his wife in a department store without any prior understanding on where to meet if they get separated, the chances are good that they will find each other. It is likely that each will think of some obvious place to meet, so obvious that each will be sure that it is "obvious" to both of them. One does not simply predict where the other will go, since the other will go where he predicts the first to go, which is wherever the first predicts the second to predict the first to go, and so *ad infinitum*. Not "What would I do if I were she?" but "What would I do if I were she wondering what she would do if she were wondering what I would do if I were she … ?" (Schelling 1960: 54)

Schelling is describing a *coordination problem*, where the married couple needs to coordinate such that they both go to the same place (although in this case it doesn't matter exactly where that place is, just that they both get there). For this problem to be solved, it is not enough to represent simply where that place might be, but it is also necessary to represent the spouse's knowledge of what the place might be, and the spouse's knowledge of where the first spouse believes the meeting place is, and so on. The solution must involve, in Schelling's terms, that they 'must "mutually recognise" some unique signal that coordinates their expectations of each other' (*ibid.*).

This sets common knowledge apart from mere mutual knowledge. In mutual knowledge, people know the same thing: we may all know that the game will be shown in the park. But mutual knowledge can fall short of solving the coordination problem of deciding where to go tonight, because you may not know whether other people know that the game is on in the park, and this may matter to you because you don't want to end up in the park alone, or at home while everyone else goes to the park. So you need to also know that others know that the game is on in the park. But of course if you only know that others know that, then they might not go because they might not know that you and others know about the game in the park, or indeed that you know that they know that you know, and so on. In fact, to solve the coordination problem, an infinite hierarchy of knowledge about each other's knowledge must be established. What establishes this hierarchy is not an actual infinite series of mental states in each person's brain but Schelling's unique signal that is mutually recognised. This signal can be very many different things. In the department store example, it might be knowledge that the spouses would each find it amusing if they found each other in the wine store, in the park example it might be a particular tweet.

In other cases, it might be something as simple as eye contact. In a well-rehearsed example, two friends enter a full bus but end up sitting at opposite ends of it. At a stop halfway through the ride, a third person, also a friend, calls out from the street to ask whether the two on the bus would like to come for a drink. This initiates a coordination problem for the two friends on the bus: both want to get off the bus together to get the drink, and if not that then they both want to stay on the bus, foregoing the drink; but neither wants to leave the other behind. The key here is whether each of the two friends on the bus knows that the other heard the third friend's invitation and knows of each other that they heard this, and so on. This knowledge, and thus common knowledge, can be established if they both look up at the same time and their eyes meet, whereupon they are assured that the message was heard, and that they both know it, and know that they know it, and so on, and they therefore both alight the bus to get the drink. Thus, while the difficulty in consciously holding in mind multiple levels of the hierarchy of knowledge states required for common knowledge is an argument against the behavioural relevance of this concept, our brains may all the same be tuned to recognise cues that establish common knowledge efficiently.

In general, a proposition P is common knowledge for S and S' if and only if, S and S' know that P, S knows that S' knows that P, and knows that S' knows that S knows that P, and so on; and similarly for S'. There is a very sizable literature on common knowledge, and different formalisations, interpretations, and applications of it (for a classic statement, apart from Schelling, see Lewis (1969); for a review, see Vanderschraaf and Sillari (2009); we stress that in this chapter we avail ourselves of the concept of common knowledge, we do not wish to contribute to the technical debate about, e.g. what it takes to establish the infinite hierarchy of reciprocal beliefs).

We want to make the observation now that common knowledge manifests pervasively and that insults to the ability to establish common knowledge will have profound and variegated effects on one's communal function. Straight off, the kinds of cases where common knowledge is useful can seem rare and recherché. It does not seem central to the human endeavour to finesse with common knowledge our ability to find each other in department stores, to alleviate awkward situations when the waiter spills the soup, or to have a convention for who should call back (the caller or the called) when the phone lines go dead (Lewis 1969). But, of course, common knowledge is everywhere, for social creatures like us who live in close quarters with each other and whose trajectories constantly cross. A good example is the convention to drive on the left (or the right as the case might be). We don't just have mutual knowledge that driving is on the left, we have common knowledge: I would not go on the roads if I didn't know that you know that driving is on the left, and you know that I know, and so on.

Driving is an example where there are two equilibria, namely where we all drive on the left or all on the right. We don't care which it is as long as we all do the same thing and we are confident that this is established as common knowledge. These cases are not rare but it is important to observe that there are cases as well where we do care which of several equilibria we end up deciding on. The stag hunt is one such case. In this classic example, two hunters can each hunt rabbit or stag. There are two equilibria, namely where we both hunt rabbit or we both hunt stag. Each hunter is not interested in the scenario where he or she goes stag hunting alone, because it is impossible to kill a stag without collaboration. Importantly, both hunters are more interested in sharing the stag than getting a rabbit each, because this way they individually get more to eat. Common knowledge helps with the navigation of this scenario because the hunters need to set up mutual expectations that they are going to do the same thing. Similarly, in the example with the two people on the bus, they both had a preference for getting off to get a drink, but only if they both get off.

So common knowledge plays a role in the great many endeavours where we jointly engage in some activity: particularly in situations where it matters that we do the same thing, that we together achieve an outcome that is optimal for each of us individually, and that we all know what others know, and so on. This even applies to simple, everyday matters such as cooking dinner. Even though the family members all know dinner is at 7, you will not be enthusiastic about cooking dinner for everyone unless you know that they know that dinner is at 7 and that they know you know that they know that dinner is at 7 – if they don't know this, then they will not expect dinner to be at 7 after all. Moreover, even though there are many solutions to the coordination problem of all being at the dinner table when dinner is served, members of the family will all prefer the final decision to be that dinner is at 7 because that's when they are hungry. Common knowledge is essential not only in cases where we need to establish awareness of a specific individual's intentions, but also for the function of shared rules and interpretations.

Michael Suk-Young Chwe (1999, 2000, 2001) has developed a set of intriguing analyses of cases involving common knowledge. These analyses are important in part because they anchor common knowledge in a very wide set of social contexts. For example, Chwe analyses the decision to revolt in terms of common knowledge. He notes that people will have a threshold for when they will revolt, that is, they will revolt only if a certain number of other people also revolt. But of course it matters to your decision not only what your threshold is but also what other people's thresholds are. You might be prepared to revolt if 2 others do so, but everyone else might only want to revolt if there is a million on the street already; if you know their thresholds, then you know that your low threshold is pretty immaterial. There will also be cases where meta-mentalising is crucial. If three people communicate their thresholds of three to each other, and they know that this has been communicated, then they know that they occupy a world where the three of them have a desired equilibrium – and so they can each revolt.

If four people each have a threshold of three then we should expect revolt to occur – but this in fact depends on the shape of their social group and whether this shape is itself common knowledge. If their communication is organised in a *square*, then the revolt will not happen, because in this case common knowledge is not engendered. In a square, Person 1 communicates her threshold with 1 and 4 but not 3; similarly, Person 2 communicates with 1 and 3 but not 4, and so on. This means that

Person 1 cannot rule out that Person 3 has a threshold of five, and therefore she cannot rule out the possibility where Person 2 and 4 will not revolt, so she will not herself revolt. The key here is that the knowledge she misses is knowledge about what her neighbours know. Similar cases hold for all four people, so the revolution doesn't happen because they each do not have knowledge of what other people know.

If instead the group was organised as a *kite*, that is, a triangle made up of Persons 1, 2, and 3, with person 4 dangling at the tail, then the revolt will happen, albeit with only three people. This is because now each of the three in the triangle knows what each other's threshold is and knows that they each know this, and so on. The fourth person is unable to revolt due to an inability to establish common knowledge.

Importantly, under this analysis the shape of the social network must itself be common knowledge such that the participants must know whether they are organised in a kite or a square. That is, they must know who communicates with whom and how. In other words, mentalising and meta-mentalising must proceed under models of the wider social landscape, including models of whom the people you talk to talk to.

Chwe discusses a number of interesting elements to this kind of analysis. One element is the distinction between *strong* and *weak* links that can exist between participants in a social network (Chwe 1999). Strong links differ from weak links in how probable it is that the friends of your friends are your friends too. If the probability of this is low, then the network is more a network of acquaintances than of close friends. When an individual passes a message in a network of strong links, they know that the likelihood of others in the network receiving the message, and the likelihood that others know that the rest of the network has received the message, is increased due to the shared knowledge that the network is highly interconnected. Chwe's analysis shows that strong links are good for ensuring participation (in revolt, etc.) when thresholds are low, because strong links ensure good communication in small groups. On the other hand, weak links are better for participation when thresholds are high, because information traverses weakly linked networks more quickly (because links tend to disperse away from each node). Common knowledge scenarios therefore depend on an interaction between thresholds and weak vs. strong links; conversely, the shape of social networks can be expected to reflect the common knowledge scenarios they focus on (small, strongly linked scenarios might involve cases like when to make and come for dinner, and larger, weakly linked scenarios might involve cases like fashion trends or, indeed, revolution).

A second element is the notion of *bandwagons* and their fragility (Chwe 1999). A bandwagon is, for example, a situation where Person 1 has a threshold of 1, so revolts, Person 2 has a threshold of 2, so revolts on knowing that Person 1 has a threshold of 1, and Person 3 has a threshold of 3 so revolts on knowing about the thresholds of the first two, and so on and so forth for the rest of the people in the group. Bandwagons are very dependent on the thresholds and reciprocality of the first few links. If Person 1 and 2 both have a threshold of 2, then nothing will happen across the whole group of people if communication is one way only between Person 1 and Person 2. If communication is reciprocal in such a way that common knowledge is established, however, then the bandwagon can get going. Roughly put, this means that without reciprocality, one will be less engaged in taking initiatives for social collaboration and will be left more to one's own devices.

A third element concerns the formation of *cliques* and the flow of information between cliques (Chwe 2000). For example, a leading clique might be a group of three people each with a threshold of three, organised in a triangle. This clique will revolt, and this will be known to a follower clique of two people each with threshold 5, who will revolt, knowing about the leading clique. Notice that here the follower clique needs to model the shape and common knowledge properties of distinct groups and at the same time model their own group in relation to this. That is, they need to interpret their own local knowledge in a more global network of groups. Being too 'myopically' focused on one's own group means that the behaviour of leading cliques will be missed and one's own group will fail to join the collaborative action.

In addition to discussing these elements of common knowledge networks, Chwe (2001) offers many examples where common knowledge is crucial for the way groups are organised and interact. Common knowledge thus becomes a key element in the understanding of ritual, advertising, and the organisation of public fora. Ritual dancing, for example, is interpreted as a tool for ensuring joint attention on the common knowledge signal and easy detection of those who fail to attend. This ensures that the participants know that everyone got the message and that they know that everyone knows that they got the message, and so on.

There are methods other than ritual to ensure people's attention to a common knowledge signal. In general, creating a signal with much redundancy helps because then it is more likely that many people will notice it and also notice that many people notice it, and so on. With this in mind, one can look at important events that initiate common knowledge-based processes. The revolts of the Arab Spring, for example, purportedly began with the tragic self-immolation of the Tunisian street vendor and protester Mohamed Bouazizi. Though there may have been many protesters before him, the act of self-immolation is a signal that carries immense redundancy and as such many people would see it and see that many people see it.

Interestingly, Chwe broadens the discussion of common knowledge to include objects too. That is, some objects exist in such a way that for most people they are represented in a manner that involves common knowledge. Chwe's main example is the marketing of the mouthwash product Listerine. Listerine was originally an antiseptic, and few would consider putting it in the mouth. But through blanket marketing that focused on the medically sounding term 'halitosis' for bad breath, the makers of Listerine made it common knowledge both that halitosis was widespread and that your friends will not tell if you suffer from it. The thought is that you will be more inclined to buy Listerine if you know that other people are likely to have halitosis, that they are likely to know about halitosis and its 'treatment' through Listerine, that they are not likely to tell you about your halitosis, and that they know that you know about all this. Even though blanket marketing is in many ways characterised by redundancy, the redundancy helps create the common knowledge that sells the product. This means we can reasonably classify Listerine as a common knowledge object, or as a social object. Its representation is embedded in a functional role that involves what other people know, what other people know about what other people know, and so on. Chwe analyses Kotex, HIV tests, and Macintosh computers in a similar vein. Expanding the common knowledge conception to objects is important because it underscores the point that common knowledge is pervasive in our everyday lives.

The picture so far is then that common knowledge is a pervasive element of social cognition and that social cognition is to be understood as causal inference. We mentioned that meta-mentalising is an element of what makes social causal inference stand apart, and it is clear that meta-mentalising is a crucial part of common knowledge endeavours. We do not want to claim that metacognition is needed for all and only common knowledge, but it is tempting to think that they are closely related nevertheless. That is, in some instances it may be useful to model other's mental models of one's own mental model, even if common knowledge is not in the offing. This may be the case in deception, for instance. But even in these cases perhaps it is useful to model precisely to check whether or not common knowledge can be established. For example, it may be that you stand to gain more by not joining collaborative action: perhaps you know that your fellows are poor stag hunters so you will gain more by knowing that they will be off hunting the stag while you scoop up the rabbits.

The proposal is then that the mentalising and meta-mentalising that comes with common knowledge processing is a pervasive and central part of the causal inference involved in social cognition. This includes all the different elements identified by Chwe, from the uptake of Listerine to the discerning of social network shapes like kites and squares. With this proposal in mind, we next turn to the ways in which common knowledge formation can be challenged and disrupted.

12.4 Challenges to Common Knowledge

Common knowledge requires, in Schelling's formulation, a unique signal that is mutually recognised such as to coordinate expectations. We have seen that this signal may take many forms: eye contact, communication about thresholds, blanket advertising, self-immolation, etc. The context in which this signal is delivered matters. If delivered during ritual dancing, attention may be ensured, and if delivered through mass events (like the NFL Super Bowl), uptake can be ensured. Also, the context of social groupings, such as cliques, will matter for how signals are processed, as will issues like communication reciprocity in relation to thresholds for bandwagons. We have also seen that there is a varied class of events and objects to which common knowledge signalling is relevant.

This means there is a rich tapestry of situations where common knowledge can be challenged and disrupted, where such situations will pertain to the processing of Schelling's unique signals.

A classic example of this is the *Byzantine Generals' Problem*. Two generals, each situated on a separate hill, want to attack a city in the valley between them. They must attack together to succeed, or not attack at all, since a lone attack will be disastrous. The first general sends a messenger through the perilous valley with a message to attack at dawn but will of course only attack if receiving confirmation from the second general that he or she has received the first message. But the second general will not be happy to attack unless receiving a message confirming the first confirmation was well received. And so on. The consequence is that the attack never happens. The problem concerns the uncertainty about whether the messenger got through the enemy lines down in the valley. It would be solved if the signal could be made unmissable, for example, by agreeing to have a massive signal fire on each hill top – but in this scenario this would alert the city below too. This problem will arise whenever a signal isn't known to carry perfect information. Of course the stakes are not always as high as in the case of the generals, so often sending just a few messages will be deemed good enough. But the quality of the communication channel is a challenge to solving coordination problems.

Notice that in this case, it is the reliability of the communication channel that matters – how well it carries information about the mental states of the sender. Across different kinds of cases, this would be a matter of degree. Some communication channels are more precise than others. This means the severity of the problem will differ from case to case. But similarly, the severity of the problem will depend on the participants' expectations about the reliability of the communications channels. If a participant expects the communication channel to be very unreliable, then little trust is placed on the incoming message and the urge bigger to enter a new round of messaging. This is a simple point that corresponds to the urge to sample for longer when one expects variability. Mismatches are then bound to occur when the communicators have different expectations for the precision of the signal. In particular, if one party believes the signal is as clear as a beacon on a hilltop but the other party thinks that it is as unreliable as a messenger sent through volatile territory, then we should expect common knowledge to suffer.

The notion of expectations of precision is essential to causal inference. A given hypothesis about the cause of sensory input will have different strengths if the signal in one case can be trusted to be very reliable and in other cases not. Uncertainty in the signals we base our inferences on is state-dependent, that is, it may vary according to the context in which the signal occurs. This means that levels and regularities of uncertainty must be learned and inform causal inference in the shape of expectations for uncertainty or precision. This holds for all types of causal inference, including the kind that the Byzantine generals each engage in when trying to decipher the mental state of the other general from the context and the signals sent.

The occurrence and robustness of common knowledge also depends on the degree of *alignment* between the participants. Alignment should here be understood as the degree to which different individuals share their initial beliefs about the world and the present situation in particular, including the probabilities assigned to those beliefs. This matters because the more aligned participants are, and the surer they know this, the more they can be sure that a new message, when sent, will also be interpreted in the predicted way. Alignment is then a tool for reduction of uncertainty in message passing for the purposes of common knowledge. Perhaps we can add to Chwe's account of the role of ritual here: not only is ritual used to ensure attention to the signal, it also serves to shape the prior expectations of the participants, such that there is less uncertainty about whether they interpreted the message in the right kind of way.

This means that misalignment is a challenge to common knowledge. Knowledge regarding what other participants know (and what they know about others), on the basis of a unique signal, is undermined if we are not sure that the participants employed the right frame of reference to the signal.

The list of challenges to common knowledge also extends to the notion of bandwagons. We noted that they are sensitive to the thresholds and reciprocality of the first few links. In particular, having reciprocal communication and common knowledge at the first links can do much to ensure that a bandwagon gets started. This requires a level of sophistication in the causal inference at play. For example, when Person 2 receives a message from Person 1, then it may be fruitful to engage in turn-taking where a message is sent back. This requires inference of not only Person 1's threshold but also of that person's representation of Person 2's threshold. If this level of representation is challenged, then bandwagons may get stuck.

Finally, we make the general point that the causal inference required for common knowledge is context-dependent and hierarchical. It is rare that signals are as unequivocal as beacons on the top of hills or self-immolations. Mostly, signals are imbued with a degree of uncertainty and ambiguity. Confident inference then requires tools for reducing uncertainty and for resolving ambiguity. In order to do this the participant needs to appeal to prior knowledge and to active probing of the situation. That is, if you are not sure how to interpret a signal, then you can down-weight the character of the signal itself and instead begin to appeal to your prior conceptions about the situation and the likely way the message was meant. Of course, these prior conceptions will involve prior beliefs about the degree of alignment too. This process attempts to reduce uncertainty by taking the wider context into account, namely in the shape of longer-term, learned regularities about what to expect. Similarly, a vague idea about what the best hypothesis might be can be tested actively, by predicting what the interlocutor would say in response to a particular question, were the hypothesis in fact correct ('if she said her threshold is three, then she will confirm she will revolt when I tell her that myself and my neighbour will revolt if she does'; this is neural hermeneutics, see Wentzer and Frith (forthcoming) or, more generally, a social version of active inference (Friston et al. 2011)).

Notice that both of these tools for disambiguation of the signal depend on the expectations for the precision of the signal, which we mentioned before. If one expects much precision in the signal, then one will sample it for longer before appealing to prior conceptions and longer-term regularities; vice versa for the case where imprecision is expected. Similarly, if one expects much precision, then one will sample for longer before resorting to actively testing a given hypothesis.

For all these challenges to common knowledge, there is the prospect of interactions and cascading effects. For example, if there is a unilateral problem with trusting a signal, then common knowledge is not established and bandwagons may fail or misalignment result, which again results in more difficult common knowledge consumption. Similarly, if an individual is expecting more than normal precision in a situation loaded more than usually with uncertainty, then the distance between that person and others in terms of their ability to make sense of signals is going to be compounded.

There is therefore ample scope for challenges and disruptions to common knowledge. We have presented this in terms that lend themselves to both the social deficits seen in ASD and theories about which sensory deficits may be present in this disorder; we now turn to this issue.

12.5 Causal Inference Differences as a Common Cause of Sensory Differences and Common Knowledge Differences

We first presented social cognition as a matter of causal inference, then we described common knowledge as a major ingredient in social cognition and outlined types of challenges to common knowledge. We now want to bring these elements together, using ASD as the key test case.

There is a very direct way to relate ASD and common knowledge: begin by positing mindblindness (i.e. a local deficit to a specialised mentalising circuit in the brain), then observe that common knowledge requires mentalising, and predict widespread difficulties with common knowledge processing in ASD. We believe this explanatory strategy is uninformative because it misses important aspects of the nature of both mentalising and ASD. If mentalising is just another type of causal inference, then mentalising deficits should be associated with a problem with causal inference; this direct strategy is blind to such issues. Similarly, this strategy ignores the presence of a wide class of nonsocial sensory differences in ASD, which are now so well recognised that the upcoming fifth edition of the *Diagnostic and Statistical Manual of Mental Disorders* will for the first time include sensory dysfunction as a diagnostic criterion for ASD (i.e. 'hyper- or hypo-reactivity to sensory input or unusual interest in sensory aspects of environment' (American Psychiatric Association 2013)). It is hard to understand why there should be differences in very basic sensory processing if ASD is just a domain-specific deficit in mentalising (or indeed why a social deficit could cause a difference in the ability to perceive, e.g. visual illusions).

Above, we advocated a common cause model of the sensory differences and social deficits in ASD such that the same underlying aspect of causal inference causes both. We believe this explanatory strategy is more promising. It has the potential to explain constellations of traits in the ASD spectrum in more detail than an account of a local mentalising deficit. It also has the potential to create a deeper understanding of the nature of mentalising and social cognition more broadly: we can present social cognition as a type of cognition in general, rather than a somehow specialised module, and we can present social cognition as the upshot of causal inference.

Notice that the explanatory strategy that we favour also differs from an approach that begins with the sensory differences and explains the social deficits as caused by them. On our account it is a deeper aspect of causal inference that underlies both. The challenge in adopting this strategy is to explain why the social deficits in ASD are so prominent in the clinical picture and the sensory differences less so. It is in order to discharge this explanatory burden that we appeal to the intricate causal inference involved in common knowledge processes. We think that there is a type of difference in causal inference that can explain both relatively subtle sensory differences and prominent social deficits.

The underlying factor in causal inference that we will focus on is what we mentioned in the previous section, concerning the expectations for the precision of sensory input. This is a key ingredient in the idea that the brain processes its sensory input by minimising prediction error (or more generally, free energy; Friston and Stephan 2007; Feldman and Friston 2010; Friston 2010; Brown et al. 2011). It is of particular interest for mental illness and developmental disorders like ASD because differences in this factor have the potential to regulate the relative weighting in causal inference of top-down prior expectations and bottom-up sensory input. That is, when sensory precision is expected, top-down priors are weighted less relative to bottom-up signals, and when imprecision is expected, they are weighted more. In general, having such a mechanism is crucial to causal inference because it ensures the reasonable principle that one should base one's causal inference on reliable evidence or retreat to priors when reliability drops off.

This is then also related to people's tendency to sample either more or less in sense perception, to shift attention, attend to detail, and to be sensitive to overall context – all aspects that are implicated in ASD. Expected precision, as we have mentioned, is related to learning of state-dependent levels of noise and uncertainty. This means that different levels of expected precision for different people can be expected to manifest differently for different contexts, giving rise to the varied landscape of sensory differences and perhaps the heterogeneity of symptoms on the autism spectrum.

The specific proposal is that as individuals get higher and higher on the autism spectrum, they tend to expect more and more precision in their sensory input (this proposal is worked out in some detail in Hohwy (2013)). Heightened expectations for precision can be beneficial for some tasks because it is related to heightened attention and increased sampling. But similarly, it can be detrimental in other tasks, when the signal in fact is deteriorating and when the context should be used to squash uncertainty. Because the concept of expected precision is very basic to all kinds of causal inference, and with a potential to cascade into many kinds of inference, it is conceivable that a domain-general trait bias in expectations for precision, which is very different from the majority, will present clinically. Thus, while for typical individuals the degree of precision expected from sensory input during causal inference should vary across contexts, here we suggest that expectations for precision are consistently high in ASD.

From a statistical point of view, expectations for precisions are related to the confidence of causal inference. As such they are part of second-order statistics. This means that more drastic problems with optimising one's expected precisions can be very hard to rectify. It is basically a type of inference that is itself meant to ensure the reliability of first-order inference, so ensuring its own reliability requires going to a third level of statistics, and so on. This comes with metabolic costs and danger of regress that we don't think the brain can comfortably encompass. This aspect of expected precision then speaks to the recalcitrance of mental, developmental disorder such as ASD (and schizophrenia, see Hohwy (2013)).

This proposal finds a natural partner in the *weak central coherence account* of autistic perception (Frith 1989; Happé and Frith 2006), which suggests a processing style focused on local perceptual features and a diminished tendency to integrate perceptual features into a coherent whole. The idea that we suggest is that differences in expected precisions is the mechanism behind weak central coherence and that it is able to explain the varied landscape of enhanced and diminished ability in ASD, which the weak central coherence account cannot so easily accommodate. (The proposal is also related to ideas from Mitchell and Ropar (2004), from Qian and Lipkin (2011)), and from Brock (2012); Pellicano and Burr (2012); Friston et al. (2013); Van Boxtel and Lu (2013); and Van de Cruys et al. (2013, submitted).)

The proposal is new and evidence is needed to substantiate it. Our own research is providing data that is consistent with it, in the context of sensorimotor processing and multisensory integration. Our key model is the rubber hand illusion, which has all the required elements to trigger differences in expected precisions. The rubber hand illusion occurs when a visible rubber hand and one's own hidden real hand are touched in synchrony, giving rise to the startling experience that the touch one can feel is located on the rubber hand (Botvinick and Cohen 1998). We assess the varying effects of this illusion on proprioception (perceived arm position) and also introduce a reach-to-grasp task after experiencing the illusion, which must then be performed under the uncertainty-inducing context of the rubber hand being experienced as the locus of touch.

We find that patients with ASD differ from controls and that individuals with ASD-like traits differ from those low on ASD-like traits. Specifically, participants with ASD and ASD-like traits have more accurate proprioception, suggesting they do not integrate under a more global model, which would pull their proprioceptive estimate towards the (illuded) visuotactile estimate. This is consistent with an upregulation of bottom-up sensory estimates regarding arm position due to higher expectations for precision in sensory input compared to the control groups. Moreover, people low on ASD-like traits reach with much tentativeness and uncertainty after experiencing the illusion, which is not seen in individuals with high ASD-like traits, suggesting that the latter group expect more precision in the proprioceptive and kinesthetic input they will receive as movement unfolds (Paton et al. 2011; Palmer et al. 2013).

This idea is also worth pursuing as the variability of findings for ASD in the sensory domain may be better explained by appealing to differences in the presence and absence of uncertainty-inducing contexts in specific experimental set-ups.

The question we wish to address now is whether expectations for high precision of sensory input would cause the kinds of challenges we have outlined for common knowledge and thereby on social cognition.

It seems clear that someone with expectations for high precision will present differently in scenarios that invoke versions of the Byzantine Generals' Problem. Under conditions of uncertainty (i.e. not a beacon on a hill but a more subtle signal), people with higher expectations for precision should trust the signal more and sample the signal for longer in order to arrive at the expected precise estimate. People who expect less sensory precision should be quicker to appeal to prior expectations (e.g. rely on known alignment) to overcome uncertainty and should not sample for as long. This should manifest such that those expecting precision will sometimes act on a misinterpreted signal because they trust it more than the context mandates they should (compare: reach less tentatively and more smoothly) and might fail to a larger degree to integrate the signal under a model of (aligned) mental states of the sender; alternatively, they may sample for longer than neurotypical collaborators and thus not act when everyone else is acting – missing the boat and failing to learn common knowledge truths.

At the outset, we noted that social cognition is special because it involves metacognition, that is, representation of other's mental representation of one's own and other's mental states. This occurs not only in one's attempt at representing other's mental states but also in extracting information about the shape of social networks and who is telling what to whom (e.g. 'is this a *square* or a *kite*?'). This was noted to be a special kind of non-linear, causal interaction and was identified as a requirement for common knowledge. Non-linearity is what introduces ambiguity in causal inference because it makes it difficult to match cause and effect in one-one relations. Multiple, nested levels of non-linearity are then especially difficult to deal with and require especially well-honed balance of trusting the signal and relying on prior knowledge. In other words, we expect meta-mentalising to be especially challenged when expectations for precision are not optimised. Specifically, expecting too much precision means being more stuck in low-level signal processing and less inclined to fit represented causes in with more global models. This would predict that highly interacting causes are missed, in particular those that relate to meta-mentalising.

This overall picture of lessened representation of high-level, interacting causes would then cascade to other areas. For example, if meta-mentalising is less prevalent, then there will be less inclination to offer information about one's own threshold, which could feed into other's model of oneself. This impedes the reciprocality that we saw was often needed to take initiative and get a bandwagon rolling. Likewise, we can expect such problems to cascade into lessened alignment and reduced concern about being aligned with others. The result of these mechanisms is that not only does the person with expectations for high precision in sensory estimation fail to represent other's mental states with much depth, they also will tend to fail to be able to learn, and they will be marginalised in common knowledge efforts.

It thus seems to us that the quite simple proposal that individuals with ASD have problems with optimising their expected precisions quite quickly can cause profound and widespread problems in common knowledge, with wide ramifications for social cognition at large.

Compared to typically developing children, those with ASD tend to show developmental delays on tasks designed to test for the basic ability to attribute mental states (reviewed in Happé (1995)). Many individuals with ASD, however, especially older children and adults, are able to pass the classic tests of this faculty, instead showing more subtle behavioural and neurophysiological differences in tasks that have been suggested to more specifically elicit automatic mental state attribution, rather than allowing for inference via explicit reasoning or other strategies (Klin 2000; Castelli et al. 2002; Senju et al. 2009). It has thus been proposed that a deficit in the automatic and intuitive ability to attribute mental states can be compensated for, just not to the extent that everyday social difficulties can be avoided (Happé 1995; Frith 2004). Understanding mentalising with respect to coordination problems and differences in expected precisions may therefore be useful in characterising the extent to which individuals can compensate, or fail to compensate, for deficits in automatic processes involved in mental state attribution.

We will end this section by noting how the proposed differences in expected precisions could dynamically impact on social interaction. This stems from the trivial observation that communication is a 'two-way street' where the quality and quantity of an individual's participation depends on what the interlocutors offer up. On our proposal, we predict restricted messaging *to* individuals with ASD from other people (something that of course will be especially detrimental to learning during development). Common knowledge depends on everyone knowing what messages were received by whom and how they were interpreted. If interlocutors can see that some participant is consistently not paying attention (e.g. literally out of step in ritual dance or engulfed in increased sensory sampling), then it may not be worth sending messages to that person. Thus Schelling's unique signal may become less and less available to individuals with ASD because the rest of us are less inclined to include them. At the same time, there may be restricted messaging *from* individuals with ASD to other people. If such an individual does not engage in much meta-mentalising and does not represent social networks and reciprocal communication channels correctly, then they will be less inclined to divulge information about their thresholds in the right way in the right circumstances, and then they will be gradually dealt out of common knowledge generation (e.g. treated as the tail of kites or as one-person cliques).

Once upon a time, ASD was explained with the sexist and now entirely discredited cold mother hypothesis, namely that it was caused by emotionally cold mothering. With our proposal comes a different kind of social interaction model, where a simple deficit in expected precisions leads to a cold social network, where fewer messages are being communicated both ways and where people with ASD are increasingly in danger of being marginalised.

12.6 Concluding Remarks

The agenda in this chapter has been to throw light on the notion of social cognition by aligning it with causal inference in general and common knowledge in particular. We have used ASD as a test case to bring out how basic, simple differences in the optimisation of expectations of the precision of sensory input could challenge common knowledge and thereby social cognition in ASD. The proposal is ambitious in the sense that it posits a single deficit in causal inference as underlying ASD. This may seem unlikely, given the heterogeneity of ASD symptomatology, and it is certainly hostage to empirical fortune. However, the proposed deficit is motivated specifically because deficits in precision optimisation are capable of manifesting in a surprising number of ways, often of particular relevance for ASD; further, it is quite likely that a range of different genetic and developmental factors can go together to explain a variety of different impairments to precision optimisation.

This differs from many other accounts of ASD because we do not think people with ASD have a specific inability to represent mental states of other people. The problem does not arise because those states of the world are mental. It arises instead because the causal inference required to extract these causes, from the sensory input one receives, is especially sensitive to exquisite optimisation of expected precisions. This has to do with the requirement to meta-mentalise to engage in common knowledge exchanges.

If this kind of challenge to causal inference in the social domain occurs early in developmental processes, then it is possible that a deep-seated and incorrigible deficit in mentalising ensues a profound mindblindness that impedes language learning and many other social aspects of normal life. But in principle, people with ASD should be able to represent mental states, since they are just causes in the world, on a par with other, nonmental causes, which they are able to discern. One interesting possibility here is what happens if people with similar, skewed expectations for precisions communicate with each other (e.g. on Internet forums). We expect that mentalising will be more likely when people share expected precisions and also that it will be easier for common knowledge to arise because problems like the Byzantine Generals' Problem, the bandwagon issues, and the cold social network issues we have discussed all to some degree depend on people having differences in such expectations and misaligned priors.

Lastly, there is a clear programme here for further, empirical study on two fronts. Firstly, one could study whether it is the case that people with ASD and high on ASD-like traits do expect more precision in their sensory input, how this plays out in sensory contexts under differing levels of uncertainty, and how this may impact on social cognition (see Van de Cruys et al. (submitted)). Secondly, one could study whether common knowledge is a main contributor to social cognition and whether it is especially challenged in ASD, in the ways that we have outlined. Such empirical study could look at, for example, the relative uptake of common knowledge objects like Listerine and Macintosh computers; studies could focus on the relative participation in common knowledge activities such as revolts and compare this with pure preference-based activities; and studies could focus on participation and performance in collaborative games such as the stag hunt (see Yoshida et al. (2010)). Finally, studies could investigate whether intra-autistic communication in fact has improved social cognition, mentalising, and common knowledge, but perhaps with a different timbre, scope, and depth than that seen in the general population.

Acknowledgements Thanks to the audience at the Aarhus-Paris Conference in Social Ontology and Social Cognition at Aarhus University, especially John Michael, Mattia Gallotti, Andreas Roepstorff, and Chris and Uta Frith; thanks also to the staff and students at Tokyo University's Centre for Philosophy, in particular, Yukihiro Nobuhara, Iizuka Rie, and Kataoka Masa.

References

al-Haytham, I.A. ca. 1030; 1989. *The optics of Ibn al-Haytham* (trans: Sabra, AI). Warburg: Warburg Institute.

American Psychiatric Association. 2013. *Diagnostic and statistical manual of mental disorders: DSM-5*. Arlington: APA.

Apperly, I.A., D. Samson, and G.W. Humphreys. 2005. Domain-specificity and theory of mind: Evaluating neuropsychological evidence. *Trends in Cognitive Sciences* 9(12): 572–577.
Botvinick, M., and J. Cohen. 1998. Rubber hands 'feel' touch that eyes see. *Nature* 391(6669): 756.
Brock, J. 2012. Alternative Bayesian accounts of autistic perception: Comment on Pellicano and Burr. *Trends in Cognitive Science* 16(12): 573–574; author reply 574–575.
Brown, H., K.J. Friston, and S. Bestmann. 2011. Active inference, attention and motor preparation. *Frontiers in Psychology* 2.
Call, J., and M. Tomasello. 2008. Does the chimpanzee have a theory of mind? 30 years later. *Trends in Cognitive Science* 12: 187–192.
Castelli, F., C. Frith, F. Happe, and U. Frith. 2002. Autism, Asperger syndrome and brain mechanisms for the attribution of mental states to animated shapes. *Brain* 125(Pt 8): 1839–1849.
Chwe, M.S.-Y. 1999. Structure and strategy in collective action. *The American Journal of Sociology* 105(1): 128–156.
Chwe, M.S.-Y. 2000. Communication and coordination in social networks. *The Review of Economic Studies* 67(1): 1–16.
Chwe, M.S.-Y. 2001. *Rational ritual: Culture, coordination, and common knowledge*. Princeton: Princeton University Press.
Dayan, P., G.E. Hinton, R.M. Neal, and R.S. Zemel. 1995. The Helmholtz machine. *Neural Computation* 7(5): 889–904.
Feldman, H., and K. Friston. 2010. Attention, uncertainty and free-energy. *Frontiers in Human Neuroscience* 4(215).
Friston, K. 2010. The free-energy principle: A unified brain theory? *Nature Review Neuroscience* 11: 127–138.
Friston, K. 2011. What is optimal about motor control? *Neuron* 72(3): 488–498.
Friston, K., and K. Stephan. 2007. Free energy and the brain. *Synthese* 159(3): 417–458.
Friston, K., J. Mattout, and J. Kilner. 2011. Action understanding and active inference. *Biological Cybernetics* 104(1): 137–160.
Friston, K.J., R. Lawson, and C.D. Frith. 2013. On hyperpriors and hypopriors: Comment on Pellicano and Burr. *Trends in Cognitive Science* 17(1): 1.
Frith, U. 1989. *Autism: Explaining the enigma*. Oxford: Blackwell.
Frith, U. 2004. Emanuel Miller lecture: Confusions and controversies about Asperger syndrome. *Journal of Child Psychology and Psychiatry* 45(4): 672–686.
Gallagher, S. 2007. Logical and phenomenological arguments against simulation theory. In *Folk psychology re-assessed*, ed. D. Hutto and D. Ratcliffe. Berlin: Springer.
Gallese, V., and A. Goldman. 1998. Mirror neurons and the simulation theory of mind-reading. *Trends in Cognitive Science* 2: 493.
Gopnik, A. 1993. How we know our minds: The illusion of first-person knowledge of intentionality. *Behavioral and Brain Sciences* 16(1): 1–14.
Gopnik, A., and A.N. Meltzoff. 1997. *Words, thoughts and theories*. Cambridge, MA: MIT Press.
Gregory, R.L. 1980. Perceptions as hypotheses. *Philosophical Transactions of the Royal Society of London, Series B, Biological Sciences* 290(1038): 181–197.
Happé, F.G. 1995. The role of age and verbal ability in the theory of mind task performance of subjects with autism. *Child Development* 66(3): 843–855.
Happé, F., and U. Frith. 2006. The weak coherence account: Detail-focused cognitive style in autism spectrum disorders. *Journal of Autism and Developmental Disorders* 36(1): 5–25.
Heal, J. 1986. Replication and functionalism. In *Language, mind, and logic*, ed. J. Butterfield. Cambridge: Cambridge University Press.
Helmholtz, Hv. 1867. *Handbuch der Physiologishen Optik*. Leipzig: Leopold Voss.
Hohwy, J. 2013. *The predictive mind*. Oxford: Oxford University Press.
Hutto, D. 2008. *Folk psychological narratives: The sociocultural basis of understanding reasons*. Cambridge, MA: MIT Press.
Jackson, F. 1999. All that can be at issue in the theory-theory simulation debate. *Philosophical Papers* 28(2): 77–96.

Kersten, D., P. Mamassian, and A. Yuille. 2004. Object perception as Bayesian inference. *Annual Review of Psychology* 55(1): 271–304.
Kilner, J.M., and Chris D. Frith. 2008. Action observation: Inferring intentions without mirror neurons. *Current Biology* 18(1): R32–R33.
Kilner, J., K. Friston, and C. Frith. 2007. Predictive coding: An account of the mirror neuron system. *Cognitive Processing* 8(3): 159–166.
Klin, A. 2000. Attributing social meaning to ambiguous visual stimuli in higher-functioning autism and Asperger syndrome: The social attribution task. *Journal of Child Psychology and Psychiatry* 41(7): 831–846.
Lewis, D.K. 1969. *Convention: A philosophical study*. Chichester: Wiley-Blackwell.
Meltzoff, A.N., and J. Decety. 2003. What imitation tells us about social cognition: A rapprochement between developmental psychology and cognitive neuroscience. *Philosophical Transactions of the Royal Society of London Series B-Biological Sciences* 358: 491–500.
Mill, J.S. 1865. *An examination of Sir William Hamilton's philosophy*. London: Longmans.
Mitchell, P., and D. Ropar. 2004. Visuo-spatial abilities in Autism: A review. *Infant and Child Development* 13: 185–198.
Mumford, D. 1992. On the computational architecture of the neocortex. II. The role of cortico-cortical loops. *Biological Cybernetics* 66: 241–251.
Neisser, U. 1967. *Cognitive psychology*. New York: Appleton.
Palmer, C.J., B. Paton, J. Hohwy, and P.G. Enticott. 2013. Movement under uncertainty: The effects of the rubber-hand illusion vary along the nonclinical autism spectrum. *Neuropsychologia* 51(10): 1942–1951.
Paton, B., J. Hohwy, and P. Enticott. 2011. The Rubber hand illusion reveals proprioceptive and sensorimotor differences in Autism Spectrum Disorders. *Journal of Autism and Developmental Disorders* 1–14.
Pearl, J. 2000. *Causality*. Cambridge: Cambridge University Press.
Pellicano, E., and D. Burr. 2012. When the world becomes too real: A Bayesian explanation of autistic perception. *Trends in Cognitive Sciences* 16: 504–510.
Perner, J., M.C. Mauer, and M. Hildenbrand. 2011. Identity: Key to children's understanding of belief. *Science* 333(6041): 474–477.
Qian, N., and R.M. Lipkin. 2011. A learning-style theory for understanding autistic behaviors. *Frontiers in Human Neuroscience* 5.
Schelling, T.C. 1960. *The strategy of conflict*. Harvard: Harvard University Press.
Senju, A., V. Southgate, S. White, and U. Frith. 2009. Mindblind eyes: An absence of spontaneous theory of mind in Asperger syndrome. *Science* 325(5942): 883–885.
Van Boxtel, J.J.A., and H. Lu. 2013. A predictive coding perspective on autism spectrum disorders: A general comment on Pellicano and Burr (2012). *Frontiers in Psychology* 4: 19.
Van de Cruys, S., L. de-Wit, K. Evers, B. Boets, and J. Wagemans. 2013. Weak priors versus overfitting of predictions in autism: Reply to Pellicano and Burr (TICS, 2012). *i-Perception* 4(2): 95–97.
Van de Cruys, S., K. Evers, R. Van der Hallen, L. Van Eylen, B. Boets, L. Lee de-Wit, and J. Wagemans. Submitted. Precise minds in uncertain worlds: Predictive coding in autism.
Vanderschraaf, P., and G. Sillari. 2009. *Common knowledge*. In *The Stanford encyclopedia of philosophy*, Spring 2014 ed, ed. Edward N. Zalta. http://plato.stanford.edu/archives/spr2014/entries/common-knowledge/
Wentzer, T., and C.D. Frith. In press. Neural hermeneutics. In *Encyclopedia of philosophy and the social sciences*, vol. 1, ed. B. Kaldis. Sage.
Wolpert, D.M., K. Doya, and M. Kawato. 2003. A unifying computational framework for motor control and social interaction. *Philosophical Transactions of the Royal Society London B* 358: 593–602.
Woodward, J. 2003. *Making things happen*. New York: Oxford University Press.
Yoshida, W., I. Dziobek, D. Kliemann, H.R. Heekeren, K.J. Friston, and R.J. Dolan. 2010. Cooperation and heterogeneity of the autistic mind. *Journal of Neuroscience* 30(26): 8815–8818.

MIX
Papier aus verantwortungsvollen Quellen
Paper from responsible sources
FSC® C105338

If you have any concerns about our products,
you can contact us on
ProductSafety@springernature.com

In case Publisher is established outside the EU,
the EU authorized representative is:
Springer Nature Customer Service Center GmbH
Europaplatz 3, 69115 Heidelberg, Germany

Printed by Libri Plureos GmbH
in Hamburg, Germany